The Zeppelin Reader

The  Zeppelin

Reader

Stories, Poems, and

Songs from the Age

of Airships

Edited by Robert Hedin

University of Iowa Press Ꝑ Iowa City

University of Iowa Press

Iowa City 52242

Copyright © 1998 by the

University of Iowa Press

All rights reserved

Printed in the United States of America

Design by Richard Hendel

http://www.uiowa.edu/~uipress

Printed on acid-free paper

Library of Congress Cataloging-in-Publication Data

The Zeppelin reader: stories, poems, and songs from the

   age of airships / edited by Robert Hedin.

       p.   cm.

    Includes index.

     ISBN 0-87745-629-1 (pbk.)

     1. Airships—Literary collections.   I. Hedin, Robert,

  1949–   .

PN6071.A57Z46   1998

808.8'0356—dc21   97-52974

98 99 00 01 02 P 5 4 3 2 1

For my brother, Douglas

And we shall see old planets change

And alien stars arise

—Rudyard Kipling

Contents

Introduction

Size is often the first thing that comes to mind when we recall the great airships of the past. And indeed they were huge, dominating the imagination like no other objects of their time. For many people, they were bigger than life itself, bright and wondrous apparitions that engendered a religious-like awe. To this day, they are still the largest crafts ever to be launched into the skies. The *Hindenburg*, for example, was nothing if not colossal. Weighing 236 tons, it was thirteen stories tall and was nearly three football fields long. The 7,062,100 cubic feet of hydrogen that it carried was enough to run an ordinary kitchen stove for several hundreds of years.

But the *Hindenburg* was by no means the only airship of gargantuan size. All of them were enormous beyond imagining. German peasants in the early 1900s often described the first zeppelins in terms traditionally reserved for supernatural creatures. Of the R 101, the ill-fated British airship, it was estimated that the intestines of a million oxen were used to make the ship's seventeen enormous gasbags. Even airship hangars defied imagination. The Goodyear-Zeppelin hangar in Akron, Ohio, considered to be the largest structure in the world without interior supports, occupied some eight and a half acres. The doors alone each weighed 600 tons. So huge, in fact, was the structure that clouds were often reported to form near the ceiling and, at times, rain would quietly begin to fall.

The story of the airship is a story of grand proportions and one that involves a large cast of inventors, rogues, and occasional geniuses. Names such as Henri Giffard, Alberto Santos-Dumont, Ferdinand von Zeppelin, and Hugo Eckener loom large in the world of early dirigibles. It was Giffard who guided the world's first navigable airship over Paris in 1852. Powered by a small but hazardous three-horse-power steam engine, the balloon was 144 feet long, with sharply tapered ends, and was able to navigate only in calm weather. Giffard's pioneering flight was followed by *La France*, a 165-foot-long, electrically powered dirigible designed by Charles Renard and Arthur Krebs, whose initial voyage was carried out over the balloon park at Chalais-Meudon in Paris in 1884. After the invention of the gasoline engine in 1886, Alberto Santos-Dumont of Brazil built fourteen non-rigid airships and made several celebrated flights over the French capital, ultimately capturing the famed Deutsch Prize in 1901 when he guided his rickety *Santos-Dumont No. 6* from Saint-Cloud to the Eiffel Tower and back, a flight that lasted thirty minutes, covered a distance of seven miles, and gained an international following for the tenacious aviator.

At the same time, in Germany Count Ferdinand von Zeppelin began constructing the first navigable airships with a rigid internal structure, a skeleton comprised of rings, girders, and a maze of wires that allowed the ship to maintain its streamlined shape despite variations in hydrogen pressure. This boldly conceived structure dramatically altered the future of airships, transforming them into viable tools in exploration, in transportation, and in the military. Of all of Zeppelin's early ventures, it was the flight of the LZ 4 that caused the greatest stir. Though destroyed in a storm on its trials for the army, it made the longest flight yet attained by an airship, a feat for which Zeppelin won wide acclaim and financial support from both the German people and the government.

Bolstered by such enthusiastic support, Zeppelin formed the German Airship Transportation Company in 1910 and, along with Hugo Eckener, constructed more than twenty-six zeppelins. In three years of service prior to World War I, Zeppelin's four passenger airships— *Schwaben*, *Viktoria Luise*, *Hansa*, and *Sachsen*—made 760 flights and carried over 14,000 passengers without any serious injuries. By the time World War I broke out, Zeppelin's dynamic rigid airships had eclipsed all other designs and made it possible in the succeeding decades for such beautiful and beguiling crafts as the *Graf Zeppelin* and the *Hindenburg* to take command of the skies.

During the course of World War I, more than eighty-eight zeppelins were constructed, each one larger than the last. What once had been looked upon as essentially an aerial curiosity was transformed into a military tool that terrorized London and other British cities. All total, during the war German zeppelins carried out over 4,700 military missions, attacking the enemy on two hundred separate occasions. Of these, fifty-one raids were made against England, with London being bombed twelve times. In all, zeppelins dropped 9,000 bombs, leaving 1,500 people dead and 3,500 wounded. Though zeppelins ultimately proved to be ineffective military weapons, they nevertheless haunted the British imagination, proving that no nation, however isolated, was exempt from twentieth-century aerial technology. In more ways than one, their raids over England helped pave the way for the devastating Nazi blitzes of London during the Second World War.

In the years following World War I, the role of airships expanded dramatically into areas of exploration and transportation. In 1919, the British-made R 34, a ship patterned after the long-distance German raiders of World War I, became the first aircraft of any kind to cross the Atlantic Ocean in both directions. In 1924, the American-built *Shenandoah* made a record-breaking 9,000-mile voyage across the United States, and two years later the *Norge*, an Italian-built semi-rigid airship under the command of Umberto Nobile, made the first successful flight across the North Pole.

Of the many remarkable feats performed by airships during the twenties and thirties, none surpassed those of the *Graf Zeppelin*, a magnificent ship that measured 775 feet in length, carried a crew of forty, and had room enough for twenty passengers to travel in Pullman-style luxury. In 1929, the *Graf* accomplished the first circumnavigation of the globe by an airship, a feat for which its famed commander, Hugo Eckener, received the National Geographic Society's coveted Gold Medal. In 1930, it provided regular mail and passenger service to Rio de Janeiro and, in 1931, made a dramatic journey to the Arctic to rendezvous with the Russian icebreaker *Malygin* before heading back to Berlin. In its nine years of service, the *Graf Zeppelin* logged 17,178 hours in the air, covered more than 1,000,000 miles, and carried 16,000 enthralled passengers to some of the most exotic places on earth.

Indeed, by the 1930s, zeppelin life had undergone a virtual renaissance. Cruising at speeds of eighty miles an hour, airships made little or no noise and, unlike airplanes and ocean liners of the time, created no sensation of movement. Passengers, often a who's who of the world's upper classes, marveled at the unearthly, almost angelic lightness they experienced while in flight. With splendid promenades and large slanted windows, the airships were a sightseer's dream, offering unbroken panoramas of fifty miles in all directions, views that were previously unimaginable.

Furthermore, the excitement generated on the ground by airships was remarkable. When they passed overhead, whole cities ground to a halt, thousands of people gazing up through the gray industrial haze in wonder. In rural flatlands, farmers and ranchers climbed to the tops of their windmills in hopes of gaining a better view. In fact, for many people during the Great Depression, these majestic ships represented something free and unencumbered and, upon seeing them, people often felt strangely privileged, if not somehow blessed. Even animals seemed in awe of their wondrous presence. When airships passed over farmlands, for example, herds of livestock bellowed and bolted, and chickens flapped about wildly. At sea, flocks of pelicans followed them as though they were gods, and whales often played with their enormous shadows.

Despite the grandeur of the era, however, it was a volatile time. From beginning to end, one airship after another was lost, destroyed, or suffered some ignominious fate due to faulty design, mismanagement, or the vagaries of hydrogen, war, or weather. In World War I alone, Germany lost a total of thirty-five ships to enemy fire. Another twelve were destroyed by explosions, and several others were either damaged in their sheds or lost to storms. British and American airships suffered similar fates. In 1930, the R 101 crashed on its first voyage near Beauvais, France, effectively putting an end to Britain's airship dreams. In America, the *Shenandoah* broke in two over Ohio during a violent thunderstorm in 1925. The *Akron* sank off the New Jersey coast during a storm in 1933, and the *Macon* went down dramatically in the Pacific Ocean off Point Sur, California, in 1935.

Ultimately, it was the disaster of the *Hindenburg* on May 6, 1937, at Lakehurst, New Jersey, that marked the end of the era. Though only thirty-six passengers and crew perished and the disaster itself lasted a mere thirty-four seconds, it quickly assumed mythical proportions in the mind of the public, largely because it was the first such disaster ever to be recorded on film and radio. Within days newsreel footage of the explosion was seen by millions of people in theaters all over the country. And Herb Morrison's account of the disaster for WLS radio came to represent the haunted awe and hysteria that we now tend to associate with disasters of any kind. Today, some sixty years later, listening to Morrison's stricken voice or watching the fiery hull of the *Hindenburg* go down in grainy newsreels is still a darkly captivating experience. In effect, one is witnessing the collapse of an entire era in thirty-four apocalyptic seconds.

Soon after the disaster of the *Hindenburg*, the *Graf Zeppelin* and the *Graf Zeppelin II* were grounded, and, except for an occasional spying mission by the *Graf II* off the English coast prior to World War II, they never flew again. On May 6, 1940, their great sheds at Frankfurt were blown up by the Nazis, and both ships were eventually turned into bombers and fighters for the Luftwaffe during the war. In 1944, Allied bombing destroyed the airship hangars at Friedrichshafen, and the Zeppelin Company turned its attention to producing parts for the v-2 rocket. At present, fewer than thirty airships remain in the world. Employed largely for scientific purposes or by companies to hover over weekly sporting events, they still inspire a certain awe and curiosity. None, however, compare to the colossal majesty of their beguiling, unpredictable ancestors.

Tracing the history of the airship era from its beginnings in the nineteenth century to its fiery conclusion in 1937, *The Zeppelin Reader* brings together some of the finest writings of what the era was like in both fact and spirit. Included in the volume are accounts by such legendary figures as Ferdinand von Zeppelin, Hugo Eckener, and Alberto Santos-Dumont, as well as numerous selections from memoirs, logs, journals, and diaries by commanders, crew, explorers, journalists, and survivors of ill-fated flights.

Selections such as "The Flight of the LZ 4" by Karl Schwarz, "Through Heavens Hitherto Unsailed" by Alberto Santos-Dumont, and the excerpt from *Chauffeur of the Skies* by Roy Knabenshue describe early flights. Harrowing and at times unwittingly comical, the essays reveal the kind of tenacity and temerity that it took to make these early, almost suicidal ventures into the air. The volume also presents accounts by several World War I zeppelin commanders and crewmembers. Included are stories by Ernst A. Lehmann, Heinrich Mathy, and August Seim—all of whom vividly describe their spartan lives aboard the cramped, cold, and lethal wartime ships. The book also gathers eyewitness accounts by Winston S. Churchill, D. H. Lawrence, Arnold Bennett, William Mitchell, and others who were in France or England during the daring zeppelin raids.

Other authors in the book write of airship journeys to exotic areas. Lincoln Ellsworth details the famous flight of the *Norge* to the North Pole, while journalist Junius B. Wood describes in loving detail the *Shenandoah*'s record-making cruise across the United States, an odyssey that marked for one of the first times the rendering of the breadth and magnitude of the American landscape from such dizzying heights. Hugo Eckener writes of the *Graf Zeppelin*'s voyage to Egypt and the Holy Land, and John R. McCormick offers a poignant portrayal of a farmboy and his grandmother witnessing the passage of the *Graf* over their small Illinois farm on the last leg of the ship's acclaimed around-the-world tour in 1929. Other essays—"The Violent Death of America's Last Dirigible" by Harold B. Miller and the excerpt from *The Millionth Chance: The Story of the R 101* by James Leasor—capture the drama, grandeur, and volatility that marked the close of the era.

In addition, *The Zeppelin Reader* gathers a wide range of poems about airships by some of the finest modern and contemporary poets from Europe and the United States. Poems such as "The Zeppelin" by Laurence Binyon and "Zeppelin Nights" by D. H. Lawrence— both written during World War I—constitute some of the first ever written about the advent of military aerial technology, and for this reason alone they bear historical importance. Displaying a quintessentially modern sensibility, they portray the airship in decidedly demonic terms as a senseless, death-dealing machine capable of destroying the pastoral tranquility of England.

Other poems in the volume depict the airship in very different ways. In "By Chanctonbury" by Edmund Blunden, "The Week the Dirigible Came" by Jay Meek, and "Phenomena" by Robinson Jeffers, the airship is rendered in grand, omniscient terms as a dreamy counterpoint to the irremediable realities of the human world or simply as a divinely inspired creation easily assimilated into the great harmonies of nature. Still others—"The Zeppelin Factory" by Rita Dove, "The Hangar at Sunnyvale: 1937" by Janet Lewis, "An Elegy" by Yvor Winters, and "A Complaint for Mary and Marcel" by Kay Boyle—memorialize such ships as the *Akron*, *Macon*, and *Hindenburg*. Furthermore, the volume presents an abridged version of Turner Cassity's lengthy "The Airship Boys in Africa," perhaps the finest, most comprehensive poem ever written about an airship. It is based on what is certainly one of the most extraordinary aviation events in all of World War I, the famous voyage of the L 59 to Africa. In Turner's hands, the entire journey is resurrected in all of its truly fantastical proportions.

Also included in *The Zeppelin Reader* is a rich sampling of airship music. Gathered are waltzes, ballads, blues, marches, polkas, and children's songs from Germany, France, Great Britain, and the United States. Some, such as "Come, Take a Trip in My Air-Ship" by Ren Shields and George Evans, were composed prior to World War I, and their moods of innocence and playful flirtation reflect a time when airship travel seemed more dream than reality. Others in the volume—"Fly, Zeppelin: A Children's Song" by an anonymous author and "The Zeppelin Polka" by Victor Léon—embody the spirit of World War I German nationalism and suggest the immense pride that Germany took in Zeppelin's miraculous ventures. Still others, such as "On the Z-R-3" by Sam M. Lewis, Joe Young, and Walter Donaldson, and "The Zeppelin March: 'Los Angeles' U.S.A." by Arthur Rebner, celebrate particular ships, while "The Wreck of the *Shenandoah*" by Maggie Andrews and "The *Hindenburg* Disaster" by Leadbelly devote themselves to ill-fated flights. In addition, *The Zeppelin Reader* includes several full-length musical scores.

It should be remembered that many of the songs were born out of an original innocence, at a time when the holds of gravity were suddenly loosened and, almost overnight, the heavens were opened to navigation. Though the flowering of airship music was particularly prodigious, the era did not last long enough for a unique, identifiable tradition to be formed. Few if any of the songs became naturalized into folk traditions and in most musical archives are not to be found at all. For all intents and purposes, the music has been lost to history.

Together, the lyrics and scores found in *The Zeppelin Reader* constitute a kind of recovered history and help recapture the emotional range and variety of the era's music.

Some of the essays and poems found in *The Zeppelin Reader* have been previously published in small regional magazines or in large, nationally circulated journals. Others are reprinted from texts long out of print. "I Will Not Follow the *Hindenberg*" and "If the *Hindenberg* Had Left from Las Vegas" have been written specifically for the book and appear in print for the first time. In resurrecting these many accounts, poems, and songs, I hope they will gain new life for modern audiences. All of them, in one way or another, evoke a fascinating era in the history of aviation. Through them, the great airships are allowed once again to take their rightful place over the landscape, their huge ghostly outlines filling the skies as well as the imagination in uniquely palpable ways.

Respectfully dedicated to
MRS MARGARET J. REGAN
ST. LOUIS.

The AIR SHIP.

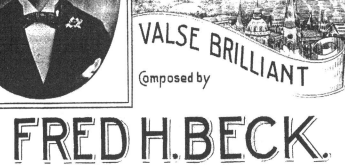

VALSE BRILLIANT

Composed by

FRED H. BECK.

PUBLISHERS

JOS. PLACHT & SON.
ST. LOUIS, MO.

THE AIR SHIP.

VALSE BRILLIANTE.

By FRED. H. BECK.

Andantino.

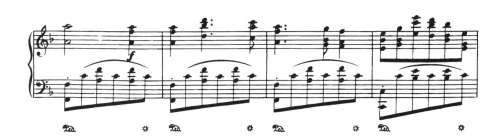

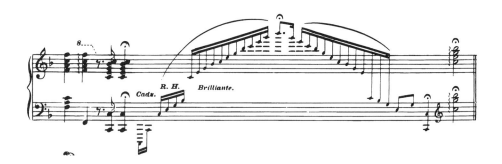

Valse.

Each Power Car has a 300 H.P. Packard Motor

Ge
An

U.S.

The Control Car with 1000 mile Radio Outfit

Fore Power Cars

Pneumatic Bumper

Af
Po

Observation Pla by Ladder from Keel

Interior of Hull, depicting relative position of Gas Bags, extent of Keel Corridor etc...

Outer Cover of Cotton Cloth, treated with Aluminized Dope

Metal Cone for securing Ship to Mooring Mast

Gas Cell

Gas Cell

Girder construction of sectional, triangular Duralumin

High tension wire bracing throughout frame

Shaft

Navigat
Ro

tail Amidships of the Keel Corridor...
(*Longitudinal Section*)

Water Line

Gas Cell

I. "Let Go All the Ropes!"

Whenever the airship flew over a village, or whenever she flew over a lonely field on which some peasants were working, a tremendous shout of joy rose up on the air towards Count Zeppelin's miracle ship which, in the imagination of all those who saw her, suggested some supernatural creature.

– Thüringer Zeitung

I had just sat down at the terrace of a café on the Avenue du Bois de Boulogne and was enjoying an iced orangeade. Suddenly I was shaken with surprise on seeing an airship come right down in front of me. The guide-rope coiled around the legs of my chair, and M. Santos-Dumont got out. He then called for an apéritif, drank it down, got on board his airship again, and went gliding off into space. I am glad that with my own eyes I have been able to contemplate the bird-man.

—André Fagel, *L'Illustration*

Report to the King of Württemberg, 1887

If airships are to be of any real use for military purposes, it is imperative that these airships must be able to navigate against very strong air currents; they must be able to remain in the air without landing for at least twenty-four hours, so that they can perform really long reconnoitering tours. These airships must also be built so that they can carry a heavy weight of men, supplies and ammunition. These three demands would necessitate extensive balloon compartments for the gas which would be required. In other words: *large* airships will be needed.

Following are the main factors in the development of dirigible airships: the shape of the airship best suited to cut through the air must be determined; a way must be found of rising in the air without being forced to throw off ballast; a way must, equally, be discovered of descending without being forced to let out (and thus waste) quantities of gas. If it is possible to solve these problems, the importance of airships in the future will certainly be immeasurable. Not only will they become important in warfare; they will be used for civil transportation as well (airships would represent the shortest journey across mountains, across the sea, or between any two given points). They will also be used on expeditions of discovery (to the North Pole, to Central Africa).

The hull of the *U.S.S. Akron* under construction at the Goodyear-Zeppelin Airdock, 1930–31, Akron, Ohio. Courtesy of the University of Akron Library.

Through Heavens Hitherto Unsailed

In the middle of September 1898 I was ready to begin in the open air. The rumour had spread among the aeronauts of Paris, who formed the nucleus of the Aéro Club, that I was going to carry up a petroleum motor in my basket. They were sincerely disquieted by what they called my temerity, and some of them made friendly efforts to show me the permanent danger of such a motor under a balloon filled with a highly inflammable gas. They begged me instead to use the electric motor—"which is infinitely less dangerous."

I had arranged to inflate the balloon at the Jardin d'Acclimatation, where a captive balloon was already installed and furnished with everything needful daily. This gave me facilities for obtaining, at one franc per cubic metre, the 180 cubic metres (6354 cubic feet) of hydrogen which I needed.

On September 18th my first air-ship—the "Santos-Dumont No. 1," as it has since been called to distinguish it from those which followed—lay stretched out on the turf amid the trees of the beautiful Jardin d'Acclimatation, the new Zoological Garden of the west of Paris. To understand what happened I must explain the starting of spherical balloons from such places where groups of trees and other obstructions surround the open space.

When the weighing and balancing of the balloon are finished and the aeronauts have taken their place in the basket the balloon is ready to quit the ground with a certain ascensional force. Thereupon aids carry it toward an extremity of the open space in the direction from which the wind happens to be blowing, and it is there that the order: "Let go all!" is given. In this way the balloon has the entire open space to cross before reaching the trees or other obstructions which may be opposite and toward which the wind would naturally carry it. So it has space and time to rise high enough to pass over them. Moreover, the ascensional force of the balloon is regulated accordingly: it is very little if the wind be light; it is more if the wind be stronger.

I had thought that my air-ship would be able to go against the wind that was then blowing, therefore I had intended to place it for the start at precisely the other end of the open space from that which I have described—that is, downstream, and not up stream in the air current with relation to the open space surrounded by trees. I would thus move out of the open space without difficulty, having the wind against me—for under such conditions the relative speed of the air-ship ought to be the difference between its absolute speed and the velocity of the wind—and so by going against the air current I should have plenty of time to rise and pass over the trees. Evidently it would be a mistake to place the air-ship at a point suitable for an ordinary balloon without motor and propeller.

And yet it was there that I did place it, not by my own will, but by the will of the professional aeronauts who came in the crowd to be present at my experiment. In vain I explained that by placing myself "up stream" in the wind with relation to the centre of the open space I should inevitably risk precipitating the air-ship against the trees before I would have time to rise above them, the speed of my propeller being superior to that of the wind then blowing.

All was useless. The aeronauts had never seen a dirigible balloon start off. They could not admit of its starting under other conditions than those of a spherical balloon, in spite of the essential difference between the two. As I was alone against them all I had the weakness to yield.

I started off from the spot they indicated, and within a second's time I tore my air-ship against the trees, as I had feared I should do. After this deny if you can the existence of a fulcrum in the air.

This accident at least served to show the effectiveness of my motor and propeller in the air to those who doubted it before.

I did not waste time in regrets. Two days later, on September 20th, I actually started from the same open space, this time choosing my own starting-point.

I passed over the tops of the trees without mishap, and at once began sailing around them, to give on the spot a first demonstration of the air-ship to the great crowd of Parisians that had assembled. I had their sympathy and applause then, as I have ever had it since; the

Parisian public has always been a kind and enthusiastic witness of my efforts.

Under the combined action of the propeller impulse, of the steering rudder, of the displacement of the guide rope, and of the two sacks of ballast sliding backward and forward as I willed, I had the satisfaction of making my evolutions in every direction—to right and left, and up and down.

Such a result encouraged me, and, being inexperienced, I made the great mistake of mounting high in the air to 400 metres (1300 feet), an altitude that is considered nothing for a spherical balloon, but which is absurd and uselessly dangerous for an air-ship under trial.

At this height I commanded a view of all the monuments of Paris. I continued my evolutions in the direction of the Longchamps racecourse, which from that day I chose for the scene of my aerial experiments.

So long as I continued to ascend the hydrogen increased in volume as a consequence of the atmospheric depression. So by its tension the balloon was kept taut, and everything went well. It was not the same when I began descending. The air pump, which was intended to compensate the contraction of the hydrogen, was of insufficient capacity. The balloon, a long cylinder, all at once began to fold in the middle like a pocket knife, the tension of the cords became unequal, and the balloon envelope was on the point of being torn by them. At that moment I thought that all was over, the more so as the descent, which had begun, could no longer be checked by any of the usual means on board, where nothing worked.

The descent became a fall. Luckily, I was falling in the neighbourhood of the grassy turf of Bagatelle, where some big boys were flying kites. A sudden idea struck me. I cried to them to grasp the end of my guide rope, which had already touched the ground, and to run as fast as they could with it *against the wind*.

They were bright young fellows, and they grasped the idea and the rope at the same lucky instant. The effect of this help *in extremis* was immediate, and such as I had hoped. By the manœuvre we lessened the velocity of the fall, and so avoided what would have otherwise have been a bad shaking-up, to say the least.

I was saved for the first time. Thanking the brave boys, who continued aiding me to pack everything into the air-ship's basket, I finally secured a cab and took the relics back to Paris.

And now, 19th October 1901, the air-ship "Santos-Dumont No. 6," having been repaired with great celerity, I tried again for the Deutsch prize and won it.

On the day before the weather had been wretched. Nevertheless, I had sent out the necessary telegrams convoking the Commission. Through the night the weather had improved, but the atmospheric conditions at 2 o'clock in the afternoon — the hour announced for the trial — were, nevertheless, so unfavourable that of the twenty-five members composing the Commission only five made their appearance — MM. Deutsch (de la Meurthe), de Dion, Fonvielle, Besançon, and Aimé.

The Central Meteorological Bureau, consulted at this hour by telephone, reported a south-east wind blowing 6 metres per second at the altitude of the Eiffel Tower. When I consider that I was content when my first air-ship in 1898 had, in the opinion of myself and friends, been going at the rate of 7 metres per second I am still surprised at the progress realised in those three years, for I was now setting out to win a race against a time limit in a wind blowing almost as fast as the highest speed I had realised in my first air-ship.

The official start took place at 2.42 P.M. In spite of the wind striking me sidewise, with a tendency to take me to the left of the Eiffel Tower, I held my course straight to that goal. Gradually I drove the air-ship onward and upward to a height of about 10 metres above its summit. In doing this I lost some time, but secured myself against accidental contact with the Tower as much as possible.

As I passed the Tower I turned with a sudden movement of the rudder, bringing the air-ship round the Tower's lightning conductor at a distance of about 50 metres from it. The Tower was thus turned at 2.51 P.M., the distance of 5½ kilometres, *plus the turning*, being done in nine minutes.

The return trip was longer, being in the teeth of this same wind. Also, during the trip to the Tower the motor had worked fairly well. Now, after I had left it some 500 metres behind me, the motor was

Alberto Santos-Dumont passes the Eiffel Tower on his way to winning the Deutsch Prize, October 19, 1901, Paris. Courtesy of the National Air and Space Museum.

actually on the point of stopping. I had a moment of great uncertainty. I must make a quick decision. It was to abandon the steering wheel for a moment, at the risk of drifting from my course, in order to devote my attention to the carburating lever and the lever controlling the electric spark.

The motor, which had almost stopped, began to work again. I had now reached the Bois, where, by a phenomenon known to all aeronauts, the cool air from the trees began making my balloon heavier and heavier—or in true physics, smaller by condensation. By an unlucky coincidence the motor at this moment began slowing again. Thus the air-ship was descending, while its motive power was decreasing.

To correct the descent I had to throw back both guide rope and shifting weights. This caused the air-ship to point diagonally upward, so that what propeller-force remained caused it to remount continually in the air.

I was now over the crowd of the Auteuil racetrack, already with a sharp pointing upward. I heard the applause of the mighty throng, when suddenly my capricious motor started working at full speed again. The suddenly-accelerated propeller being almost under the high-pointed air-ship exaggerated the inclination, so that the applause of the crowd changed to cries of alarm. As for myself, I had no fear, being over the trees of the Bois, whose soft greenery, as I have already stated, always reassured me.

All this happened very quickly—before I had a chance to shift my weights and guide rope back to the normal horizontal positions. I was now at an altitude of 150 metres. Of course, I might have checked the diagonal mounting of the air-ship by the simple means of slowing the motor that was driving it upward; but I was racing against a time limit, and so I just went on.

I soon righted myself by shifting the guide rope and the weights forward. I mention this in detail because at the time many of my friends imagined something terrible was happening. All the same, I did not have time to bring the air-ship to a lower altitude before reaching the timekeepers in the Aéro Club's grounds—a thing I might easily have done by slowing the motor. This is why I passed so high over the judges' heads.

On my way to the Tower I never looked down on the house-tops of Paris: I navigated in a sea of white and azure, seeing nothing but the goal. On the return trip I had kept my eyes fixed on the verdure of the Bois de Boulogne and the silver streak of river where I had to cross it. Now, at my high altitude of 150 metres and with the propeller working at full power, I passed above Longchamps, crossed the Seine, and continued on at full speed over the heads of the Commission and the spectators gathered in the Aéro Club's grounds. At that moment it was eleven minutes and thirty seconds past three o'clock, making the time exactly twenty-nine minutes and thirty-one seconds.

The airship, carried by the impetus of its great speed, passed on as a racehorse passes the winning-post, as a sailing yacht passes the winning-line, as a road racing automobile continues flying past the judges who have snapped its time. Like the jockey of the racehorse, I then turned and drove myself back to the aérodrome to have my guide rope caught and be drawn down at twelve minutes forty and four-fifths seconds past three, or thirty minutes and forty seconds from the start.

I did not yet know my exact time.

I cried: "Have I won?"

And the crowd of spectators cried back to me: "Yes!"

For a while there were those who argued that my time ought to be calculated up to the moment of my second return to the aérodrome instead of to the moment when I first passed over it, returning from the Eiffel Tower. For a while, indeed, it seemed that it might be more difficult to have the prize awarded to me than it had been to win it. In the end, however, common-sense prevailed. The money of the prize, amounting in all to 125,000 francs, I did not desire to keep. I, therefore, divided it into unequal parts. The greater sum, of 75,000 francs, I handed over to the Prefect of Police of Paris to be used for the deserving poor. The balance I distributed among my employees, who had been so long with me and to whose devotion I was glad to pay this tribute.

At this same time I received another grand prize, as gratifying as it was unexpected. This was a sum of 100 contos (125,000 francs), voted to me by the Government of my own country, and accompanied by a gold medal of large size and great beauty, designed, engraved, and struck off in Brazil. Its obverse shows my humble self led by Victory and crowned with laurel by a flying figure of Renown. Above a rising sun there is engraved the line of Camoëns, altered by one word, as I adopted it to float on the long streamer of my air-ship: "Por *ceos* nunca d'antes navegados!" ["Through *heavens* hitherto unsailed," instead of *"Por mares nunca d'antes navegados"*—"O'er *seas* hitherto unsailed."] The reverse bears these words: "Being President of the Republic of the United States of Brazil, the Doctor Manoel Ferraz de Campos Salles has given order to engrave and strike this medal in homage to Alberto Santos-Dumont. 19th October 1901."

Stanley Spencer over London

Mr. Stanley Spencer travelled yesterday [September 17, 1902] in his airship from the Crystal Palace to St. Paul's Cathedral, but he did not return. Instead, he continued his northward course, which was the way the wind was blowing. [. . .]

Word had gone forth that the voyage really would take place during the afternoon, and thus by half-past three a goodly congregation of the public had assembled in the Palace ground, between the bicycle path and the polo ground. There they gazed upon the huge shed—a structure of no architectural distinction—which was known to contain the vessel upon which £4,000 and seven years' thought have been expended. Many enthusiasts were not content with an exterior view; they paid their sixpences and went inside to see the yellow monster in its stable. Everything was ready, and Mr. Spencer, cool and smiling, got upon the side of his basket-like car to deliver a short farewell oration. [. . .] Then, still smiling, he announced that he was about to start, whereupon the people first clapped their hands and then hurriedly made their exit, to the end that they might watch developments in the open air.

The gigantic doors of the building had already been opened, and in a little while the creature's yellow nose emerged. Moving on a trolley, the ship slowly passed down the gangway that was held by police, and so entered the polo ground. When it was well out in the centre of that arena the aeronaut's assistants actively bestirred themselves in removing ballast bags and adjusting cordage. A few hundreds of men and women gathered around the great swaying contrivance, other spectators looking down from neighbouring terraces and mounds. Interest grew keen when the monster broke out into hissings and gurglings, which, if unpleasant to hear, were at least a guarantee that the motor was amenable to its master. Presently the horrid noises ceased, but the adjustment of cordage still proceeded. At length everything appeared ready for a preliminary trial in leading strings, as one might say. Mr. Stanley Spencer entered the car, and made all ready there. Then he gave the word, and the airship gracefully floated up into the air. But men still held it in check with strong ropes, and they led it round the polo grounds. Something still was not quite right, so Mr. Spencer ordered a descent.

More adjustments were made, and then up the great monster rose again. But this time it got into trouble, for it rushed against the telegraph wires from the polo ground to the Palace. One wire broke. The airship was brought to earth once more, but was found to be uninjured. Then a third rise was made. This time the trail rope caught the telegraph wires and broke more of them. But Mr. Spencer cried out "Let go," and, throwing off the ropes, up he went. As he stood out clear in the air the spectators cheered him, and he turned his airship over their heads and won more cheers. Then he turned its head towards his destination, St. Paul's Cathedral, and away he went, soon being lost to sight in the mist.

But it could hardly have been out of sight of the spectators at the Crystal Palace before it came in view of a little party of anxious watchers, including three or four ladies, gathered in the Golden Gallery at the summit of St. Paul's Cathedral. From here, writes a representative of "The Daily News" who was present, the great roof and towers of the Palace stand out clearly on the horizon, and an excellent view was expected of the entire journey. At half-past three the sky was clear, and while the mist lay like a silver-grey pall upon the housetops, one could see the Palace splendidly. But by five o'clock the smoke had risen in the distance, and formed a dense cloud, through which not even the outline of the Palace was visible. The wind had strengthened slightly, but had become extremely cold at that elevation. It was a shivering task, and nearly all the party were perished, tired, and disappointed. Several were just on the point of giving up and returning to warmer quarters on terra firma. Then a cry went out, "Look, it's up!"

Eyes were strained into the mist. "Where is it? Where is it?" There, sure enough, it was, a dark speck amid the grey, looking no larger than a bowler hat. Just then the speck turned sideways, and we recognised the shape of the airship. The Cathedral clock had just before then chimed out the first quarter after five. For a minute or two the distant speck kept disappearing momentarily among the clouds, but each time it reappeared it looked larger, and we could see that it was coming straight for the Cathedral. The shivering waiters had suddenly grown warm with the excitement, and when the airship was seen to be performing graceful evolutions, turning slowly round and round, and curving this way and the other, a cheer of hearty recognition went up for the pluck of the aeronaut. We could see the propeller at work. We could see the ship answering readily to its helm. We could see the trail rope hanging below like a thread.

Down below we could also see the crowds. On Ludgate-hill the mass was so dense that there was only a narrow lane left for the traffic. On the southern and eastern pavements were similar throngs. The top of Cheapside was practically blocked, and the statue of Sir Robert Peel seemed to be addressing a meeting in opposition to Mr. Chamberlain's taxes-on-food proposals. Thousands were lined up in front of the General Post Office. But it was the same everywhere where we could get a glimpse of the pavement. Nor were the spectators only in the streets. Every roof in sight was occupied, from the British Museum down to the Tower, and the cage on top of the Monument appeared black with people. On the garden roof-playground of the St. Paul's Choirboys' School, near the Dean's house, the lads were keeping themselves and the servants warm by playing cricket, the boys batting to the bowling of the maids. Nurses could be seen at St. Bartholomew's Hospital, and at some of the drapery shops the customers had evidently gone out to see the airship, for the girls in their black gowns came trooping on to the roofs.

By half-past five the airship had arrived. It had reached St. Paul's. It had come steadily and gracefully. Now and again it pitched, as boats do at sea, but never so as to suggest danger. But it was at a great height. It appeared to be at least three times higher above the ground than we were in the golden gallery. At any rate, it was so far up that the lettering on the side could not be read with the naked eye, nor without glasses could we distinguish Mr. Spencer or tell whether he was alone. But there it was; it had come right from the Palace, and we had seen it heading for St. Paul's. Now and again it seemed to pause and turn, as if Mr. Spencer were desirous of showing that it was perfectly under his control. Now we saw him make for the Mansion

House or eastern side of the Cathedral, and by the sacred edifice he went with a cheer from the crowd below and a cheer from us in the gallery.

But it was then that came the anxious excitement. The airship had passed on without stopping. It was over Finsbury, and still it did not stop. It turned again and again. It manœuvered this way and that. But on it went. And beneath it we could see the smoke of the houses and factories going the same way. The wind was blowing both. Evidently Mr. Spencer was making a valiant fight to tack across the breeze, but the wind, though it seemed slight, was too much for him. Gradually the airship began to grow smaller and smaller to our eyes, and it never left the line of the smoke which the wind was blowing northwards. We still could see it turning, but no manœuver turned it out of the course of the wind, and away it blew as a mere old-fashioned balloon might have been blown. And then it became a speck again, and again became invisible in the distant clouds. [. . .]

After passing out of sight of St. Paul's, and finding that he could not defeat the wind, Mr. Spencer tried to descend in the grounds of the Alexandra Palace. Failing to accomplish that he continued his journey northwards. At half-past six Mr. Spencer safely descended on Mrs. Devan's estate, Trent Park, New Barnet. On the receipt of the message at Highbury announcing the descent a motor-car was dispatched to New Barnet to convey the aeronaut back to London.

"Come, take a trip in my Air-ship."

WORDS BY
REN SHIELDS.

MUSIC BY
GEORGE EVANS.

Tempo di Valse.

1. I love a sail-or, the sail-or loves me, And sails ev-'ry
2. One night, while sail-ing a-way from the crowds, We passed through the

night to my home. _____ He's not a sail-or that
milk-y white way, _____ Just i-dly sail-ing and

sails o'er the sea, Or ov-er the wild brin-y foam; _____ For
watch-ing the clouds, He asked me if I'd name the day. _____ And

he owns an air-ship and sails up on high, He's just like a
right near the dip-per I gave him my heart, The sun shines on

bird on the wing, _____ And when the shad-ows of
our hon - ey-moon, _____ We swore from each oth - er we

eve-ning draw nigh, He'll sail to-my win-dow and sing:_____
nev - er would part, And teach all the ba-bies this tune:_____

CHORUS.

Come, take a trip in my air - ship, Come, take a sail 'mong the

stars, _____ Come, have a ride a-round Ve - nus, Come, have a

spin a - round Mars. _____ No one to watch while we're kiss - ing,

No one to see while we spoon. _____ Come, take a trip in my air -

ship, And we'll vis-it the man in the moon. _____ moon. _____

Roy Knabenshue

from Chauffeur of the Skies

FIRST SUCCESSFUL DIRIGIBLE FLIGHT IN USA

For many years I heard of a man named Thomas Scott Baldwin. He had in his youth left home and joined a circus, became a trapeze and tight rope performer and was considered very good in his line. He later became interested in the balloon business. He and his brother, Sam, had a balloon factory in Quincy, Illinois; I purchased two balloons from them. However, lately Tom had worked mainly on the Pacific Coast and I had not seen him for some time. But I was sure he would want to take part in this world renowned exposition [St. Louis World's Fair, 1904].

Baldwin's advance guard, Ed Carpenter, arrived first. We met and discussed the aerial events to be performed.[. . .] Their intention was to be paid for all flights made. He asked my advice as to who to see, who had the authority to make such a contract. I introduced him to Mr. McGarvey, the Director General of Publicity for the Fair.

Carpenter quickly made a contract with the Exposition officials to make five flights, one flight per day for five days. I did not learn the figure, but assume it was to be $1,000 per flight.

And then Tom Baldwin himself arrived. His outfit consisted of a small flat trunk containing a silk balloon and netting, a small crate containing a motorcycle engine and a long crate containing the propeller shaft. These three articles were the makings of a dirigible airship—Baldwin's *California Arrow.*

Baldwin knew of my reputation as an aeronaut and soon after his arrival we had several discussions about the airship he designed and built in California. After going over the many problems to be met, we made a verbal agreement that we would work together. I was to do all the hard work, make the gas, build the propeller, the rudder, the undercarriage or framework and, in fact, I was to build and assemble the airship in addition to flying it. In payment, he was to give me one half of the net profits, after all expenses were paid. As I had nothing to lose, I accepted.

Baldwin was a typical showman, knew all the tricks of the profession, was genial and kindly and soon won the admiration and good will of everyone connected with the fair.

Assembling the Baldwin airship, the *California Arrow*, was not an easy matter. We had no blueprints, but used instead some sheets taken from the *Scientific American*, illustrating the Santos-Dumont airship. Some spruce lumber was purchased and roughed out into shape, these strips served as longerons and uprights. We used piano wire for the bracing. On being assembled we gave it a coat of aluminum paint which improved the appearance. The next step was to inflate the balloon with hydrogen gas. Using wooden casks furnished by the fair as generators, the balloon was filled to capacity. The car or framework was then placed under the balloon and the cords leading from the netting were secured to the frame. The propeller and rudder were then secured in place.

When all was declared to be shipshape, Baldwin mounted the frame, and we found that with all the gear and a two hundred foot trail rope in place, the ship would not lift him. There was a difference of about 100 pounds in our weight; I could carry about 90 pounds in sandbags as ballast.

Then came the instructions. Baldwin did not think that I knew anything about the show business, and told me I must listen to him and be guided by his advice. He told me that he did not believe Santos-Dumont had made the flights with which he had been credited, that he had tried his ship at Idora Park at Oakland, California, and that he was unable to steer the machine. Therefore, I was to start the flight, go over the big fence, shut off the motor and make a quick landing. We would then lead the ship back to the hangar and be ready for a flight on the following day. Whatever happened I must not lose the gas.

He repeated these instructions whenever we were alone, until he finally became convinced that I would do as he wished. He did not believe it was possible to make good and give an honest performance, but instead believed in faking a flight as the oldtime showmen would do if they had an airship.

Baldwin told me that he had purchased a Curtiss motorcycle from a young man in San Francisco, had a mechanic make the necessary repairs on the motor, then mount it on a frame and connect it to the propelling mechanism. The sprocket on the motor was connected to a counter shaft by a small bicycle chain, and from this counter shaft to the propeller shaft was also a small bicycle chain. On attempting to crank the motor, these chains would sometimes break, especially with motor backfire.

The propeller was made with four ash sticks in pairs, two near the bearing and the other two at the end of the shaft. These ash pieces were fitted around the shaft and held in place by two flat pieces of steel which passed through the shaft. These sticks were set at an angle of seventeen degrees, which gave the necessary pitch to the propeller. Spaced eight inches apart were two inch strips of spruce, securely fastened to the ash by wood screws and glue. Each blade was covered with a heavy grade of muslin. The whole structure was painted with several coats of aluminum paint. A very crude propeller, but it served our purpose.

Baldwin purchased some bamboo poles with which we made the rudder. It measured ten feet long by six feet wide. This structure was covered with muslin. At the king post we lashed a crossbar of bamboo from which the steering rope was attached. This rope extended from the rudder to about five feet forward of the motor, and passed through a pulley at this point. The pilot was able to steer from any point on the frame that he found he was able to keep an even keel. When completed, the ship was a very crude affair, with a motor that was anything but reliable.

The fair management looked on the proceedings with mixed interest. If it proved to be a failure, it would not be good for the fair, every delay added to the tension, but on the other hand if it proved to be a success, the fair management would be credited with producing another great first.

"When do you think you will be able to make a flight?" This question was asked a thousand times, not only by the management, but by interested patrons, some of whom had traveled considerable distance just to see an airship make a flight. The answer was always the same, "When we get the ship ready, the public will be notified in advance."

As our preparations neared completion, the public became interested and patronage increased daily. Newsmen from not only St. Louis but from out of town papers were represented at the fair. We had reporters with us daily, and the public was well informed as to our progress.

On October 24, 1904, Baldwin notified the fair officials that on the following day, weather conditions permitting, there would be a public demonstration. Newspapers carried the announcement. One printed a proposed triangular course of some twenty miles on each leg. Several thousand persons gathered at the Aeronautic Concourse to witness the demonstration.

Baldwin again walked me beyond earshot and once more repeated his instructions. He explained that if anything happened to cause the loss of the balloon full of gas, it would about ruin our prospects of making a profit on the first flight, that the only sensible thing to do would be to go over the fence and come down immediately. We would then tow the ship back and be ready for a flight on the following day.

I promised to do my best to faithfully carry out his instructions. We walked back into the hangar and made final preparations for the flight. The gasoline tank was filled, oil was added to the crankcase, steering was tested, extra knots tied in the cordage where it joined the frame, the motor was warmed up and then stopped. Finally the big doors were opened and, while the crowd cheered, we walked the ship out of the hangar and set it down on two saw-horses made for the purpose, being high enough to permit the propeller to swing clear of the ground.

Baldwin secured a four inch board and lashed it to the two lower members of the frame and told me to get up in my place and to be sure to stand on that board. The mechanic was ready to start the motor, but Baldwin started the motor himself. It started with a roar and vibrated so badly that it was difficult to remain standing on the plank or board. I shouted for him to stop the motor for it was apparent that it was out of tune or poorly timed. He did not hear me, and without warning he called to everybody to let go. And, we were off.

My troubles began. First I managed to clear the thirty foot fence by throwing overboard a sack of sand, then the ship headed straight for the dome of the Brazilian Building. By handling the rudder ropes,

I found to my surprise that the ship responded. I worried about the motor, it was putt-putting away and belching out red flames from both exhaust pipes together with black smoke, which indicated a very poor mixture. From my position on the frame, I could do nothing about it. To move forward toward the motor would cause the bow or nose to point downward which in turn would bring the ship down. I was too low or near the ground to risk it. I continued to worry.

Having missed the Brazilian Building by inches, the ship now headed for the center of the big Ferris Wheel. I was in real trouble this time. What could I do if the ship plunged into the spokes of this giant wheel. Here again I found to my delight that it was possible to steer around it. Finding I could steer and control the ship, I headed for the big Transportation Building and, after passing over it, turned toward the Aeronautic Concourse. Everything seemed to be working all right, the red flames and black smoke had disappeared. I could see the faces of the people waiting to see the finish of this flight.

I was delighted. This was to be a success after all. However, after passing the French Pavilion, the motor blew out black smoke and stopped. Now I was in real trouble, I must make a landing at once. I must not lose the gas, but the wind was blowing and I could not see any place where a landing could be made. The ship was light and immediately started to rise. I released some of the hydrogen gas and then managed to keep a level position.

I found by this time the wind had carried me to the east and going strong toward downtown St. Louis. I remembered Baldwin's instructions and was worried as to just what effect this flight would have on our relations. After what seemed to be hours, the ship passed over St. Louis and then crossed the great Mississippi River.

I finally succeeded in making a safe landing on a farm which belonged to Harry Gardner, a farmer living near East St. Louis. He was engaged to haul the ship back to the fair for a fee of ten dollars. Such lavish expenditure of money further increased the awe in which both the aeronaut and the airship had been held. After deflating the ship, Mr. Gardner hitched a team of horses to a hayrack and we loaded the outfit on it and started back for the fair. To further increase the speed of the workers who were assisting me, I promised refreshments for all when we should reach East St. Louis. This announcement and the novelty of seeing a real airship served to draw a big crowd. They followed us to East St. Louis, the men flanking the wagon like a platoon of police.

While the ship had not been injured, I was still worried as to Baldwin's attitude over the loss of the hydrogen gas. When we reached the bridge, there appeared a number of newspaper reporters seeking interviews. One of these men drew a picture of me as we progressed toward the fairgrounds and to my surprise it was a good likeness. After a long and slow ride we finally reached the grounds and were met at the gate by Baldwin, together with some of the fair officials.

I started to explain what happened and why it was necessary to do as I had done. Baldwin caught me in his arms and exclaimed, "You did just right; you followed my instructions to the letter." I was relieved to say the least. We unloaded the frame and the propeller and left them at the "Under and Over the Sea" show on the Pike with a Mr. Donovan, a friend of Baldwin, and the balance of the outfit we unloaded in the hangar. [. . .]

I was asked over and over again, "How did it feel? What was it like to be the first man in America to successfully fly in an airship?" I believe my feelings were well expressed by the *St. Louis Dispatch*, October 26, 1904, when it reported:

> I asked Knabenshue how he liked his first sail through the air. "Glorious," he said, not ecstatically, but in a hushed way, and in his face was a sort of afterglow of the glories of the hour he had spent above the earth: "I don't suppose I could make anyone feel what I felt when, for a short time, I made that airship obey every touch of my hand, when for a few splendid moments I controlled the upper world. It seemed like this to me: Life, motion, everything was untrammeled, without limitation, pathless, all mine." This young poet of aeronautics shivered a little bit and turned his coat collar up and pulled his cap down over his eyes as he sat curled up in a chair in the big cold aerodrome.

The *St. Louis Globe Democrat* reported: "KNABENSHUE'S PERIL," and quoted me as saying, "At one time a gust of contrary wind caught my airship dead in the center and tilted it up to a dangerous degree. I was forced to leave the four inch plank on which I stood and crawl out on the framework in order to right the craft. This experience, at a height of a mile, was anything but pleasant."

The interest of the schools was portrayed in the following story from the *St. Louis Globe Democrat*, October 26, 1904:

SCHOOL CHILDREN AIDED AERONAUT TO ALIGHT!
G. S. Brooks, roadmaster of the St. Louis Terminal railway, was superintending a force of men employed at work on the St. Louis Valley division of the Iron Mountain railway, southeast of East St. Louis yesterday afternoon, and saw Knabenshue alight in his airship. He stated that Knabenshue selected a corn field near the old Kahokia graveyard in which to alight. As he neared the spot he was sailing down slowly and, dropping a line to the ground, he called to some school children and their teacher, who had been watching him, and was assisted by them in bringing the ship to the ground. He landed at four o'clock. Neither Knabenshue nor the airship was hurt or damaged.

The therapeutic effects of my flight were told in a dispatch in the *St. Louis Dispatch*, December 26, 1904, captioned: SIGHT OF AIRSHIP PROVES BETTER THAN MEDICINE!

Unsuspected tonic and recuperative properties resident in an airship were developed by the flight of the Baldwin ship over the city Tuesday afternoon. These properties were manifested at Rebekah Hospital, Grand Avenue and Caroline Street.

Dr. Albert Stenier was at the hospital using all of his skill to improve the condition of the patients when the airship hove into sight. The effect on the patients was electrical. The lame, the halt and the deaf forgot their infirmities and stampeded for the open air, and even the blind groped their way after the rest, eager to be told about it by those who could see.

The airship was watched as long as it could be seen, and for quite half an hour afterward the patients were so interested in talking about what they had seen that they had no time to think of their aches and pains. The improvement in the cases of some of them seems to have endured.

In view of the evident effect wrought by the appearance of one airship over the hospital it is thought that a regular airship regiment would accomplish wonders!

Yes, I was now a famous aeronaut! I had been the first in the United States to successfully fly a dirigible. But my only thought was to do it again! To perfect the next flight! To return the ship to the starting point! I, after a good night's sleep, returned to work and began readying the dirigible for the next flight. This came two days later.

Record of flight made by the *Arrow* from the *St. Louis Republic,* October 26, 1904:

Starting point: Aeronautic Concourse, World's Fair grounds.

Finish: near Chartrand School, St. Clair County, Illinois, three miles south of East St. Louis and three and one half miles east of Mississippi River.

Distance in bee line from start to finish: eleven miles.

Distance traversed by airship approximately: fifteen miles.

Time of start: 1:52 P.M., Tuesday, October 25, 1904.

Time of finish: 3:23 P.M.

Length of time of flight: one hour and thirty-one minutes.

Average rate of speed: 10 miles hourly.

Airship: The *California Arrow,* invented by Capt. Thomas S. Baldwin.

Navigator in yesterday's voyage: A. Roy Knabenshue of Toledo, Ohio.

Length of gas bag: 52 feet.

Diameter of gas bag: 17 feet.

Capacity of gas bag: 8,000 cubic feet.

Wooden frame substructure: 40 feet long.

Weight of gasoline motor: 66 pounds.

On October 27, after advertising a flight would be made, a very large crowd assembled. Interest was tremendous, as the public was beginning to realize that the flying machine had arrived, and that it was only a question of time when it would be possible to fly from one point to another. About three o'clock we were ready and the machine was walked out of the hangar and placed on the sawhorses previously mentioned. Baldwin had secured the services of an expert to go over the motor, and it was with more confidence that we listened to the purring of the two exhausts.

Baldwin made a speech, in which he explained to the crowd that he would make a short flight, as a result of which he would issue to me further instructions. He had fastened a twenty foot rope to the frame just forward of the motor, and he told me to run along under the ship and to not let go no matter what happened. We started along the side of the hangar. With the trail rope interfering together with resistance of the rope I was holding, he could not possibly steer; the result was a broken propeller. We placed the machine back on the sawhorses and I proceeded to make repairs on the propeller. It was a piece of patchwork and to make it look better I daubed aluminum paint over the repairs. I used glue, small thin pieces of spruce held in place by soft iron wire and screws. I had something new to worry about. If this work of art managed to come off in flight, I could see where it was possible to have quite a serious accident.

After making another speech, explaining that we had learned something from the attempt he made, and that Mr. Knabenshue would now make a flight and come back to the starting point, the motor was started and he gave the word and the start was made. This time everything was under control. Every maneuver was made including circles, figure eights, diving and climbing. After circling the field several times, we landed.

The crowd was wildly enthusiastic. Some of the boys pulled me off the frame and carried me around the field on their shoulders, while Baldwin was having all he could do to hold the ship on the ground. Finally, the excitement subsided and the ship was placed in the hangar.

Baldwin and I had been living in quarters in the hangar. We now moved to Epworth League Hotel, just outside the fairgrounds. I was able to secure a hot tub bath, had a good dinner and good night's rest. The public was now thoroughly aroused. It had been demonstrated that directional flight had been accomplished and that further development along the same general design was in order. These demonstrations had dispelled the doubt and suspicions that Santos-Dumont could not fly, but it was too late to do anything about that matter. Inventors turned their attention to this new problem.

Very few books had been printed on the subject, no textbooks were available, and the beginner had to either buy his information from professional balloonists or figure it out by himself.

The next day, October 28, we repeated the exhibition but this time I made my landing on the field used by Pains Fireworks. We then carried the machine back and placed it in the big hangar. Tom explained to the crowd that this precaution was taken to avoid the risk of losing the machine. On the previous day, the men who had helped us had all they could do to hold the dirigible on the ground after I had been dragged off the frame.

Again, on the following day, October 29, we made another flight which was successful in every way. The motor seemed to respond to our hopes and ambitions and chug-chugged with little vibrations. We had the good fortune to have found a man who seemed to know about engine maintenance. I was amused at Tom when this man started to make repairs. Tom guarded the motor much as one would a watch which had been handed down as a family heirloom. When the motor was taken apart he looked as though he were suffering from pain. But our mechanic was skillful and the motor performed perfectly to everyone's great relief.

HIGH TENSION WIRES

On the last flight I had bad luck, October 30. Passing over a high tension line as the airship approached the grounds for a landing, the trail rope came in contact with the wires. There was a flash and we passed beyond the wires. I noticed a tiny flame creeping up the rope toward the frame. Hoping that an increase of speed would extinguish it, I advanced the spark on the motor, but the temperamental motor only stopped.

We were almost over our grounds, but not near anyone who could reach the rope. By dragging the rope through the trees, the branches had extinguished the blaze. The ship rose steadily and drifted with the wind. I tried several times to make a landing but found a high tension wire directly in my path. Eventually, I came down in an open pasture some twelve miles from the fair. No one was to be seen but soon several automobiles arrived. With help I succeeded in getting the motor started and then started for the exposition grounds. But the motor had become temperamental again and refused to function. Before I could make another landing we had traveled twenty miles away. It was nearing darkness and I was wondering if I should deflate when Tom arrived in a car. We then decided to tow the airship back to the grounds. I tied the trail rope to the frame in order to have two separate lines one hundred feet long. When we reached high tension or other wires, I would throw one rope over and it would be fastened to the automobile after which the other line was released and I would pull it up and be ready for more wires. We passed over many different electric power lines before arriving at the outer fence of the fair.

We hoped that our troubles were over as it seemed a simple matter now to pass over the fence and then walk the machine into the hangar. But we were mistaken. A trolley line had to be passed over. We attempted it in the dark with the aid of six men. Fortunately I had dismounted, for suddenly the machine became loose and disappeared in the darkness. Just how it had managed to get away we were not able to determine, but after some unhappy speculation about where it would go, we did the only sensible thing and went to bed and had a good night's rest. The following day we recovered the ship about twenty miles away. It had settled gently in a corn field and a farmer had tied the rope to a tree just as he would have done with a horse. [. . .]

The Lost *La Patrie*

On Saturday, November 30 [1907], after having sailed from Paris to Verdun, *La Patrie* was being employed in reconnoitering from Verdun when the engine became disabled through the mechanic's clothing catching in the gearing. It was thought the repair could be made quickly and the ship was allowed to drift before the wind. Dusk came on, however, before the work was finished and it was decided to make an immediate descent, which took place at Souhesmes.

Work on the engine was commenced the following morning and continued all day, being only completed about quarter of eight at night.

The wind had been increasing in force and by eight o'clock had assumed the proportions of a gale. It would seem that 180 men would be sufficient to hold an airship, but in an exceedingly heavy gust of wind the ship tore itself loose from the restraining ropes and sailed away to the westward. An officer tried to reach the ripping cord but was unsuccessful in the attempt.

During the night the ship sailed across France towards Saint Lo, across the English Channel and was seen over South Wales at eight o'clock the following morning. After leaving Wales, *Patrie* turned northeast, passing above Lloyd's Signal Station at Torr Head, opposite the coast of Argyllshire, at about four o'clock on Sunday evening. Later in the day the ship touched the ground near Ballysallough, County Down, Ireland. During the course of its erratic wanderings, it seems that the *Patrie* collided with a hill, and, after tearing up the ground for some little distance, finally sailed through a farmyard wall, shedding in its passage a propeller and sundry tins of oil.

Lightened by the loss of these articles, the ship "rose again and ascended into Heaven," and was last seen heading for the North Atlantic, there no doubt to travel about [. . .] until it finds a grave. [. . .]

EN DIRIGEABLE

pour PIANO
par H. DEUTSCH (de la Meurthe)

EN DIRIGEABLE

Souvenir du *"VILLE-DE-PARIS"*

1907-1908

H. DEUTSCH (DE LA MEURTHE)

CHANGEMENT DE DIRECTION

ARRÈT.—LANCEMENT DES GUIDE-ROPES

a Tempo

ATTERRISSEMENT

a Tempo

Plus lent—Maestoso. RENTRÉE AU

HANGAR

Max Reger
Lyrics translated from the German by
Friederike von Schwerin-High and Jeffrey L. High

For Zeppelin

Dedicated to His Excellence Count Ferdinand von Zeppelin

You who bravely leads mankind
to soar over rifts with pride
have triumphed, now your toils behind
you, aloft in the sky so wide,
lead us higher on your path!
to destinations afar
you German eagle, with God, God leads the way
and upwards to the stars
and upwards to the stars.

Hand set firmly on the helm,
eyes focused on the goal forever
forward you go, and never back!
Slowed perhaps, defeated never.
Like proud phoenix from the ashes rise
on up to gleaming stars of pride,
the emperor's and the empire's prize,
and upwards to the stars
and upwards to the stars.

As if at play, you forced the way,
progress itself should progress!
A way whose ultimate goal, today
we can't even venture to guess.
How to achieve the highest perfection,
that is what you've taught us.

Heavenward into the ether
your ship has proudly brought us
and upwards to the stars
and upwards to the stars.

The Flight of the LZ 4

The long-distance flight of the LZ 4, which was to last for twenty-four hours and was a condition of the purchase of the ship by the military department, was set for July 15, 1908. But when the new tug-boat *Weller* was pulling the LZ 4 out of the floating hangar, the tow-rope broke, and the southwest wind dashed the helpless airship against the walls of the hangar, damaging the propeller, the elevator rudder, and two gas-cells. The steamer *Königin Charlotte* helped rescue the injured giant, and the Imperial Commissioners departed.

The LZ 4 was repaired, and the Imperial Commission returned. The members of the Commission were Privy Councilors Hergesell and Mischke, Major Sperling of the Mechanized Division, and Captain von Jena, who later became the commander of the army airship Z 1 (LZ 3). Shortly after day-break on August 4, 1908, we took our posts on the LZ 4. Count Zeppelin piloted the ship, with Chief Engineer Dürr operating the elevator helm, and Lau and Captain Hacker at the rudder. Engineer Stahl and Baron von Bassus were with us in the aft gondola. Mechanics Laburda, Kast and myself tended the two 110-horsepower Daimler motors. When we took off, at about seven o'clock, there was no wind; but when we were under way it became sultry and close, and during the midday heat, over Strassburg, the ship ascended to a high altitude and thus lost gas. At six in the evening, over Nierstein, a cog-wheel slipped off the forward motor, and until it was replaced, the ship sank almost to the Rhine. We landed on a peaceful tributary, near Oppenheim, where a local wine-merchant gave us a bottle of fine Niersteiner which we shared with Count Zeppelin. While I repaired the damage to the forward motor, the LZ 4 was relieved of all superfluous weight, especially the gasoline tins; and Captain Hacker and Baron Bassus were sent ashore.

At 10.30 at night, the LZ 4, with the aid of a Rhine steamer and a company of Sappers, took off and continued the journey to Mainz, where we put about. Shortly afterward the foremost of the two four-

Z 4 „Echterdinger Schiff." 190

The LZ 4 and its floating hangar, 1908. Courtesy of the National Air and Space Museum.

cylinder motors went dead; a connecting-rod bearing had burned out. But we flew on with one motor and finally reached an altitude of 6,000 feet. Near Echterdingen, we made a forced landing to repair the forward motor again, and to replenish gas and gasoline.

We had been on duty for twenty-four hours without any relief and we were dead tired. The clamor of the hundreds of thousands of people in cities and villages, the steamer sirens, the ringing church-bells—all were drowned out by the deafening roar of our motors. And when the first groups of people ran toward us and spoke to us, we couldn't hear a word they said. But they understood we needed help, and they grabbed on with a will. The cable holding the bow of the ship like a bear's nose-ring was secured with a heap of earth; and not content with that, we buried a whole farm-wagon and fastened the cable to it. But even that later proved to be insufficient.

Soldiers arrived from Cannstadt and helped us arrange the ship so that it would be free to swing into the wind. From Untertürkheim, Daimler sent out a wrecking car with a portable workshop, and the damaged motor was taken out, repaired and reinstalled. Meanwhile, the news of our forced landing caused a veritable migration. By train, in carriages and automobiles, on bicycles and on foot, more than 50,000 people gathered on the field during the course of the forenoon. Count Zeppelin had gone to rest at the local hostelry at Echterdingen; the other members of the party were having their midday meal in the village. I remained in the aft gondola, the only one—as I thought—on the ship. I did not know that in the forward part of the ship, my comrade Laburda and one of the soldiers were still replenishing the water ballast.

At two in the afternoon, a storm came up, one of those savagely furious storms, like the one which caused the fire at Donaueschingen. The force of the wind overturned the airship and tossed it high in the air. The ground crew, fearing to be dragged along with it, released the tow-ropes. I saw somebody (it was a mechanic from the Daimler Works, who had been repairing the motor) leap from the forward gondola, and I ran along the catwalk as fast as I could to get to the forward gondola and pull the gas valves. My only thought was to bring the runaway airship back to earth. The individual valve-levers are placed beside each other on the control panel, and I took one in each finger and pulled with all my strength.

The gas escaped, but the ship continued to drift. The crowd faded away beneath me, and I found myself about half a mile away from the anchorage. I did not know whether the drifting ship had grazed a tree or the earth, but at any rate it seemed to me that I heard a cry of "Fire!" The airship was on an incline, with the bow sinking down; I leaned over the rail of the gondola. Within the airship envelope there was a suspiciously bright light which seemed to grow and come closer. And suddenly I knew. Fire. The airship was burning. I cannot say that I was either very frightened or prepared to die. Again, I had only one thought, and that was "watch for your chance to jump!" I released the valve knobs which I had been holding tightly in my hands, and waited for my chance to jump. But the distance to the earth was still too great, and the burning ship was being driven along at a fast speed. Fifteen thousand cubic meters of hydrogen gas were burning, and the ballonettes were bursting with our reports. The rings, supports and struts of the metal frame were glowing, bending and breaking; the envelope was being torn apart in blazing shreds; and soon the flames were eating through to the gasoline tanks. The heat was becoming unbearable; it was Hell itself in which I was burning alive.

If you ask me how long this lasted—I do not know. At such a moment, time has no meaning, and a second is longer than years or decades. There must have been a crash, the ship must have struck a tree; for suddenly I lay outside, flat on my face. Gas-cells, the envelope, and the whole net of girders crackled in livid red above me. As well as I could, I protected my head, breathing fire and trying to sit up and look around. Just then another mass caved in upon me. At such moments, one has terrific strength—I pushed the burden high, wound myself like an eel through the bent girders, slipped under the net of cloth covering me like a shroud, and I did not even feel the flames tonguing at me from all sides. I came free, stumbled to my feet and said grimly to myself, "Now, run like hell!"

My lungs were filled with smoke and I gasped for breath. Falling as much as running, I nevertheless got about a hundred feet away from the ship. When I looked back, the proud giant airship was no more; the terrifying pyre had burned itself out, and only a few weak flames rose from the stern of the smoking ruin. A man in a singed uniform leaped toward me from the wreck, ran around blindly for a few seconds, and then stopped and stared. I got to my feet. He was a soldier. 'Where did you come from?' I asked. He fought for breath, and then said, 'I was in the airship; there's someone else back there.' I looked in the direction toward which he pointed, and saw another man lying near the edge of the ruins. It was my comrade Laburda. I stumbled toward him, and with the aid of the soldier dragged the unconscious form out of danger. Blood was running in two red streams from his nose. The impact had thrown him and the soldier out of the gondola, just as it had me. But Laburda was unfortunate and was knocked unconscious.

While I was still working over him, an excited crowd of people gathered to stare with dumb horror at the pitiful jumble of ruins which, only a few minutes before, had been a triumph of human endeavor and the symbol of German aspiration. Internes, taking the injured man from my care, wanted me to go along, but I refused and only then realized that my head and hands were badly burnt. In Echterdingen, the wife of the local doctor did an expert job of bandaging me.

How did I get to Echterdingen? I walked. There weren't as many autos then as there are now. Scarcely had I been bandaged, when I was again out at the scene of the disaster. There, the Stuttgart firemen were already extinguishing the remaining flames and cleaning up the wreckage. The Stuttgart Fire Commissioner, Jacobi, an efficient Berliner, had me re-bandaged by an interne, and then took me home with him in his auto. I dined with him and slept in his guest room. On the next morning, the clean new linen on the guest bed was in such a mess from my blisters that I was ashamed to face my hosts. But I couldn't help it. I looked frightful; the blisters had swelled so much that I couldn't recognize myself when I looked into a mirror.

Once more, the internes bandaged me, and at ten o'clock in the morning I took the train to Friedrichshafen, where I recuperated before flying again.

Count Ferdinand von Zeppelin (in white cap) and Orville Wright (in bowler hat) in control car of early airship, September 1909. Courtesy of the Paul Laurence Dunbar Library, Wright State University.

Walter Wellman

Aboard the *America* over the Atlantic

It was at 8 o'clock Saturday morning, October 15, 1910, that the airship *America*, with a crew of six men aboard, set out from Atlantic City over the fog-surrounded ocean, headed for Europe. That she did not cross the ocean, but did make a memorable voyage of three days and nights, beating all records of airship navigation for distance covered and duration of voyage, is now known all over the world.

When we fared forth that foggy morning we six men of the crew — myself as commander, Melvin Vaniman as chief engineer, Louis Loud and Frederick Aubert as assistant engineers, Murray Simon as navigator and Jack Irwin, wireless operator — had very little idea of what was to happen to us or where we were likely to stop.

We knew we were going to try to reach Europe; we knew we had some sort of a chance — how good or poor a chance it was we could not calculate — to do so. We knew we were engaged in a difficult and dangerous scientific experiment and adventure, one which was the more fascinating because it was difficult and dangerous; that it was a thing worth doing for itself and what it might lead to in the progress of the arts; that it was not foolhardy because all possible precautions on a large and engineering basis had been taken to assure success and our own safety — all advancement in aerial navigation is attained at some risk; that it was not merely a sensational feat, because a high and worthy purpose lay behind it; and that like many other achievements marking man's conquest of the elements, we never could know what we could do till we tried.

Despite all the precautions our experience and foresight and study could suggest, we were not unmindful of the risks to be taken, nor of what the world has been kind enough to call the daring of our unique, unprecedented venture. But we were filled with joy to have our chance for whatever it might be worth.

My first thought was one of pride in the gallant men of my crew.

Hundreds had volunteered. Letters and cablegrams and telegrams had been sent from all parts of the world by men eager to go in the *America*—aeronauts, engineers, sailors, motor-experts, journalists, men of no vocation or fitness, cooks, scientists, army officers, wireless operators. Applications had come from England, France, Germany, Russia, Cuba, Egypt, South America, a great number from the United States.

But the men who had been chosen were well fitted for their difficult tasks, were personally known to me. Vaniman had been with me in two aerial voyages, Loud in one voyage, and were men tried and true; Aubert, the youngest man in the party, I had known for years, and felt every confidence in him; Simon had come to us from the White Star Steamship Company, where he had been one of the officers of the great steamship *Oceanic,* and his long experience, his character and our personal contact with him told us he was the man we wanted; Jack Irwin, an Australian by birth, a man who had been in the Zulu and Boer wars, of late wireless operator on the steamship *St. Louis,* and the man who had received Jack Binn's famous C.D.Q. call from the sinking *Republic,* had been chosen by the Marconi Wireless Telegraph Company from among a host of volunteers, and we never doubted he would prove to be the right man in the right place.

First, the canvas doors of the balloon house were pulled back out of the way. Then the steel sea serpent, or equilibrator, weighing nearly two tons, were carried on the backs of three-score men and thrown into the sea, a few hundred yards distant. Next the lifeboat, considerably more than a ton with its cargo, was taken out and placed upon the ground in front of the balloon house. All this time the fog was still thick; there was no wind; telegrams and telephones from the Weather Bureau at Washington, with which for days we had been in almost hourly communication, brought no news of probable change. General conditions over the Atlantic Ocean were reported favorable; local conditions were right; thanks to a little patience and watchfulness our chance had come to launch the airship without danger of accident in taking her out, one of the things which from the first we had most feared, for well did we know from experience the hazard of that operation.

Then we took her out. A hundred men grasped the leading lines placed for their use, hanging down from the sides of the balloon. The $12\frac{1}{2}$ tons of material and gas composing the ship floated in the air upon such an even balance that one could push the whole mass up or down with one hand. A few hundred weight of sand bags were thrown off, the hundred men pulled enough upon their lines to compensate the upward thrust of this buoyancy, and as the crews of men walked forward at the word of command the huge ship glided gracefully out of the house in which she had been assembled and painstakingly prepared for her long voyage. The assembled people cheered as they saw her slide out into the fog. They were amazed at her great size, her graceful proportions. A small boy cried out: "My, just see how big and long she is!"

In a few moments the lifeboat had been hooked to the steel car— the shackles and fasteners were all ready. One by one we of the crew bade good-bye to families and friends; no tears were shed by anyone, though all of us felt the seriousness of the moment. The cat was placed on board amid the applause of the on-lookers. Engineer Vaniman remained on the ground to superintend the attaching of the cables which hung the equilibrator to the airship. This done, and the last remaining sand bags cut away, he clambered to his place in the engine room, and was cheered by the crowd as he did so.

The *America* was now ready. At the order of "Let go all," the hundred men holding her slipped their lines and she rose in the air, carrying the lifeboat with her, and lifting about one-tenth of the weight of the equilibrator. A line was given to a motor-launch, to tow us out through the bay over the bar to the open sea. In a moment we lost sight of the balloon shed and the people on shore; but we could hear them cheering somewhere back there in the gloom.

Moving slowly out through the mists towed by the launch, my first thought was of the equilibrator down below. It swam easily on the surface of the water. But a pity 'twas, thought we who had laboriously and carefully made the plan of all this, that the design could not have been better carried out and fully one-half of the weight of the serpent be suspended in the air at the very start. At this moment I confess I had my first forebodings of trouble; weights had overrun; the lifeboat was double the stipulated weight; apparently almost everything else had exceeded calculations; thus the ship was overloaded in a desire to carry with us enough fuel to insure a radius of action equal to the tremendous distance which lay ahead.

OUT OVER THE ATLANTIC

So off we went to the eastward, the seven of us, including the cat. In a quarter of an hour the eight-cylinder motor was started; the propellers cut the air; the *America* vibrated, responded, moved over the water with her own power. She was a real cruiser of the air. Down below through the fog we could see the equilibrator swimming along, for all the world like a great sea serpent, its head in the air, with a tortuous foamy wake. There was a gentle breeze from the northwest. The ship was making fair headway.

We all felt the exaltation of this moment, and said little but smiled at one another. All were happy, save Kiddo, the cat, and he was still sullen with the strangeness of his garret. A strange garret indeed, perched upon a frame of steel, suspended underneath a mass of silk and cotton and rubber, lifted by a ton of hydrogen, a whirring engine disturbing the silence and moving through gray space—pioneers in navigation of the atmospheric ocean which covers the world's high sea. It was no wonder that for an hour or two Kiddo's eyes stared a trifle wildly.

But we who were conscious of the fact that no man before us had attempted what we were doing—conscious that no matter what and whom we had left behind, or what we were going to, we were the first of humankind to sail these two oceans in one with a great engineered and cunning machine, designed to conquer them both together—we should have been less than human if we had not felt a strange joy, an almost uncanny fascination. Even men of the calm, cold, practical order of minds, who calculate stresses and pressures and densities, who figure and plan and construct and experiment and work logarithms on the one hand and carburettors on the other, may have a little imagination and may be permitted an occasional moment of enthusiasm. All about me were radiant faces—all save Kiddo's, it still a bit sour with strangeness; cats have no imagination, no ken of chemistry and human nature and the history of progress; no vanity in pioneering.

After we had been out two and a half hours, the motor was stopped to try the wireless. Jack Irwin was scrouched down in his corner by his instruments in the lifeboat; the wireless receivers at his ears; over them thick woolen pads to drown out the whirr of the motor and propellers. Now there is a broad, bright grin underneath the pads. We all lean forward expectantly. He must be hearing something from shore. He waves off interruptions, then seizes paper and pencil and jots down this message from Atlantic City:

"*Wellman, Airship America:* We are getting your signals. What news?"

I dictated to Irwin the reply:

"Headed northeast. All well on board. Machinery working well. Good-bye, Wellman."

And these were the first wireless messages exchanged between a station on shore and an airship navigating the sea. One world's record had at any rate been established; and again we all felt the gladness of pioneering along the path of progress.

More messages followed. Overjoyed with this strange experience of carrying on conversation with friends and families twenty miles away from our aerial perch, I wirelessed the *London Daily Telegraph*, the *New York Times* and the *Chicago Record-Herald* that we were on our way and making good progress. Mindful of our friends at Atlantic City, I sent the following to the President of the club which had built the *America*'s shelter house—and lost money in the operation:

"*Joseph W. Salus:* Atlantic City did nobly. We are doing our best to repay your loyal support."

And in his generous enthusiasm, Mr. Salus replied:

"*Wellman, Airship America:* Great work. One of the achievements of the century. God speed to you and Vaniman. J. W. Salus."

There was Vaniman, unemotional, unimaginative, a good mechanic, and seeming to live in his machines, a part of them, and as matter of fact as they. Yet Vaniman confessed afterwards that when he realized we were well out to sea and were communicating to the shore back and forth with Signor Marconi's wizard will-o'-the-wisp whisperings, through the misty miles, tears stood in his eyes. That was indeed a triumph of mind over matter—not only the far whispers, but the tears in the eyes of a stoic like our engineer.

Now Mr. Percy Bullen, American representative of the *London Daily Telegraph*, asked me from Atlantic City through the Hertzian waves:

"From your experience up to now, do you feel confident of being able to make Europe?"

My reply was: "Just started; too early to judge the outcome."

Frankly, at that moment we had no great degree of confidence, only a hope large enough to cling to and work for. Realizing how weights were overrunning, how the symmetry and balance of the original plan was being overthrown by the exigencies of construction and equipment and the impracticability of getting contracts filled to the letter—such as the life-boat weighing double the stipulation—realizing, too, that the agreed-upon quantity of fuel could not be carried and that the equilibrator was far too much in the sea and too much of a drag upon the ship, for a fortnight or more my hope had sensibly diminished. And now, with almost stunning swiftness, came trouble with the motors; and hence the caution with which my reply to Mr. Bullen was phrased.

Motor troubles came soon enough, heaven knows. Despite all our experience with these engines, all our care and expense in fitting them up and trying them out, with the best experts we could bring over from Paris, and more than two months in which to get them in perfect order, the eight-cylinder motor never gave more than one-half its normal power. Just why, I do not know even now. It worked weakly by fits and starts. The four-cylinder Lorraine-Dietrich did a little better, but during the first ten hours was not up to its mark. My log shows many entries like these: "L.D. worked 12 minutes and stopped 40 minutes. E.N.V. ran 9 minutes and it was two hours before it started again." Engineer Vaniman and his two assistants, Loud and Aubert, worked like Trojans. They did the best they could, but that unfortunately was not good enough; motors are proverbially coy and uncertain.

This first day out, with a quiet sea and a gentle wind from the right direction, when we should have been making excellent progress on our course, we had a motor running about four hours altogether, and that at a reduced output of power. And in the afternoon the eight cylinder broke down entirely, Vaniman remarking that "It was no good and could be thrown overboard as ballast." So this day was virtually wasted. By nightfall, nearly ten hours out, we were sighted and reported by the steamer *Coamo*, about eighty miles from Atlantic City, when we should have been two hundred. It was a discouraging start, and that's the truth. Blame does not fall upon any man, but it does fall upon the pesky machines, which failed us so early, despite the fact that the plan of campaign, from the first, all factors taken into consideration—the time, distance, probable winds, speed of ship, fuel supply, everything—I had expressed in these words of elementary law: "We have two good, well-tried motors; if we can keep one or other of them going all the time, we can cross the Atlantic."

It was particularly maddening, as night came on and the gas in the balloon contracted, and the ship dropped more and more of the equilibrator into the water and came nearer and nearer to the surface of the sea, to find it necessary to throw overboard, for lightening ship, the very gasoline which should have been burned during the day in the engines and converted into so many more miles covered.

Adventures in the air? Well, we had our share. It was our lot to break another record. Not only the first to navigate the atmospheric and aqueous oceans, the first to send wireless messages from airship to shore, now we were the first to be in imminent danger of collision between a ship of the air and a ship of the sea. About eight o'clock that Saturday night a cry of alarm was raised by one of our crew; dead ahead, ghost-like in the fog, was a four-masted schooner. We were almost upon her. I called to Vaniman to stop the motor, that the *America* might swing round with the wind and cut in behind the vessel. Instead, he ran forward to warn Simon at the wheel, the window at the navigating deck not affording a very clear lookout. But the alert Simon had already seen the schooner. In a moment he threw his helm hard to starboard; the *America* responded quickly, swung round to the northward, and passed astern the stranger. We all breathed more easily as her masts slipped by.

It was a close call. From the lifeboat we looked almost straight down upon the schooner's deck, where we could see men running to and fro, but the noise of our exhaust drowned their voices. If we were astonished, what must have been the feelings of the skipper and his crew when they saw a great dark, whirring, chugging thing rise like a monster upon them out of the murky air?

We would not be Americans if we failed to have our laugh over the funny side of the affair, serious as it looked for a few moments. Vaniman came down to the lifeboat, wondering what the skipper and his helmsman were thinking and saying. "I'll wager the men on deck will not dare tell their shipmates down below what they saw on their watch. And if they do, they will be unmercifully ridiculed for spinning such tipsy yarns about seeing a regular Flying Dutchman." And we all laughed with Vaniman. But the skipper of the schooner happened to be on deck, saw the apparition in the air with his own eyes, and was not afraid to tell about it when he made port. The schooner was the *Bullard*, bound for Norfork.

"We were running in a thick mist," said Captain Sawyer, "and were tooting our fog horn. Suddenly a sound like the steady grind of an engine reached our ears, and we thought some steamer was close upon us. Just over our heads we saw a light, but we thought it was only the mast of the steamer. We never thought the airship was near us. We left Boston without hearing that Wellman had sailed, and the only thing we were thinking of was a steamer. I ran aft and tooted our fog horn, and the members of my crew ran about shouting and yelling to what they believed was a steamer, hoping that its lookout might see us in time to avoid a collision.

"There was great confusion aboard the *Bullard*. We could plainly hear the steady grind of the machinery and the whirring of the motor, but we could see nothing but the light in the air. It was dark, and there was a thick fog. The light came nearer and nearer, and members of my crew said that they could hear voices. Then out of the darkness and mist shot a big aerial phantom, as we imagined, going east, and headed directly for the *Bullard*. The thing was such a big surprise for all hands that we were knocked off our pins.

"The airship, when almost on us, rose up higher, and shot out to sea. She was probably going fifteen miles an hour. The *America* was less than a hundred feet above the sea, and the topmasts of the *Bullard* are 110 feet. Had the airship hit us, she would undoubtedly have been destroyed and probably those in her would have been killed. The miss was so close that several members of the *Bullard*'s crew declare they heard the airship scraping the topmasts as she veered off."

At dawn the practiced eyes of sailor Simon and Jack Irwin, who have sailed a lot along the transatlantic steamer lanes, detected the ripples of shoal water, or tide-rips, underneath us. They concluded we were between Nantucket Lightship and Nantucket Island, and this agreed with our rough log. An hour later we reckoned we were free of land. We had escaped the humiliation of pulling up short on the coast of New England. The broad Atlantic was opening before us.

A little later the wind freshened, and seemed to be carrying us more to the north. Alarmed, we called Vaniman—he had been asleep fifteen minutes—and started the motor again to make sure of completing our victory. At eight o'clock we felt sure of having passed well east of Nantucket, and it was high time Engineers Vaniman, Loud and Aubert should have a brief rest from their arduous labors and the red-hot exhaust pipe should get a chance to cool. The big, heavy Lorraine-Dietrich had run altogether about twelve hours with only a few minutes' stoppage, had kept the *America* from 40 to 60 degrees into the wind, and had saved the situation.

The *America* had thus given gallant proof of what she could do as a cruiser. This Sunday we were now entering upon she was to be tested in another and most severe way. Early in the morning heavy gusts from the southwest struck the ship, sending her forward at tremendous speed, causing the submerged equilibrator to pull harder and harder and bearing the *America* almost down to the sea. Once or twice the lifeboat nearly touched the crest of the waves; if it had struck it would have been torn loose from its shackles, those of us in her would have been swamped or set adrift, while the members of the crew in the car overhead would have had no craft left in which to attempt an escape should opportunity offer.

Several times we thought the end had come. So great was the danger that we frequently found it necessary to lighten the ship. More gasoline, a heavy cable and various spare articles were thrown overboard one after another. The most of this day was spent in like manner, a stiff breeze from the west-southwest pushing the *America* rapidly before it, broadside to the wind, after the motor was stopped for good.

Thus we drifted an estimated 140 miles beyond Nantucket, when the wind shifted to the west-northwest, and now we drifted toward the transatlantic steamer lanes, and wondered if we should meet a ship. So great was the hazard that the lifeboat would be torn loose in the heavier gusts we took care to put the cat up in the car, where it would be safer. But it was not a very happy cat. It had little appetite, but was finally induced to eat, and whenever we of the crew could find time to snatch a few minutes' sleep puss had a way of nestling close to the face of one of us under the blanket, there sleeping soundly. Anticipating a frightful night, and increased danger of being borne down into the sea as the gas contracted with cold and the balloon lost a part of its buoyant force, we began breaking up the E.N.V. motor preparatory to throwing it overboard piecemeal.

Throughout much of this trying Sunday, and the still more trying night which followed, things wonderful were happening, things comforting, things agonizing. The air was filled with wireless whispers. Almost constantly Irwin could hear "W," "W,"—our signal letter—repeated over and over, from shore stations and ships at sea. At last we began to get an inkling of the generous, sympathetic interest the world was showing in our adventure and fate—though I must admit we did not realize it to the full till after we had reached New York. Irwin heard Cape Cod, Siaconset, Sagonapack, the Brooklyn Navy Yard, a number of ships flashing back and forth the eager, kind query: "Any news of the *America?*" And it was hard indeed to listen to all this magic questioning, and to the replies, repeated over and over: "No news!"—to know how anxious many hearts were for our welfare, and not to be able to tell them we were alive—unable to break our silence because our apparatus could not transmit through the distance which separated us from other ships or land stations. Once, indeed, we felt awed in the presence of the strange circumstances, the mysterious forces man has harnessed. This was when, far out at sea, battling with the storm for life itself, we heard the Marconi Company had just long-distance telephoned our families at

Chalfonte, Atlantic City, that they had tried very hard but could get no news of the airship, but hoped all was well!

Through this dreadful night it became apparent enough to all of us that it was a mistake to try to sail over a stormy ocean with nearly all of our heavy equilibrator floating upon the waves and dragging the airship downward. But it was equally apparent that if the equilibrator had been employed in accordance with the original design, it would have shown itself a successful device. When only half or less than half in the sea its pull upon the airship was not strong enough to lead to any trouble. How we did curse the combination of circumstances which had made it necessary for us to attempt the voyage with so much of the serpent down in the ocean that it was a hindrance instead of a help.

Still, we were not beaten — not quite. After midnight I heard Vaniman order Loud and Aubert to throw over more gasoline — to take an axe and cut a hole in the big steel reservoir and let the precious fuel run out. Against this I protested, pointing out to Vaniman that the wind was fresh from the northwest; that it was driving us toward the Azores; that we had one good motor and some gasoline left, and could probably get more gasoline up from the equilibrator tanks as soon as the sea should become less boisterous; and that it was our duty to hold fast to all the gasoline we had and prepare to make a fight for it with the engine should the conditions change in our favor.

Vaniman made no answer, but recalled the order to jettison more gasoline. I presume he would have obeyed my instructions to start up the motor and make an effort to run to the east-southeast if the weather conditions had held any length of time. But soon the wind shifted more to the north, and then to the north-northeast and northeast, and blew more strongly. In an hour it became necessary to throw over more gasoline in order to prevent the lifeboat being torn away as it struck the waves; and as I saw the gasoline streaming down into the sea I realized that the hope of reaching Europe, or at least the Azores, was practically at an end, though we were still determined to take advantage of any opportunity that might arise for a renewal of the struggle. That opportunity never came.

This was the turning point of the voyage—this shift of the wind into the northeast. And right here I wish to record a few facts: The *America* was a splendid airship. She held gas admirably, and all the predictions that we should fail through rapid loss of hydrogen, were wide of the mark. Her structural strength was superb, as was shown in these severe tests. In all respects save over-weight and lack of buoyancy due to faulty execution of the design, and in part to the poor installation of one of the motors, she was a successful airship. Had we been able to execute the work of construction fairly close to the plans, to start with plenty of fuel, the equilibrator a reserve in the air instead of a drag in the sea, and the part of it that was in the sea at the start rapidly lifted as fuel was fast converted into miles made, the *America* could have sailed three thousand miles instead of one thousand.

Under the circumstances which did exist, one motor gone and most of the fuel poured into the sea instead of into the engines, and the wind holding strong in the northeast, it was necessary to begin to think in earnest about saving our lives. All Monday afternoon we were talking about that. The wind was driving us toward Bermuda, and inspection of our chart showed the Bermudas were the nearest land.

Since leaving Atlantic City we had not been able to get a satisfactory observation of the sun, nor of any other heavenly body, for position, on account of the thick weather. But at noon on Monday we got the sun, and with the latitude thus obtained and our dead reckoning, rough as it was, we knew approximately where we were—about four hundred miles east of the Hampton roads.

Our plan was as follows: To hold the one good motor, and all the gasoline we could, in reserve for a final struggle to reach the Bermudas or the Florida coast, meanwhile permitting the ship to drift with the wind. [. . .]

It was a serious question during this Monday afternoon if we could keep the *America* afloat during the night, as the gas cooled after the sun should set. We decided to try it, hazardous as it was—hazardous because if it should come on to blow during the night, or rain, and thus drag the airship down to the ocean, we should be compelled to launch the lifeboat, no matter what the conditions. With a high wind or rough sea that would mean disaster. And it was with most anxious eyes I watched the barometer; we were approaching the area of the cyclone we had heard by wireless was coming up the coast, and which did strike Florida a few hours later with destructive force; had the glass shown any marked drop we should have taken to the lifeboat at once for fear of running into the edge of the storm.

Irwin told me that day a regular steamer left Bermuda Monday. Taking my chart, reckoning our position and course, and also the course and probable speed of the steamer, my conclusion was we should have at least a chance to pick her up Tuesday forenoon. It is always well to be an optimist. And if we had to launch the lifeboat, and run the risk of foundering and being smashed by the steel serpent, it would be pleasant to have a steamship somewhere in the neighborhood.

This third night out, a bright, full moon brilliantly illumined the waters. Wind from the northeast, about 15 to 18 miles per hour. Warmer, and the gas did not contract as much as we had feared. Not so difficult to keep afloat. Only a little lubricant and remaining parts of the motor thrown overboard. Barring the uncertainty as to how we were to get out of the dilemma, an agreeable experience. Most of the crew slept fairly well—and heaven knows they needed it. I had had more rest, and stood watch most of the night, eyes alert for signs of a ship—which I had a belief we should find. I am not a fatalist, nor superstitious, nor anything of that sort. But I had been in so many tight corners, and always getting out of them with an approximately whole skin, that not for a moment did I doubt we should get out of this one, sometime, somehow.

That Bermuda steamship would be about right. I looked for her so intently, and at times so drowsily, my eyes began seeing things in the gleaming horizon or the gloomier depths covered by passing clouds. I saw a hundred steamers, some of them full electric lighted from stem to stern; trains of cars, rushing automobiles, tall buildings shining with lights. Then I shook myself, and saw nothing at all, only to drowse again, and have more optical delusions; then rouse, and nibble, and smoke.

We ate at all times, cold ham, ship's biscuits, tinned meats, Horlick's malted milk tablets, drank much water, and not an ounce of spirits was used on the trip. The cat ate, too; now the garret was not so strange. We were all settling down to the strange life.

But we knew, each of us, this was our last night; we could keep the *America* up during the following day, Tuesday, but when night fell again, and the sun set and the gas cooled, down she must come and into the lifeboat we must go, be the conditions for launching what they might—favorable or fatal. We had not enough ballast left for another night.

AIRSHIP AND STEAMSHIP MEET

At four-thirty Tuesday morning I thought I saw the lights of a ship; but had so often deceived myself that I looked again, long and carefully, before crying out. This time it was sure. I called to my mates; told Vaniman to get out some sort of a torch or signal; roused Irwin and all the others. Vaniman soaked some waste with gasoline, lighted it, suspended the blazing mass from a wire; the steamer changed her course—they had seen us.

Irwin tried his wireless but got no response. Then he seized the electric "blinker" and with Morse dashes and dots in flashes of light signaled to the steamer. Her officers replied in the same fashion. We told them we wanted them to stand by, prepared to help us, and they said they would do so. We asked the name of the ship; she was the *Trent*—the Bermuda steamer we had been looking for! Then Irwin signaled we had wireless aboard, and in a short time Mr. Ginsberg, the *Trent*'s operator, was got out of bed. From that on we conversed freely back and forth by wireless. The *America* kept drifting, and the *Trent* followed us, having about all she could do to keep up at her topmost speed.

Strange chance that brought these two ships together—that gave us the pleasure of establishing another record, the first rescue of an airship by a steamship. If we could not reach Europe with the *America*, it seemed the fates had conspired to make our adventure as thrilling and dramatic as if a Sardou or a Belasco had written it all out for us, and we were merely rehearsing. If the *America* had drifted a few miles faster or slower, or half a point of the compass to the right or left; if the wind had not shifted to the eastward an hour or two ear-

The *America* as seen from the deck of the rescue vessel, the steamship *Trent*, 1910.
Courtesy of the National Air and Space Museum.

lier in the morning; and if the *Trent* had not on this voyage for the
first time visited a Cuban port before starting to New York, thus be-
ing out of her regular schedule, the ship of the air and the ship of the
sea would not have come together. And in that case what would have
become of us? We have not the slightest idea.

Down came the *America* nearer and nearer the sea. We gripped the
lashings of the boat, and each of us held fast to a life-preserver. No,
Vaniman had none—and called attention to the fact; so Louis Loud
and Jack Irwin promptly gave him one of theirs and shared the other
between them, though neither is much of a swimmer. Simon and
Loud held the lines which were to release the boat at a single pull.

When the water was only four or five feet from us the word was
given, snap went the two release-hooks simultaneously, up shot the
lightened airship, down into the rough sea plumped our craft. She

almost capsized, then righted herself in a twinkling. At that instant the dreaded equilibrator hit us, bruised Irwin and Loud, and stove a hole in the forward compartment of the boat, fortunately above the waterline—probably the kind fates were eager to make sure kitty had enough air—and it was all over.

Still we were not quite out of danger. Almost before we could realize it, before we had time to unship oars and get our somewhat clumsy craft under control, the *Trent* was upon us. Her prow, rising it seemed to us as high as a church, was coming straight for us at a speed of fifteen knots. Were we to be smashed to smithereens here within ten feet of safety and after escaping all these other dangers through which we had passed? Five seconds will tell the story. She is going to smash us! No, her sharp stem hits us a glancing blow on the side, we sheer off, we are running along her port quarter. We are all right. Indeed the fates are good to us this day; thrice within as many minutes they have resolved dubious chances in our favor.

But we are not yet aboard. One more chance at least one of us must run before safety is ours. As we spin along the iron sides of the big ship the sailors on deck throw us a line. Someone on our craft sings out to catch it. We all grab. I chance to be in the middle of the group of six. We all grip the line. But they have made it fast on deck, and our lifeboat is heavy, and the ship is running fifteen knots the hour. The line sings and burns through our fingers. In some way a hitch has come into the rope; the hitch is round my right hand; the others have let go, but I can't. The line winds round my fist, draws tighter and tighter, and it flashes through my mind that one of two things is sure to happen—my fingers will go with the rope, or I shall; and what chance shall I have to get out of the sea alive, dragging captive at the end of a line trailing at fifteen knots? Of course it was only a flash; for in two seconds it was all over—and strange to say, neither happened. My fingers were not torn off—I was not dragged into the sea; only a lacerated and bruised hand, that was all. Such a day for good luck!

But this was not quite all. Just behind us the sea was boiling. We were nearing the propellers. One of our men cried out that we were lost. Were we going to be cut to pieces by those rapidly revolving blades of the ship the fates had sent to save us? Into the whirlpool we drifted, and for a moment the outcome was rather doubtful; but the motion of the waters sent us safely past the propellers. The *Trent* was running away from us. We were rolling in the trough of the sea. "That must have been our ninth escape from Davy Jones' locker," quoth sailor Simon, "told you it was a good thing to have a cat along—cats have nine lives!"

At last we were safe on board the *Trent*, where we were received with amazing kindness by Captain Down, his officers and crew, and all the passengers. Soon we were again in wireless communication with the shore, and learned of the more than generous interest and sympathy the people of the whole world had felt for us during our adventurous wandering, and for which my comrades and I feel more grateful than words can tell.

Upon a printed passenger list of the *Trent* there soon appeared this postscript:

Picked up at sea, from the Airship *America*, Oct. 18, 1910:

W. Wellman	M. Vaniman
M. Simon	L. Loud
J. Irwin	F. Aubert

The last we saw of our good airship, which had carried us, under her own power and drifting, a little more than a thousand statute miles over the sea, she was floating about 800 feet high, 375 nautical miles east of Cape Hatteras. A day or two later, in all probability, she disappeared beneath the waves; the gas-valve was tied open when we left her, and the big steel gasoline reservoir, with a capacity of 1,600 gallons, had been cut open so that the sea water could enter and sink it.

Each Power Car has a 300 H.P. Packard Motor

The Control Car
with 1000 mile
Radio Outfit

Pneumatic
Bumper

Fore
Power Cars

Observatic
by Ladder
from Keel

Fin

ere
rom

ontal
Fin

Interior of Hull, depicting relative position of Gas Bags, extent of Keel Corridor etc...

Outer Cover of Cotton
Cloth, treated with
Aluminized Dope

Metal
Cone
for
securing
Ship to
Mooring
Mast

Gas Cell

Gas Cell

Girder
construction of
sectional, triangular
Duralumin

High tension
wire bracing
throughout frame

S

Na

Detail Amidships of the Keel Corrido
(Longitudinal Section)

Water Line

Gas   Cell

II. World War I:
A Sky Dark with Airships

Clouds veiled the sea again, and the long straggling wedge of airships rising and falling as they flew seemed like a flock of strange new births in a Chaos that had neither earth nor water, but only mist and sky.

—H. G. Wells, *The War in the Air*

The Zeppelin manœuvered over the Welwyn valley for about half an hour before it came round and passed Londonwards with the nicest precision over our house along our ridge tiles. It made a magnificent noise the whole time; and not a searchlight touched it. What is hardly credible, but true, is that the sound of the Zepp's engines was so fine, and its voyage through the stars so enchanting, that I positively caught myself hoping next night that there would be another raid.

—George Bernard Shaw, a letter to Beatrice and Sidney Webb, 1916

Ernst A. Lehmann
Translated from the German by Jay Dratler

from Zeppelin

On March 17, 1915, the weather improved, and the radio repeated, "Attack on London." When I arrived at the hangar to give the order to "Ready ship," I found my men at work. My officers reported; the chief engineer tested the engines; the helmsmen checked the rudder controls and elevators; the gas valves and water ballast bags were in order; and the sailmaker used a paintbrush to retouch the camouflaging of the cover. Hydrogen hissed through the inflation tubes, the gasoline tanks were filled, and the capless bombs were hung in the release mechanism.

As soon as the airship was reported clear, I took my place in the control car while the Watch Officer remained outside to direct the launching. The sandbags, which weight down the ship, were removed, and it rose from the wooden blocks on which the bumper bags rested. The ground crew grasped the handling lines, and at the command "Airship march" they drew it out of the hangar. The Watch Officer was the last to swing aboard, and the man who substituted for him, or rather for his weight, jumped out. The ship was set against the wind and after releasing water ballast was "weighed off." Then with thundering motors it climbed up in wide curves to gain altitude and took course over Ostende to the North Sea.

The air was clear and calm and we searched in vain for a cloud behind which we could slip through the English coastal defense. Under us, on the shimmering sea, cruised enemy patrol boats; I prudently ordered the lights out. The airship became a ghostly apparition. In the control car, the only light was on the dial of the machine telegraph. The two helmsmen stood like phantoms beside the wheel. In his narrow cubicle the radio operator sat with his headset over his ears, listening to the confusion of signals and voices whispering in the infinity of space. Under our keel the end-weight of the antenna followed the airship like the spawn of a mother fish. The cold penetrated the control car through the floor and open windows. Despite two pairs of underwear, and leather jackets and helmets, we were cold. The thermos bottle was passed around, and the hot coffee stimulated us.

To pass the time while waiting, von Gemmingen and I made an inspection tour. The Watch Officer and Navigation Officer remained in the control car with the helmsmen. We climbed the smooth aluminum ladder leading to the walkway inside the ship. The headwinds blew icily between the car and the body of the ship, pressing me to the ladder, and my gloved hands involuntarily clutched tighter around the rungs. It sometimes happened that a man was overcome by vertigo and slid off, falling 8500 feet into the North Sea.

Even the walkway which extended through the entire ship was no promenade. In the darkness we made our way not so much with the aid of the self-illumined plaques marking the route as by habit and instinct. On the narrow catwalk between the rigging and the tanks, we balanced ourselves as skillfully as if we were walking in broad daylight down a wide street. Like the rest, I was wearing fur-lined shoes; and this thick footwear was not solely a protection from the cold. The hobnailed army boot might have damaged the ship's metal frame, and shoes with rubber or straw soles were therefore regulation.

Near the gas-cells, which threw shadows along the walkway like giant mushrooms in a prehistoric landscape, I heard a noise. In the light of my pocket-torch I saw the sailmaker climbing about with monkey-like dexterity. In his buttonless overalls (so that he couldn't get caught on anything) he braced himself between two gas-cells like a mountain-climber in a rock chimney. He was searching for a leak in the cover. Brush and cellon pot (fabric glue) were below him, close at hand if a bullet hole in the fabric had to be temporarily repaired. The sailmaker's duties involved great responsibility and were in themselves not without danger. Under certain circumstances he could be rendered unconscious by escaping gas almost before he knew it. Consequently, he always had an assistant or a comrade to attend him during his work.

On bombing raids I had no superfluous men aboard, and there was no such thing as relief after short watches, as in peace-time service. Thus the hammocks in the crew's quarters, which were eked out between the girders, were empty now. There was only a man relieving himself of his inner feelings on the throne-seat in the background. He jumped up in fright when he recognized me; but I smilingly motioned him back. The non-com who was the cook on board, reported in the darkness; I ordered him to give all hands a plate of soup from the aluminum pot on the fireless cooker—they could use something hot as long as the enemy was not making it hot for us. We didn't carry much in the way of provisions for they would have been superfluous—either we returned in twenty hours or we did not return at all. Our food was limited to bread, butter, ham, bacon, a few eggs, some preserves, a few bars of chocolate, and tea and coffee; we permitted ourselves a swallow of cognac only when we were back on land after a fulfilled mission.

Amidships, the narrow defile of the walkway widened out. Perpendicularly below me, the sea looked like lead. In the pale glimmer coming through the hatchway, I saw the bombs hanging in the release mechanism like rows of pears; besides explosive bombs weighing from 125 to 650 pounds, there were phosphorus bombs for igniting fires in the bombarded objectives. The safety catches were not yet off, but my Bombing Officer was already lying on his stomach, staring impatiently through the open trap-door. He was a fine fellow and in peace-time wouldn't have hurt a fly, but now he was eager to spill his murderous load overboard. We were at war, and war knows only severity toward the enemy, who repays in the same coin.

While Gemmingen discussed with the Bombing Officer the cooperation between him and the control car, I continued the inspection and descended to the aft engine car, which swayed under the airship like a celestial satellite. The car was enclosed and so crowded by the two 210-horsepower Maybach motors that the two mechanics could scarcely turn around. The noise of the motors drowned out every word, and the Chief Machinist simply raised his hand, which meant that everything was O.K. The air in this nutshell was saturated with gasoline fumes and exhaust gases. I almost choked, until I opened the outlet and let the icy air stream in. To exist for hours in this roaring devil's cauldron, where glowing heat and biting cold alternated, required a stone constitution and iron nerves. Yet it was as nothing compared to the demands made upon the mechanics when, during a battle with the enemy or the elements, the lives of the entire crew depended upon the repairing in mid-air of damages to the motor or propeller.

It is self-evident that in the narrow community of the airship, where all our fates were bound together, I was intimately acquainted with my men even beyond the line of duty. The commander on board is not solely a superior officer, he is also comrade, friend, father, doctor and spiritual adviser all in one. Thus, I was familiar with the personal lives of my crew, and knew that one had a wife and child at home, another had married young, and a third was the only son and sole support of aged parents. Emotional ties bound each one of them to life. No one wanted to die—all wanted to return after the war. Yet this longing for home did not make them cowardly or fearful in time of danger, but strengthened them ten-fold in their determination to repel the overwhelming enemy forces.

Proud of being permitted to lead such gallant men into the enemy's territory, I strolled through the marvelous structure that was our weapon and our home. In the darkness behind me, the stern, with its control and rudder fins, merged with the delicate filigree of girders. I passed the shaftway which led between two gas-cells to the back of the airship, fifty feet up. There, on the platform beside his machine-gun, hunched up in the winds created by the speed of the ship, the gunner acted as look-out and reported through the speaking-tube the instant he signaled an enemy flier. He was forbidden to shoot until he had received the order to do so. For when the ship climbed, gas escaped upward, and there was danger that a volley of gun-fire might ignite the mixture of gas and air. Consequently, there could be shooting on the platform only when the ship was not releasing gas.

It was eleven o'clock when I returned to the control car. The z xii had been cruising long enough, and now I set a direct course for England. The sharp coastline, with surf foaming against it, rose out of the dip of the horizon. And suddenly we had a queer feeling, as if our nerves were tightening in an almost joyous anticipation. Would we succeed in breaking through the chain of coastal batteries and remain unobserved or at least undamaged? Strange that we could see so little of the mainland; it couldn't possibly have been that dark. The mystery was solved when we came closer, for suddenly we were in a thick fog. The island was protecting itself from the flying invaders as it had protected itself from the invasions of enemy seamen centuries ago.

I brought the heavily laden ship as high as she would go. But at 10,000 feet the fog was just as thick. We cruised in all directions, constantly hoping to find the Thames, since the clouds are generally thinner over rivers. Finally I brought the ship down almost to the earth—in vain; the great metropolis was simply not to be found. We did arouse the furious fire of an anti-aircraft battery, which we were unable to find either. We had to owe it our reply.

In order not to waste the entire night in fruitless searching, we turned and steered for Calais. Much to our surprise, the weather conditions there were actually ideal for the testing of our observation basket under fire. The clouds were 4000 feet high, and the air beneath them was clear as crystal. We could see the lights of Calais from miles away, and we prepared to attack. Gemmingen and I had a friendly quarrel because both of us wanted to get into the observation basket. Then Gemmingen pointed out that he was assigned to the airship as General Staff Officer and Observer, whereas I, the commander, was obliged to remain in the control car. I had to admit that he was right.

Before we reached Calais, we throttled the motors so that they made the least possible noise while still permitting us to maneuver. The ship dove into the clouds, and Gemmingen was lowered 2500 feet in the observation car. In the infinity of space he was suspended like a disembodied ghost. But as events were to prove, he was a dangerous ghost. When we arrived over the city, the observer hung 2500 feet above it and had a clear view, whereas his tiny gondola was invisible from below. The garrison of the fort heard the sound of our motors, and all the light artillery began firing in the direction from which the noise seemed to come. But only once did a salvo come close enough for us to hear the crash of the exploding shells. When we leaned out of the car, we saw nothing but darkness and fog, but Gemmingen directed us by telephone and set the course by compass. Following his instructions, we circled over the fort for forty-five minutes, dropping small bombs here and larger ones there on the railroad station, the warehouses, the munitions dumps and other buildings.

From time to time we noticed large oval spots on the clouds; they were the searchlights gleaming as through an outspread tablecloth.

Later we learned that a panic broke out in Calais not only as a result of the air attack, but because the airship remained invisible. There was a great deal of theorizing as to how we had succeeded in concealing ourselves. They suspected a system of mirrors and colors, although science had already proven that to be impossible. At any rate, the authorities arrested a few innocent inhabitants who had been outside the city limits with their bicycles on that night. They were accused of having signalled us with their bicycle lamps.

Back from our raid, I had brought the z XII down to 400 feet and was weighing off; that is, I had stopped the motors in order to leave the ship to its own buoyancy. Our forward motion had ceased, the elevator helmsman reported that we were descending slowly, and I was just about to start the motors again when I suddenly saw a great black smokestack looming against the sky. The weather had changed, the barometer had fallen more than ten millimeters in less than twelve hours, and the altitude gauge had indicated 325 feet too many. Before we could drop ballast, the ship touched ground. It fell on a railroad track between two factories in the vicinity of our landing-field. The forward gondola came down on a foot-bridge and the rear portion of the ship squatted on the rails. Part of the steering apparatus was torn off by a telegraph pole. I jumped out, inspected the damage and sent out a man to stop all trains. After we had moored the z XII to a number of telegraph poles, we waited for daylight and then dragged the limping giant back into its hangar, where it was hospitalized for the next fourteen days.

Apparently, we were due for a streak of bad luck during this time, for no sooner was my ship in order again than it suffered a second accident. Once more we had started for a raid on London when we struck heavy rains at night over the North Sea. The rain streamed from the hull and encumbered the ship to such an extent that the execution of our plan was out of the question. In order not to bring our bombs back home again, I took course for Dunkirk and emptied one and a half tons of explosives over the fort, which in turn plastered the air with shrapnel. Suddenly, the ship quivered, there was a crash, and immediately thereafter the crew in the aft motor gondola telephoned that the starboard propeller had disappeared. A large tear in the outer cover and a smaller one in the under side of a gas-cell betrayed the course of the propeller which had evidently been struck by a splinter. We made for home, somewhat downcast, because we had once again failed to reach our real goal.

But some of my comrades had more luck with their raid on Paris than we had with ours against London. On March 20, 1915, the commanders of the army airships z x, lz 35, and sl 2 received orders to attack the French capital on the following night. By blinking their code names, German searchlights at Douai, Cambrai, Noyon and other places served as directional beacons. The wooden sl 2, built by Professor Schütte at the Lanz works, was struck on the outward journey over the trenches and therefore dropped its bombs over the French Headquarters at Compiègne and returned to its hangar. The other two airships continued their raid on the metropolis.

Paris had been warned. Its searchlights played in all directions, and a battery to the south fired furiously at a cloud which, in the gleam of the searchlight, they mistook for an airship. For reasons best known to themselves, the French left their capital brightly illuminated, in sharp contrast to London, which always lay in darkness. My comrades could clearly see the fire from the muzzles of the heavy guns in the forts. Most of their shells fell back into the city again, and some of them struck the government quarter, where they caused considerable damage. Even the "Archie" was a failure, its shells bursting far beneath the German airships. As Commander Horn of the z x told me, he reached the French capital fighting strong head-winds and, at an altitude of only 8000 feet, cruised around for half an hour in order to drop his bombs carefully and accurately. Even the Reuter newspaper agency was obliged to acknowledge the German success, and reported that a large munitions factory had been hit. "Half of the factory operating at the time was blown to bits. The rest of it looked as if it had been struck by a cyclone. An enormous hole in the earth was filled with beams, girders and stone débris." A large power house was destroyed in the same manner.

The lz 35 likewise reached Paris, bombarded it and, upon leaving the city, was followed by motorized units of anti-aircraft guns and searchlights. Commander Masius shook off the pursuers by altering his course over the forests north of Paris. When the airship crossed the frontier it was again fired upon, but despite hundreds of holes in its outer cover, returned home safely.

The Z X was less fortunate on its homeward journey. "Dawn broke just as we were passing the front near Noyon," Captain Horn relates. "The French were waiting for us. Although we flew as high as we could, nevertheless, at an altitude of 10,000 feet, the Z X was struck by two full salvos from a battery. Shells and shrapnel burst around us, and their splinters tore through two or three cells simultaneously. A whole shell went through the ship, and two shrapnel shells missed the control car by inches.

"We escaped behind our own lines by speeding away. German planes convoyed us in case enemy fliers appeared, but the latter didn't even take off, not wanting to risk getting into the hail of shells. The Chief Engineer, who made the rounds with two mechanics, reported that no less than five cells were rapidly losing gas, and the elevator helmsman supplemented this news with the information that the Z X was losing more than five feet per second. I brought the ship down to 4,000 feet in order that the buoyant gas would be forced upward, where the cells were not so full of holes. We lightened the ship by throwing machine-guns, gasoline tanks, oil reserve tins, tools and equipment overboard. Our coats and shoes followed. And when nothing else seemed to help, we resigned ourselves to the inevitable and brought the leaking ship to an emergency landing in a field near St. Quentin, without injury to the crew."

Despite his misfortune, I envied Captain Horn, for he had been able to carry out his mission. On my third foray against England I got only as far as Harwich, where I emptied my load of explosives. Two days later the LZ 38 was over London, thus being the first airship to bombard the capital of the British Empire.

Victor Léon
Lyrics translated from the German by
Friederike von Schwerin-High and Jeffrey L. High

The Zeppelin Polka

from the musical I Traded Gold for Iron

Zeppelin, that is a man
who is second to none,
leads our flight toward victory
before the war's begun!

He soars high over everyone,
below him rages their fighting!
Buzz, a little bomb sails down
just like a flash of lightning!

And when the enemy fires back
laughs back our Zeppelin!
This little bomb brings fond regards
from Vienna and Berlin!

In Paris, people shake all over
in terror as they wait.
The count prefers to come at night,
expect him at half past eight!

Nothing is as sure as this,
yet, who would have dared to say!
The count flies air raids over Paris
and does so every day.

He commands the airforce might
like no one ever saw!
Leads Germany to a new height
and with her Austria!

A little bird comes flying by
and its name is Zeppe-Zeppelin!
A little bomb is in the beak
of this Zeppe-Zeppe-Zeppelin!

O how much they'd like to snatch
this Zeppe-Zeppe-Zeppelin!
from the sky, oh what a catch,
but snails, you'll never fell him!

August Seim
Translated from the German by Claud W. Sykes

The Rigger Tells a Tale

Every airship carries a rigger. His duties are to look after the gas-bags, but he must also be able to steer, as he has to relieve the men at the lateral and elevating controls. He must also take his turn at the look-out.

You know, the look-out man had a peculiar job. You sat up there all alone on the forward platform, for hours at a stretch, for a whole day perhaps, and all the time it was brutally cold. We generally wore thick woolen underwear, then our blue naval kit, then leather overalls, and on top of everything a fur overcoat. Naturally we had thick gloves as well, made of leather and lined with sheep's wool. We also wore thick, big felt overshoes over the ordinary boots we used in the gondola. In addition to our thick helmets we had scarves and goggles; round our necks hung our binoculars and the Dräger oxygen apparatus. Thus muffled up, we squatted down by the machine-gun on the platform. I was often up there when the temperature was 30 or 35 degrees below zero.

It was a feat in itself to climb up in all our thick clothing through the narrow shaft that led from the catwalk to the platform. One sat up there, with eyes bloodshot from frost and strain, and used a kind of telegraphic instrument connected up with the control-car; there was also a speaking tube through which one could communicate. These often provided the only intercourse that you had with any living soul during the whole trip, and not infrequently you found you had no time to go down for a bite of food and a drink from your thermos flask. And it must be remembered that a voyage generally lasted from 25 to 30 hours.

I have a clear recollection of one such trip in which I did not leave the platform for a second from the moment I climbed up on to it in Tondern until we were back there. That was on the L.22, and there was only one means of "refreshing" yourself; when the gas from the bags (which is colder than the air) blew off and evaporated, you sat in its horrible icy current for a few minutes. After that the air round you felt as warm as a hothouse, although the temperature was 30 degrees below zero! [. . .]

In spite of the trouble Germany was having with her food supplies at that time, we were fairly well fed when we were sent out on a trip that was likely to prove a strain on us. We got sausages, good butter, thermos flasks containing an extra strong brew of coffee, plenty of bread, chocolate, and 50 grammes of rum or brandy per man. We were forbidden to open our alcohol flasks until we reached a height of 3,000 metres, but, of course, we often did so. Then if the ship never went higher than 3,000 metres during the whole voyage, there was trouble ahead, for when we were in port again the commander made us hand over full flasks. Thank heavens, he never tasted the contents, which in such cases were mainly water.

We had several peculiar and very practical kinds of tinned foods, which might be described as chemical and gastronomical miracles. These were tins containing hashes and stews which were heated up by a certain chemical process as soon as you opened them. We were not allowed to cook anything on board on account of the danger from inflammable gas, and for the same reason I was forbidden to fire my machine gun on the platform just when and where I pleased. I had first to report to the control-car, so that the men down there could prevent the ship from rising up into the mantle of inflammable gases while I was firing.

When the trip was uneventful or when we were out on a mere reconnaissance affair, I was in charge of the whole commissariat. If we were likely to attack any objective, I had to get the bombs ready for action as soon as we had left the German coastline behind us. This was simply a matter of turning their ignition pins round.

But the rigger had his hardest times when we were sailing over England and the airmen were buzzing round us or the anti-aircraft batteries were throwing up shells and shrapnels by the thousand. On such occasions it was his job to climb about among the ship's wires; if a bag was hit and the puncture was anywhere within his reach, he had to patch it up again. He patched away with fingers that were often frozen stiffer than our bread and butter; his pot of cellon and his brushes were, in fact, as important on board as the ship's engines themselves.

When at last we got home safe and sound, it did not always mean that we brought the ship back in an undamaged condition. We often found hundreds of shot-holes in the envelope and bags, in which case I had to spend some seven or eight hours perhaps wandering round the ship with my cellon pot while the others were resting from their labours. As a matter of fact there was a regulation to the effect that when the ship reached port the rigger had to remain on board for several hours and supervise the refilling of the bag by the shed staff. But they knew their job so well and had so many experts among them that there were occasions when one could clear off and roll into bed. Never at any time of my life have I fallen into such deep and dreamless sleep as in those four years of war. In the daytime when you were awake— very wide awake in fact—you might have dreams or visions of the spectral glare of the English searchlights on squally nights or of other experiences, the horrors of which you could not get out of your head—but never at night.

There was one trip in the L.42, commanded by Captain Dietrich, which I shall never forget. I had four years of active service in five different ships, but that was the only time that I thought that it was really all up with me.

It happened during a voyage to England in the May of 1916. We ran into trouble while we were over the North Sea on the outward trip, for somewhere on the ship there was a valve which had not been properly closed, and consequently its bag had lost gas. My friend, Signalling Petty Officer Hellbach, and I had to go up to the platform and crawl along the ship's envelope to find that valve, clear it of ice and close it. At a height of 2,000 metres, with a terrific wind howling round us, we had hard work to hold on with our left hands to the thin wires that enclosed the envelope. With our right hands we made slight incisions in the envelope to provide footholds. It made me feel quite sick; if we had lost our holds for a second, we should have slid off to our deaths. But luck was with us; we shut the valve and climbed down some 50 or 60 metres to the platform without an accident.

When we were on the way back from England, the sky was cloudy and full of rain. Thunder-clouds collected above us, and soon we were in the middle of forked flashes and ear-splitting roars. I was sitting on the platform; Muny, the helmsman, brought me a message that I was to find out the direction from which the storm was coming. At that very moment a flash of lightning struck the platform, and I could tell quite plainly that it had hit something just over my head. As a matter of fact the flash went into our 12 centimetre dummy gun. We were the only German airship that had one of these contrivances, and we could imitate the flash from a real gun by switching on an electric light at its mouth. We often laughed about our "gun," and we thought that it might manage to scare off an English airman or two. That was all we ever expected of it.

But that lightning flash went right into the dummy gun and chased about the ship in the form of an electrical current. It looked a bad business for any tools and fittings in the catwalk that were not "earthed." In moments such as those the stoutest heart begins to quake, for the ship was so charged with electricity that sparks crackled on my fur coat and cap. But all went well, and we sailed our boat home at a height of 200 metres because the storm prevented us from climbing higher. But we were all rather quiet, and our faces were white. At last we managed to get out of that storm somewhere round about Skagen.

They had given us up in Nordholz, but we sent them a wireless message to say that we were still alive, whereupon they opened the big revolving shed for us. When I examined the ship afterwards, I found a number of holes on the top surface of the envelope. This part of the envelope must have been red hot, as well as all the ribs and bracing wires, but the bags remained intact. It was a lucky thing for us that no gas escaped.

After a long examination we found the place where the lightning went out of the ship—along the propeller of the port engine.

Anonymous

Fly, Zeppelin: A Children's Song

Fly, Zeppelin,
Help us in the war,
Fly to England,
England will be destroyed by fire,
Fly, Zeppelin!

Raids on London

AUGUST, 1915

As the sun sank in the west, we were still a considerable distance out over the North Sea. Below us it was rapidly getting dark, but it was still light up where we were. Off to one side another Zeppelin was visible in the waning light against the clear sky, gliding majestically through the air. A low, mist-like fog hung over the spot in the distance where England was. The stars came out. It grew colder. We took another pull at our thermos bottles and ate something. As we neared the coast I set the elevating planes to go still higher, in order that our motors might not disclose our presence too soon. The men went to the guns which fight off fliers should we be attacked, and the others each to his post. It was a cold, clear night, with no moon—one of those nights when the distances of objects, in looking toward the sky are illusive, and it is difficult to get the range on a rapidly moving object, while our instruments tell us exactly how high we are.

The mist disappeared. Off in the distance we could see the Thames River, which pointed the way to London. It was an indestructible guide-post and a sure road to the great city. The English can darken London as much as they want; they can never eradicate or cover up the Thames. It is our great orientation point from which we can always get our bearings. That doesn't mean that we always come up along the Thames, by any means. London was darkened, but sufficiently lighted on this night so that I saw the reflected glow on the sky sixty kilometers (37 miles) away shortly before 10 o'clock.

Soon the city was outlined, still and silent below in the distance. Dark spots stood out from blue lights in well-lit portions. The residence sections were not much darkened. It was the dark spots I was after, and bore down on them, as they marked the city. There was no sign of life, except in the distance—the movement and the light of what were probably railroad-trains. All seemed very quiet, no noises ascended from below to penetrate the sputtering motors and whir-ring propellers.

Then, in the twinkling of an eye, all this changed. A sudden flash and a narrow band of brilliant light reached out from below and be-gan to feel around the sky; then a second, third, fourth, fifth, and soon more than a score of criss-crossing ribbons ascended. From the Zep-pelin it looked as if the city had suddenly come to life and was wav-ing its arms around the sky, handing out feelers for the danger that threatened it, but our deeper impression was that they were tentacles seeking to drag us to destruction. First one, then another and another of those ribbons, shooting out from glaring search-lights picked us up and then from below came an ominous sound that deadened the noise of motors and propellers, little red flashes and short bursts of fire, which stood out prominently against the black background. From north and south, from right and left, they appeared and following the flashes rolled up from below the sound of guns.

It was a beautiful and impressive but fleeting picture as seen from above, and probably no less interesting from below, with the grayish dim outlines of the Zeppelins gliding through, wavering ribbons of light and shrapnel cloudlets which hung in the sky, with constant red flashes of many guns from coal-dark sections. At any moment we might be plunged below in a shapeless mass of wreckage. When the first search-lights pick you up and you see the first flash of guns from below, your nerves get a little shock, but then you steady down and put your mind on what you are there for. I picked out St. Paul's and, with that as a point of orientation, laid a course for the Bank of England. There was a big search-light in the immediate vicinity of St. Paul's and a battery of guns under cover of the church, as I could plainly see from the flashes as they belched shrapnel at us. Altho we had been fired upon from all sides, we had not yet dropt a bomb.

When we were above the Bank of England, I shouted through the speaking tube connecting me with my lieutenant at the firing appa-ratus: "Fire slowly!" Mingling with the dim thunder and the vivid flash of guns below, came explosions and bursting flames from our bombs. I soon observed flames bursting forth in several places. Over Holborn Viaduct and the vicinity of Holborn Station we dropt several bombs. From the Bank of England to the Tower is a short distance. I tried to hit London Bridge, and believe I was successful,—to what extent in damage I could not determine. Flashes from the Tower showed that the guns placed there were keeping up a lively fire. Maneuvering and arriving directly over Liverpool Street Station, I shouted "Rapid fire" through the tube and the bombs rained down. There was a succession of detonations and bursts of fire, and I could see that we had hit well, and apparently caused great damage. Flames burst forth in several places in that vicinity.

Having dropt all the bombs, I turned for a dash home. We had not been hit. Several times I leaned out and looked up and back at the dark outlines of my Zeppelin, but she had no holes in her gray sides. Ascending and then descending until we found a favorable wind current, we made a quick return. The main attack was made from 10.50 to 11 P.M. It lasted just ten minutes.

SEPTEMBER 25, 1916

After nightfall we flew over the English coast, the seven older ships turning northward, the three new naval airships taking course along the coast for the southern districts of London. The thermometer showed twenty-six degrees (Fahrenheit); pretty low for the crew of a military airship lacking conveniences, but welcome despite that. For with every degree the thermometer fell, the ship gained in climbing ability. On the upper platform, the machine-gunners had taken their posts and were keeping a sharp look-out for enemy fliers. In the darkness, the three naval airships lost sight of each other, and each was left to its own resources to act as an independent unit. From time to time I told my men what cities we were over, and each man marked the course on his map of England.

The minutes stretched into hours. My Watch Officer reported a searchlight to the stern; it was evidently newly installed. I marked the discovery on my map and flashed the news out into the fog. Shortly thereafter my Radio Officer intercepted an English wireless message warning London of our approach. The alarm was repeated by a number of stations. The effect was instantaneous. All the villages below us were immediately darkened, and the beams of huge searchlights shot upward to explore the sky. One of the searchlights, further away than the others, caught us. A series of thunderclaps from close by revealed an anti-aircraft battery. The L 31 banked sharply, the rays of the searchlight slid off her, and, although the "Archie" continued to fire, the prey escaped.

At midnight, the three Zeppelins reached the city of London from different directions. The English could darken the metropolis as much as they liked, but they couldn't conceal the Thames. They even placed false streetlights in Hyde Park and similarly marked out the whole city-districts on the outskirts. But the airship officers were not deceived; the course of the Thames betrayed the ruse.

I prepared for the attack. Almost the entire available water ballast was released in order to bring the L 31 as high as possible. A tug on a wire from the control car opened the sliding panels under the ship, where the bombs hung suspended side by side. The Watch Officer reported everything ready; the motors were running full speed ahead. In the dark sky, the searchlights crossed like bared swords.

My own experience—I was over London for the fifth time—had taught me that the capital had a weaker defense in the south than in the north and northeast. So I made a wide circle in order to come from the south and leave the city by the north. When, half an hour after midnight, we crossed the Croydon defense zone, the L 31 was caught in the merciless beam of a searchlight. But we outwitted the enemy. We dropped parachute flares, whose bright light made it temporarily impossible for the defenders to see the airship, and, in addition, confused them because they mistook the flares for the signals of an English flier. In such a case, the flares meant "Cease firing." At any rate, we had soon disappeared into the darkness again and we received no more fire until we began to bomb the city. But even then the searchlights were unable to find us. The L 31 laid a line of explosive and incendiary bombs right across London without suffering the slightest damage. This is only to be explained by the fact that the other two Zeppelins drew the entire attention upon themselves.

Suddenly, the sky burst into fire as if a stroke of lightning had split it apart. The L 32, commanded by Naval-Lieutenant Peterson, who was over England for the eleventh time, was overtaken by Fate. Peterson had described a narrower curve than we and crossed the Thames further east, where the defense was stronger. An English combat-squadron had climbed over the L 32 and sent phosphorus bullets into its envelope. We in the L 31 saw the ship catch fire. First the bow burned, and then the flames tongued over the whole envelope. The aft gondola broke off, and the wing cars followed. For eighteen terrible seconds the blazing ball hung like a fateful planet in the sky; then it burst asunder. A glowing mass with a tail of whirling flames fell like a comet on Billerichy, east of London.

Millions of Englishmen witnessed the catastrophe, for the blaze was visible all over London and far into the countryside. The Britons, apparently so even-tempered and composed, broke out into frenzied cheers and danced like mad in the darkened streets. The ships on the Thames sounded their sirens. It was one o'clock in the morning, and noisier than on New Year's Eve.

Meanwhile, in Essex, at the scene of the crash, the fire department was attempting to recover the bodies and extinguish the flames of the airship, part of which hung in some trees. Two hundred yards away, covered by his grey army coat, lay the commander of the airship, Lieutenant Peterson. He must have jumped or fallen from the control car. The enemy was generous enough to accord him, too, a funeral with military honors.

The third ship of our naval trio, the L 33, under Lieutenant-Commander Böcker, had approached from the east and hovered over London parallel to the Thames. Hundreds of guns opened fire at it; but in the midst of a hail of bursting shells, Böcker steadfastly followed his course. Now, his bombs were striking. Great fires sprang up under the airships and covered the city with a cloud of smoke that obscured the rays of the searchlights. Another searchlight groped through the smoke and illuminated the control car. Flaming incendiary rockets hissed by on all sides and the shells kept bursting closer and closer.

But the L 33 continued on its way. Over the eastern industrial quarter of the city, Böcker dropped the rest of his bombs. Factories blew up into the air, and flames leaped up to complete the work of destruction. Then a thin layer of clouds came to the aid of the hard-pressed ship. When the L 33 turned homeward, a narrow line of fire marked its pathway over the city. But the crew had no time to look backward, for an inspection revealed that the gas-cells were leaking.

Böcker sent every available man inside the ship to repair the damage as well as they could; meanwhile, all unnecessary weight was thrown overboard. But, while it was still within range of the British guns, the airship continued to sink down, the few cells that remained unharmed scarcely sufficing to keep it aloft. After intense effort, the L 33 left the English coast at half past one in the morning and began to struggle home. But soon Böcker was obliged to wireless that he could not even reach Holland. He determined to turn around and land somewhere in England. A few miles from Colchester he set the L 33 down in an open field, all twenty-two of the men jumped out and one of the officers shot Very lights into the hull. Despite every effort, however, the wreck could not be ignited, so that it remained practically undamaged in all vital parts.

from The World Crisis

When the war began the whole of the military aeroplanes went to France at once with the Expeditionary Force, and not a single squadron or even an effective machine remained to guard British vulnerable points from German aerial attack. The Admiralty was, however, found provided with a respectable force of its own which immediately took over the protection of our dockyards and patrolled our shores in connection with the coast watch.

As the Germans overran Belgium and all the Channel ports were exposed, the danger of air attacks upon Great Britain became most serious and real. Zeppelins had already cruised over Antwerp, and it was known that London was in range of the Zeppelin sheds at Düsseldorf and Cologne. To meet this danger there was nothing except the naval aeroplanes the Admiralty had been able to scrape and smuggle together. On September 3 Lord Kitchener asked me in Cabinet whether I would accept, on behalf of the Admiralty, the responsibility for the aerial defence of Great Britain, as the War Office had no means of discharging it. I thereupon undertook to do what was possible with the wholly inadequate resources which were available. There were neither anti-aircraft guns nor searchlights, and though a few improvisations had been made, nearly a year must elapse before the efficient supplies necessary could be forthcoming. Meanwhile at any moment half a dozen Zeppelins might arrive to bomb London or, what was more serious, Chatham, Woolwich or Portsmouth.

I rated the Zeppelin much lower as a weapon of war than almost any one else. I believed that this enormous bladder of combustible and explosive gas would prove to be easily destructible. I was sure the fighting aeroplane, rising lightly laden from its own base, armed with incendiary bullets, would harry, rout and burn these gaseous monsters. I had proclaimed this opinion to the House of Commons in 1913, using the often-quoted simile of the hornets.

I therefore did everything in my power in the years before the war to restrict expenditure upon airships and to concentrate our narrow and stinted resources upon aeroplanes. I confined the naval construction of airships to purely experimental limits, and in April, 1915, when the slow progress and inferior quality of our only rigid experimental airship were manifest, I gave orders that it should be scrapped, the plant broken up and the labour and material devoted to increasing the output of aeroplanes. Had I had my way, no airships would have been built by Great Britain during the war (except the little "Blimps" for teasing submarines). After I left the Admiralty this policy was reversed, and forty millions of money were squandered by successive Boards in building British Zeppelins, not one of which on any occasion ever rendered any effective fighting service. Meanwhile the alternative policy of equipping the Fleet with aerial observation by flying aeroplanes off warships or off properly constructed carriers, lagged pitifully, with the result that at the Battle of Jutland we had no British airships and only one aeroplane in the air.

The hornet theory, at one time so fiercely derided, was, of course, ultimately vindicated by the war. Zeppelins were clawed down in flames from the sky over both land and sea by aeroplanes until they did not dare to come any more. The aeroplane was the means by which the Zeppelin menace was destroyed, and it was virtually the only means, apart from weather and their own weakness, by which Zeppelins were ever destroyed.

F. L. Mayhew

Report from Royal Engineers

Our main job was to keep the searchlights in good order—because Zeppelin raids weren't at all frequent. There was always the possibility, but as a rule weather conditions were so abnormal that the Zeppelins couldn't operate. When the alarm came I was lucky enough to be the operator and to pick up the Zeppelin. It's an extraordinary sight! A Zeppelin in a searchlight beam looks just like a goldfish in a bowl and one could follow it quite easily. The gun was a thirteen-pounder mounted on a three-ton Daimler lorry and it could fire to about sixty degrees. After that, the angle would be so steep that the recoil would have knocked the bottom of the lorry out. On this particular occasion, after holding the Zeppelin for a few minutes, the gun fired four or five rounds and then the angle got too steep for further gunfire so we were out of action and we had to shut down.

To "shut down" we used to use a copper lid to cover up the beams, but the lamps remained lit under it and a little later the guns thought they should be in action again, so we opened out. Quite by chance I'd sort of mentally followed the Zeppelin and, when we opened out, I was able to pick it up straightaway. But we scored no hits and we had to pass the target on to some other lights.

Mrs. Holcombe Ingleby

from A Letter to Her Son, August 1915

I was here alone with Mrs Lewis and Skinner the night of the raid. It was a most thrilling and wonderful sight. I was dead tired but hardly had I got to bed when I was roused by the sound of an aircraft and the rushing of motors a few minutes after so I turned out of bed and looking up saw just above us 2 Zepps. The search lights were on them and they looked as if they were among the stars. They were up very high and like cigar shaped constellations they kept pulling away from the search lights only to be found out and caught again. It was lovely and I ran upstairs from where I had a lovely view. Then the Guns began and the whole place was full of smoke but not much where I was. It all made an infernal row and all the time I felt as in a dream. Can this be London? The wonderful part of it was that no one seemed frightened, the omnibuses were going past just as usual only there were quantities of motors rushing about and a great many people in the streets.

D. H. Lawrence

from A Letter to Lady Ottoline Morrell, September 9, 1915

Last night when we were coming home the guns broke out, and there was a noise of bombs. Then we saw the Zeppelin above us, just ahead, amid a gleaming of clouds: high up, like a bright golden finger, quite small, among a fragile incandescence of clouds. And underneath it were splashes of fire as the shells fired from earth burst. Then there were flashes near the ground—and the shaking noise. It was like Milton—then there was war in heaven. But it was not angels. It was that small golden Zeppelin, like a long oval world, high up. It seemed as if the cosmic order were gone, as if there had come a new order, a new heaven above us: and as if the world in anger were trying to revoke it. Then the small, long-ovate luminary, the new world in the heavens, disappeared again.

I cannot get over it, that the moon is not queen of the sky by night, and the stars the lesser lights. It seems the Zeppelin is in the zenith of the night, golden like the moon, having taken control of the sky; and the bursting shells are the lesser lights.

So it seems our cosmos has burst, burst at last, the stars and moon blown away, the envelope of the sky burst out, and a new cosmos appeared; with a long-ovate, gleaming central luminary, calm and drifting in a glow of light, like a new moon, with its light bursting in flashes on the earth, to burst away the earth also. So it is the end—our world is gone, and we are like dust in the air.

Arnold Bennett

from The Journals of Arnold Bennett,
October 18, 1915

Capt. K. and Capt. B. stationed here, recounted the Zeppelin at-
tack on their camp in Epping Forest. It was apparently brought on by
a light in the Officers' Mess. It seems that the Zeppelin hung over the
camp. It dropped several (4 or 5) explosive bombs right in the camp,
a few feet (under 20) away from where K. actually was. None of these
bombs exploded. They buried themselves 10 feet in the earth. They
were excavated without accident. K. said the soldiers used pick and
shovel in digging them out with perfect indifference to the danger.
[. . .] K. said he could not assert that he actually saw the Zeppelin. He
said the men saw whole fleets of Zeppelins. Apropos, Richards related
last night that Webster came across a crowd in the centre of which
was a man pointing to the sky and raging excitedly: "There she is!
She's hit! She's hit!" Webster said: "You think that's a Zep, but it's the
moon." The crowd dissolved.

from Report of the Royal Buckinghamshire Hussars, September 25, 1916

It had been a very peaceful day and we were all in bed—except for the people with late passes or the people who'd taken a night off without them. Suddenly there was a whirring noise overhead and we all rushed out and stood looking up and watching. We could see the silhouette up in the sky—a huge cigar-shaped thing caught in a searchlight. Presently we heard the noise of one of our own aeroplanes coming along behind it and the tracer bullets went from the aeroplane to the Zeppelin [L 32] and the Zeppelin burst into flames and began to fall. It was so huge that it looked as though it was just about half a mile or a mile away.

Some of the fellows rushed in and put on their boots and trousers and started off to see it. There were dozens of them jumping over the fence but most of us stayed behind watching the flare and it was such a blaze that we could even hear the crackling noise from it. While we were watching, the bugles started to sound the alarm and the order to saddle up and get going to where the Zeppelin had come down. [. . .]

We were to put a guard round the Zeppelin. It had actually fallen some distance away, outside a village just before you get into Billericay. It was much further away than we thought but when we got there it was still burning and it burnt well into the early hours of the morning. What a sight it was! What a sight!

The worst bit was gathering up the crew. The ground was very soft where they fell and when we picked them up there were indentations in the soft soil of the shape of their bodies, arms, legs, everything—a mould of the bodies really. We carried them to the farmhouse. We picked up wicker chairs, loaves of German bread and bits of burnt silk and pieces of aluminum—all sorts of stuff. It kept us in beer for months! Everybody wanted souvenirs and, when the officers weren't looking, we were selling them to the crowd for half a crown and two bob a time. It was a good morning. Special trains came down with London sightseers and they were all begging us to get souvenirs for them, so those that weren't actually on guard duty were able to get inside the guard-line without the officers noticing and bring out pieces of burnt silk and broken aluminum. You nipped in, got a piece, tucked it up your tunic and then broke it up into small pieces and sold it for about two bob a time. [. . .]

We did two hours guard at a time and the field kitchen even cooked our Sunday dinner for us there. We had beef, roast potatoes and York-shire pudding. Some of the sightseers were envious! Some of them said, "Your dinner smells good, Tommy!" They were starving. They'd been there for hours and hours, some of them, and all day more were arriving. It had been seen for thirty miles around and those that hadn't seen it for themselves had heard about it. It was a fantastic thing—so huge you wouldn't believe it. The wreckage stretched across two fields.

W. J. Tempest

from Report on the Downing of the L 31, October 1, 1916

About 11:45 P.M. I found myself over southwest London at an altitude of 14,500 feet. There was a heavy ground fog on and it was bitterly cold, otherwise the night was beautiful and starlit at the altitude at which I was flying. I was gazing overhead toward the northeast of London, where the fog was not quite so heavy, when I noticed all the searchlights in that quarter concentrated in an enormous pyramid. Following them up to the apex, I saw a small cigar-shaped object, which I at once recognized as a Zeppelin, about fifteen miles away and heading straight for London. Previous to this I had chased many imaginary Zeppelins, only to find they were clouds on nearing them.

At first I drew near to my objective very rapidly (as I was on one side of London and it was on the other, and both were heading for the center of the city): all the time I was having an extremely unpleasant time, as to get to the Zepp I had to pass through a very inferno of shells from the A.A. guns below.

All at once it appeared to me that the Zeppelin must have sighted me, for she dropped all her bombs in one volley, swung round, tilted up her nose and proceeded to race away northward, climbing rapidly as she went. At the time of dropping the bombs I judged her to be at an altitude of 11,500 feet. I made after her at full speed at about 15,000 feet altitude, gradually overhauling her. At this period the A.A. fire was intense, and I, being about five miles behind the Zeppelin, had an extremely uncomfortable time. At this point misfortune overtook me, for my mechanical pressure pump went wrong and I had to use my hand pump to keep up the pressure in my fuel tank. This exercise at so high an altitude was very exhausting, besides occupying an arm, thus giving me one hand less to operate with when I commenced to fire.

As I drew up with the Zeppelin, to my relief I found that I was free from A.A. fire, for the nearest shells were bursting quite three miles away. The Zeppelin was now nearly 15,000 feet high and mounting rapidly. I therefore decided to dive at her, for though I held a slight advantage in speed, she was climbing like a rocket and leaving me standing. I accordingly gave a tremendous pump to my fuel tank, and dived straight at her, firing a burst into her as I came. I let her have another burst as I passed under her tail, and flying along underneath her, pumped lead into her for all I was worth. I could see tracer bullets flying from her in all directions, but I was too close under her for her to concentrate on me.

As I was firing, I noticed her begin to go red inside like an enormous Chinese lantern, and then a flame shot out of the front part of her and I realized she was on fire. She then shot up about 200 feet, paused, and came roaring down straight on to me before I had time to get out of the way. I nose-dived for all I was worth, with the Zepp tearing after me, and expected every minute to be engulfed in the flames. I put my machine into a spin and just managed to corkscrew out of the way as she shot past me roaring like a furnace. I righted my machine and watched her hit the ground with a shower of sparks. I then proceeded to fire off dozens of green Very lights in the exuberance of my feelings.

I glanced at my watch and I saw that it was about ten minutes past twelve. I then commenced to feel very sick and giddy and exhausted, and had considerable difficulty in finding my way to the ground through fog and landing, in doing which I crashed and cut my head on my machine gun.

Michael MacDonagh

from In London during the Great War,
October 1, 1916

I saw last night what is probably the most appalling spectacle associated with the war which London is likely to provide—the bringing down in flames of a raiding Zeppelin [L 31].

I was late at the office, and leaving it just before midnight was crossing to Blackfriars Bridge to get a tramcar home, when my attention was attracted by frenzied cries of "Oh! Oh! She's hit!" from some wayfarers who were standing in the middle of the road gazing at the sky in a northern direction. Looking up the clear run of New Bridge Street and Farringdon Road I saw high in the sky a concentrated blaze of searchlights, and in its centre a ruddy glow which rapidly spread into the outline of a blazing airship. Then the searchlights were turned off and the Zeppelin drifted perpendicularly in the darkened sky, a gigantic pyramid of flames, red and orange, like a ruined star falling slowly to earth. Its glare lit up the streets and gave a ruddy tint even to the waters of the Thames.

The spectacle lasted two or three minutes. It was so horribly fascinating that I felt spellbound—almost suffocated with emotion, ready hysterically to laugh or cry. When at last the doomed airship vanished from sight there arose a shout the like of which I never heard in London before—a hoarse shout of mingled execration, triumph and joy; a swelling shout that appeared to be rising from all parts of the metropolis, ever increasing in force and intensity. It was London's *Te Deum* for another crowning deliverance. Four Zeppelins destroyed in a month!

On getting to the office this morning I was ordered off to Potter's Bar, Middlesex, where the Zeppelin had been brought down, about thirteen miles from London. These days trains are infrequent and travel slowly as a war economy. The journey from King's Cross was particularly tedious. The train I caught was packed. My compartment had its twenty seats occupied and ten more passengers found standing room in it. The weather, too, was abominable. Rain fell persistently. We had to walk the two miles to the place where the Zeppelin fell, and over the miry roads and sodden fields hung a thick, clammy mist.

I got from a member of the Potter's Bar anti-aircraft battery an account of the bringing down of the Zeppelin. He said the airship was caught in the beams of three searchlights from stations miles apart, and was being fired at by three batteries also from distances widely separated. She turned and twisted, rose and fell, in vain attempts to escape to the shelter of the outer darkness. None of the shells reached her. Then an aeroplane appeared and dropped three flares—the signal to the ground batteries to cease firing as he was about to attack. The airman, flying about the Zeppelin, let go rounds of machine-gun fire at her without effect, until one round fired into her from beneath set her on fire, and down she came a blazing mass, roaring like a furnace, breaking as she fell into two parts which were held together by internal cables until they reached the ground.

The framework of the Zeppelin lay in the field in two enormous heaps, separated from each other by about a hundred yards. Most of the forepart hung suspended from a tree.

The crew numbered nineteen. One body was found in the field some distance from the wreckage. He must have jumped from the doomed airship from a considerable height. So great was the force with which he struck the ground that I saw the imprint of his body clearly defined in the stubbly grass. There was a round hole for the head, then deep impressions of the trunk, with outstretched arms, and finally the widely separated legs. Life was in him when he was picked up, but the spark soon went out. He was, in fact, the Commander, who had been in one of the gondolas hanging from the airship.

With another journalist I went to the barn where the bodies lay. As we approached we heard a woman say to the sergeant of the party of soldiers in charge, "May I go in? I would like to see a dead German." "No, madam, we cannot admit ladies," was the reply. Introducing myself as a newspaper reporter, I made the same request. The sergeant said to me, "If you particularly wish to go in you may. I would, however, advise you not to do so. If you do you will regret your curiosity." I persisted in my request.

Explaining to the sergeant that I particularly wanted to see the body of the Commander, I was allowed to go in. The sergeant removed the covering from one of the bodies which lay apart from the others. The only disfigurement was a slight distortion of the face. It was that of a young man, clean-shaven. He was heavily clad in a dark uniform and overcoat, with a thick muffler round his neck.

I knew who he was. At the office we had had official information of the identity of the Commander and the airship (though publication of both particulars was prohibited), and it was this knowledge that had determined me to see the body. The dead man was Heinrich Mathy, the most renowned of the German airship commanders, and the perished airship was his redoubtable L 31. Yes, there he lay in death at my feet, the bugaboo of the Zeppelin raids, the first and most ruthless of these Pirates of the Air bent on our destruction.

William Mitchell

from Memoirs of World War I,
October 19, 1917

Early one morning in October I went over to Nancy from Toul, where I had been inspecting airdromes and had spent the night. Entering the Café Stanislas to get some breakfast, I was greeted in a very excited manner by the headwaiter. "Colonel, have you seen the Zeppelin, have you seen the Zeppelin?" he kept repeating. On my answering no, he said that one had passed a short while before with its engines stopped and drifting in the direction of Lunéville.

Without stopping for breakfast, I proceeded toward Lunéville in my car, the fastest one we had; it was said to be the German Mercedes that won the last French road race at Lyons in 1914, just before the war. I could get ninety miles out of it on a clear road, and as this road was fairly open, I made good time. At Lunéville, they told me the Zeppelin had gone in the direction of St. Clement, toward which I headed with all speed. As I neared the town, I saw a great fire, which was the Zeppelin burning, and soon came up to where it had gone down. A group of French soldiers had just arrived to take charge of the debris.

The Zeppelin had been hit at an altitude of sixteen thousand feet by an anti-aircraft projectile and set on fire. Undoubtedly its engines had been frozen, as the atmosphere at that altitude was very cold. None of the crew had been saved; all had hit the ground in the vicinity of the wreck, with arms and legs extended, as is nearly always the case when a man is thrown from an airship or an airplane. (In some places the imprint made by the bodies in the earth was later filled in with concrete, to preserve these gruesome marks for posterity.)

The officer of the guard to whom I spoke told me it was rumored that there were other Zeppelins over France, which had passed during the night, but it was not known whether they were disabled or were proceeding on a raid. After looking over the twisted members of the giant Zeppelin's frame and noticing that there were only three machine guns on board and that she carried bomb dropping equipment, I started back for my headquarters at Chaumont. As I passed through Neufchâteau, another French officer told me that several Zeppelins had passed over France, going from northeast to southwest, and they were all apparently in distress.

At Chaumont, I was immediately informed by my information officer that a Zeppelin, practically intact, had landed at Bourbonne-les-Bains, some thirty miles to the west. After snatching a bite to eat and getting some gas in the car, I took Adjutant Fumat and started, arriving there in less than an hour. I had never actually seen an un-damaged Zeppelin before, although I was thoroughly familiar with their construction. The first impression I got from the monster ship was almost indescribable. Approaching it, we rounded a little hill which formed one side of the valley of a small stream. As I looked up, I thought I saw another hill, but on looking again, I saw that instead of a hill, it was the Zeppelin.

The ship, about five hundred and fifty feet long and seventy feet in diameter, had lodged squarely across the valley. Few people were on the scene as the Zeppelin had only been down a little while. I immediately climbed through it and inspected it from end to end. It was one of the latest models and was in a perfect state of preservation, except that all the engines were frozen. It had been forced down on this account and from loss of gas, not from the action of French airplanes. Several pilots from French squadrons in that vicinity had attacked the great ship on its way down and fired innumerable bullets into its envelope, many of them incendiary, but with little effect.

I carefully inspected the holes made by these bullets in the envelope and in the gas bags which they had punctured. Only .30-caliber guns had been used, and these bullets carried so little inflammatory substance in them that I think they were put out by the outer envelope. It would take a great many bullets from machine guns to cause enough loss of gas to bring one of these monsters down.

There were some thirteen gas balloons, made of gold-beaters' skin, in the interior of the ship, each independent of the other. Some were almost empty. As the ship had landed, two or three pine trees had pushed their way through the outer casing and projected into the interior for twenty or thirty feet. The appearance of the inside, with these Christmas trees sticking up and the partly filled ballonets among the wires and aluminum framework, was grotesque and strange.

I was much impressed with the wireless equipment, which was far superior to anything we had. It was said to send and receive for more than one thousand miles. Only a couple of machine guns were carried on this ship, which showed how little they feared airplanes.

I wondered why the crew had not destroyed the ship on landing, when an old man there, the one who had really saved the ship, told me his story.

He, with five or six others, had been hunting wild boar in the valley of the little stream when the Zeppelin came down. They were all much startled of course but this old fellow kept his composure and shouted to his companions to rally around him. The French airplanes swooped over the Zeppelin until it landed, firing their machine guns incessantly so that the old men were afraid they would be hit; but this one made them stand their ground. As the ship came to rest, one of the crew started to climb up from the front control cabin into the body of the ship. He had a Very pistol in his hand with which to shoot into one of the gas bags and set the whole structure on fire. The old man divined his intention and, covering him with his shot gun, ordered him to get back into the cabin or be killed. The other old fellows covered the rest of the crew, some twenty-one in number, making them descend from the cabins and holding them prisoners until the troops arrived. Very little news or information had been extracted from them.

While there, I was joined by Major Dodd of my staff who had come out to meet me and look over this Zeppelin, the L-49. Dodd had been delayed a little, because he had gone to visit a place where the third Zeppelin, the L-51, had come down. Its front cabin had hit the top of a tree and been torn off, and the Zeppelin, being rid of this weight, had risen again and disappeared. Dodd reported that two men had been found dead in the cabin and an examination of their effects disclosed the orders that had sent the Zeppelins on their mission, to-

The wreckage of the L 49 at Bourbonne-les-Bains, 1917.
Courtesy of the National Air and Space Museum.

gether with a complete journal of the trip up to a couple of hours before the accident. We translated these and for the first time knew just what had happened to the Zeppelins.

They had formed part of a squadron that had attacked England; it was the Germans' greatest single Zeppelin raid. Thirteen of these huge ships had been ordered to rendezvous over Belgium and attack certain industrial and shipping centers in Great Britain, including London, Birmingham, Liverpool, Sheffield and others. At the point of rendezvous, two of them had engine trouble and turned back; the other eleven proceeded in a gathering storm to Great Britain and dropped their bombs at the places designated. Then they got together again over the English Channel, but there encountered terrific winds from the northeast and were unable to make sufficient headway against them to keep from being blown into France.

In the morning, they found themselves over French territory, exposed to both air attack and the fire of anti-aircraft artillery. Their orders definitely stated that they should not rise above the hail line, which at that time was about fourteen thousand feet, otherwise they would get into such cold temperatures that their engines would freeze. The hail line is where the moisture in the air turns from a liquid state into ice, its altitude varying according to the sort of storm encountered and the time of year. If this squadron of Zeppelins stayed lower than the hail line, they would certainly be shot down, so their only alternative was to go up high and take the chance of freezing their engines, as there was an attendant possibility that the winds would change and allow them to get back into Germany. This did not happen, however, and one after another of the Zeppelins had their engines frozen and became helpless, no better than free balloons.

The French aeronautical authorities made complete drawings of this ship, which I arranged to have forwarded to the United States. It seemed to me that if the French had brought up a little gas and filled the ballonets of this ship, it could have been flown to the southern part of France, landed and repaired there, and subsequently used against the Germans. This was not done, however.

D. H. Lawrence

Zeppelin Nights

Now, will you play all night!
Come in, my mother says.
Look in the sky, at the bright
Moon all ablaze!
Look at the shaking, white
Searchlight rays!

Tonight they're coming!
It's a full moon!
When you hear them humming
Very soon,
You'll stop that blooming
Tune—

(Children sing on unheeding:)
Sally go round the sun!
Sally go round the moon!
Sally go round the chimney-pots
On Sunday afternoon!

Laurence Binyon

The Zeppelin

Guns! far and near
Quick, sudden, angry,
They startle the still street.
Upturned faces appear,
Doors open on darkness,
There is a hurrying of feet,

And whirled athwart gloom
White fingers of alarm
Point at last there
Where illumined and dumb
A shape suspended
Hovers, a demon of the starry air!

Strange and cold as a dream
Of sinister fancy,
It charms like a snake,
Poised deadly in the gleam,
While bright explosions
Leap up to it and break.

Is it terror you seek
To exult in? Know then
Hearts are here
That the plunging beak
Of night-winged murder
Strikes not with fear

So much as it strings
To a deep elation
And a quivering pride

That at last the hour brings
For them too the danger
Of those who died,

Of those who yet fight
Spending for each of us
Their glorious blood
In the foreign night.—
That now we are neared to them
Thank we God.

Edmund Blunden

By Chanctonbury

We shuddered on the blotched and wrinkled down,
So gaunt and chilled with solitary breeze.
Sharp stubborn grass, black-heather trails, wild trees
Knotting their knared wood like a thorny crown—
Huge funnelled dips to chalklands streaked with brown,
White railway smoke-drills dimming by degrees.
Slow ploughs afield, flood waters on the leas,
And red roofs of the small, ungainly town:
And blue fog over all, and saddening all—
Thus lay the landscape. Up from the sea there loomed
A stately airship, clear and large awhile:
Then, gliding grandly inland many a mile,
It left our Druid height that black graves plumed,
Vanishing fog-like in the foggy pall.

I Know a Blithe Blossom in Blighty

I know a blithe blossom in Blighty
Whom you (I'm afraid) would call flighty
  For when Zepps are about
  She always trips out
In a little black crêpe de chine nighty.

A damsel who dwelt on La Tortue
Said 'George dear, do you think we ortue?'
  George replied, 'My dear girl
  My head's in a whirl
Ought or oughtn't be hanged, pull the dortue.'

from The Airship Boys in Africa

To the Crabbes: George and Buster

TIME: 1917

Readers will recognize that I have based the journey of my
fictional L-58 very closely on the actual journey of L-59, and
have relocated the destination from East Africa to Southern
Africa. My reason is that I do not know East Africa at all and
know Southern Africa well. I am also aware that Germans
refer to airships in the masculine, but for the sake of an
idiomatic English I have chosen to ignore it.—T.C.

STAFF HEADQUARTERS, BERLIN

"Send a gas bag."
                      Prompt to punctuate,
The cross of light hangs on the monocle,
And the ornate baton slams on the map.
"But My Dear General . . . it is a trip
Of quite five thousand miles. Count Zeppelin
Himself would not propose it." Short, the Aide
Bestrides the narrow world with compass-legs.
"Count Zeppelin has plans to bomb New York;
If, that is, Wilson leaps. The point is this:
If we are driven into conference,
At least one colony still in our hands
Is that much leverage. All of that sand
May not be worth much, but to reinforce
Samoa, say, might strain even the Count."

Above the wide green blaize, the shaded globe
Stirs in a draft. The tall old Adjutant
Stands up, to pull it lower. He replies:
"Not reinforce. Re-take. The only fort
In Southwest still in our hands is Namutoni.
What do you propose, a daily bag,
To feed them like Elijah's ravens?"
                                    "Not,
Hubertus, more than one. You lack all sense
Of drama. As I should not have to say,
The vulgar have turned restless. We shall mount,
Therefore, an action they can understand.
Envision: thirst, beleaguered garrison,
Late rescue . . . it will be an episode
Worthy of Karl May. Both the colony
And ship are ideal for our purposes.
They lack tone equally. The mob,
I am afraid, find it rather difficult
To live vicariously through our own class."
Inferiority and high stiff collar
Jerk the Naval Liaison awake.
"Samoa," he recovers smartly, "fell
In 1914."
            "We are grateful, Herr Schütze,
For the Navy. You may tell that lunatic,
Count Zeppelin, to have his prototype
Put in production, and inform Herr Strasser—
I forget his rank; the Chief of Airship
Operations—that the enterprise
Will be upon his shoulders. Baron Uhl,
Of course, will be the nominal command,
And is to have the credit."
                            Pink and pleased,
The six-foot Baron, patently with strain,
Has turned his torso toward the Liaison.
"If it will ease your way, do use my name."

"Shut up, you fool. We cannot have the Staff
Held liable if this does not succeed.
Herr Schütze, you may leave us now. Good Day."
Herr Schütze, knock-kneed, clicks his heels almost,
And, bowing more expertly, takes his leave.
Beyond the oceans of the Empire map,
The General is beast in the abyss.
"We are surrounded by the parvenu.
Prince Bismarck was in error. Having fleets
Is worse than having colonies. However,
We are now *chez nous.* The merest break
In our agenda cannot harm. In short,
The Baron has agreed to dance again.
Stop pouting, Poldi, and costume yourself.
Will you be long?"
                        "Not long. I have my stays
On underneath my uniform."
                        "So. Rug
Here, cello here." In the revealed parquet,
Inverted boots move out. The soft cigars
Come forth, and over Empire thick smoke drifts.
". . . a few machine guns, medical supplies;
The fort need not expect the whole of Krupp."
"If that poor colony exists at all,
It's Aristophanes. Nothing but frogs
And croaking natives. Brek-a-ka-kex . . ."
Astride the cello, Egk, the luckless Aide,
Has had a sign. He draws his horsehair bow,
Transfixing a rare swan. Tutu and wig,
The Baron Leopold von Uhl, on point,
Negotiates his entrance. All applaud,
Except the Adjutant, who, when the swan
Nears, viciously says in his ear "Remember;
Keep the right wing strong." Counting aloud,
That vain bird may or may not hear. Arms high,
She draws out her conservatory death.

Impatient with the lengthening retards,
Accompanist and bow remain unmoved.
"The slow swan-boat from Pomerania.
Die and get it over with." On cue,
Swan vanishes, and, in convulsions, Uhl,
Face purple, thrashes on the loud block floor.
All true identities revealed, the cello,
Don Quixote, dies midway in scale.
A long hold, then pandemonium
Breaks out in jack boots. "Get him on the table;
No no—face up . . . Not Lukas, idiot;
A doctor who is one of *us:* call Hess . . ."
In the engraved baton, authority
Is caught beneath the victim's head. Unmanned,
The General takes hold. He drags it free,
Along with the gardenia and wig.
A man combating a tarantula,
He lays about the spider with the scepter.
The Baron, laid out Cape to Cairo, sighs
Colossally, and stiffens his whole length.
"Loosen his stays."

     Alert to intervene,
Controlled of voice, the Adjutant contests.
"No. He will die, and it will fall on us,
Dear Friends, to put his uniform back on."
"He is in fact dead." Mouth turned aside,
Still drooling in the delta of the Nile,
The many-summered dies without a song.
Damp eyes and eye-glass fogged, the General
Picks up the wig. "I knew him thirty years."
The free hand rests on zero latitude.
Then, rising to his full field marshall's height,
And to his highest pitch of eloquence,
He vows: "The expedition *will* succeed.
It is to be his monument—his song." [. . .]

Ahead of rainfall, smelling of wet sand,
The wind springs up across the scrubby flats.
High gun ports catch the scent of game; the rope
Stands out upon its flagpole. By the wall,
The short palmettos slap the stucco. Nude
Upon the crenellated balustrade,
Legs hanging over, hands upon the edge,
The fit young man stares downward in the dark.
Behind him, from the fort's enclosed parade,
A demi-nudist mounts the wooden steps.
"Don't swim the moat, Benno, before it's dug."
"It's going to rain. I want to be all pore."
"You are. Be careful of the guard. This watch
Shoots naked savages on sight."
                              "Not many,
I should think, are left. We botched that, Man;
The English would have done it better."
                                    "Better?"
"They'd have *shot* the Kaffirs quick enough,
But they'd have had them 'poisoning the wells.'
We shot them just because they used the wells.
Speaking of poison, what's your bottle there?"
The hale, the heavier, the not so fit
Fingers a neat beard, finding no firm jaw.
"Shampoo. I've hoarded this for fifteen months."
"You'll have your rain."
                        "You territorials.
You smell it, like the Bushmen."
                                "Certainly.
Before the war it rained three times a year.
You see the Pan? Flamingoes used to pink it
Halfway toward the fort. We ate their tongues.
It was like being Nero."
                        "Right of birth?"
"Oh no. By choice. Hamburg-Amerika

Bled Father fifteen years. Before the end
He could have had us on for half the fare;
He wouldn't make us go through quarantine.
I guess we did all right. In 1910
We had the only four-wheel bathing machine
In Swakopmund."

        "That, Benno, somehow jars.
One does not see you in the stripes and wool.
You will not think it treachery, I hope,
If I maintain that Namutoni, too,
Demands some lesser rag. The tricolor
To it is what your body is to you."
"Then join the Legion, Berndt."

        "After the war
We no doubt shall."

        "What are our chances?"

        "Poor.
If we can hold out till the French collapse,
The Boere will approach with terms. If not,
Cape Town will bow to London. In that case
They will intern us, and in Togoland.
I do not have to say what that will mean.
Our former subjects have their own weird tastes."
"Not all that weird. Outside of Grootfontein,
In droughts, we hunted Bushmen for museums.
They brought in rather more than karakul."
"So little, Man, would benefit so much.
A few machine-guns, medical supplies . . .
Rust and big game: the kiss of tetanus."
"Forget it. Naked territorials
Have an old saying: 'Hoard your own shampoo.'"
Insipid lightning shows the flat thorn trees;
The wind veers sharply. It is blowing now
Hard off Etosha Pan. High sheets of rain,
The false horizons of their reedy shallows,
Undulate and section, part and close.
Rain-beaten surface throws back second rain.

Itself and after-image—green, delayed—
Chain lightning forms. In two great thunderclaps
The torrent strikes. The tin roofs pour their rust,
Becoming in the process snare drums. Deep
Below, iron cisterns thunder while they fill.
Too sudden for the gutters, cataracts
Leap out the crenellations. Dusty streams
Repeat wet muscles, outline streaming hair.
"Don't stand so near the storm drain, Berndt;
You'll have your soapsuds in the drinking water."

STAAKEN, OUTSIDE BERLIN

A formal group beside the hangar door,
The new crew musters for a photograph.
In front, the Captain, the Executive.
On either side of them, Chief Engineer
And Navigator. Ranged behind, the rest:
Two petty officers to man the rudders,
Two more for the elevators. One,
"Sailmaker," or so called, who has in charge
All sixteen gas cells, and the outer cover.
Two to man the radios, and two,
Machinist's mates, on every engine. All,
Good looking uniformly—even teeth,
Straight hair—are peering past the camera
In some unlikely, earnest search for fame.
"Is this a time exposure?" whispers one.
His like (straight mouth as little moved) replies:
"Flash powder under all that hydrogen?
Are you insane?" Above them and behind,
The vaulted hangar rises out of sight.
In its efficient gloom, a sketchy shape
Assembles. Like the full scale diagram
Of such geometry as it employs,
So large as to invite astrology

Yet myth so pure as to subsume it whole,
The giant airship waits its cover. Braced
Rings, graceful longitudinals, high fins
Make clear the stresses they oppose, the weight
They must reduce. Two gas cells, filled for testing,
Bring, to abstract science, bloat with peril.
Seven hundred forty-four feet long,
L-58 almost exceeds her shed.
The photograph will show her as a dim,
A somewhat overcomplicated nimbus,
High above the crew that, three weeks hence,
Will put her in commission. These, fame caught
And time exposure done, may now relax,
In the degree that separates "Hold still"
From "At attention." Stepping out of frame,
The still posed Captain, notebook still in hand,
Tries, mentally, the house acoustics, sets
His volume, and begins: "In Africa
We are to be cannibalized. That is,
The ship will be. What cargo we can take
Is in the neighborhood of fifteen tons.
This will consist of ammunition, mail,
Guns, bandages, and, most important, tools."
A Stuttgart Greek professor's only son,
The seasoned veteran of London raids,
Of wreck, and of the dull North Sea patrol,
Paul Theiss at twenty-nine assumes the picked,
The envied, the Homeric African command.
"On landing, preferably not before,
We pull ourselves apart. The cover, cells,
The fabric of the gas shafts . . . all our cloth
Goes into uniforms or into tents.
We hope the Territorials can sew.
They'll also have to rivet. Stand the frame
On end and there's your radio antenna.
If we can land with any fuel left,
We'll have the power for them too." Face blank,

Eyes bored, Executive Leo von Meien
Listens, then represses. Truth will out,
However, and at once. "Dear God," he thinks,
"It's *Swiss Family Robinson*." Vain, Junker
To his cheekbones, he has out of spite
Preferred the Navy: socially, a coup;
He dines out on the story. In Berlin
He has his waiting list of the appalled.
"I am a second son of second sons.
That means the Army, where the first-born are,
Or scavenging the countryside for Poles,
To help grand-uncles harvest. Faced with that,
I find the Navy not bourgeois at all.
My family, of course, behave as though
One had brought home La Belle Otéro. Ships
May have their humble origins; they are,
In fact, quite mean. But airships, zeppelins . . .
Well after all, the old man *is* a count."

The distant hangar shines in morning fog;
The wide steel doors slide open in the calm.
Not really visible, the unseen pearl
Implicit in deep shadow of the shell,
Forepeak and hull reflect upon the lintel.
Drilled insects, the mute ground crew emerge.
As if these parodied the fate they serve,
They offer, each to each, the weighted rope.
The handling lines grow taut; the great pearl moves.
It is the planet and the idol; god,
And the deceptive image of the god—
The captive, sympathetic spell of Heaven,
And the Devourer carried in procession;
Hive and all-collective energies,
The idle queen replete with death and honey.
Enthralled balance, mate, complementing sign,
In that same motion full sun moves aloft.
Prime morn, so dazzling on the silver dope

That solid mass is transformed into light,
Becomes, in the slow physics of a dream,
Itself, and moves to meet itself: the arc
Forever struck, the terminals made one.
The god is levitated by the light;
The carried idol bears the flying god.
The reborn queen will mate; the sign ascend.
Lighter than air, freed form, pure vehicle,
The wheel of Juggernaut floats free of Earth.

STAAKEN

"How many sandbags in the ground crew, Sir?"
Binoculars around his neck, forearms
Along the sill, in the front gondola
Paul Theiss has overseen the take-off. Calm,
Neat, confident, he sees the ground recede,
The tired men on the mooring lines foreshorten.
Narrowly, the long rear gondola,
Swung well below the hull, has cleared the field,
As has the bottom tail fin. Fully trimmed,
All engines idling, on her static lift
L-58 ascends. Unhurriedly,
Her Captain, leaning out the window, waves
Approval to his Engineer, who, distant
By four hundred feet, is in command
Of two men in the after gondola.
("We are the dinosaur's poor second brain.")
Theiss shuts the isinglass, and then takes up
His flight post by the engine telegraph.
Von Meien, stationed by the ballast toggles,
Sees and notes. "No fidget, anyway."
He smiles. "An airship, Uncle, is not flown.
It is commanded." Fond of the perverse,
He must acknowledge it has triumphed. He
That volunteered from pique remains for love.

"I cannot give it up. If the war is lost,
There's still the peace. Excursion flights—who knows?—
The Count may have his transatlantic line.
In that case, talents of a second son
Should merit purser, at the very least.
It's social ruin, but it's under gas."
In the seclusion of the voyeur's friend;
That is, behind the shadow of his visor,
Theiss appraises his Executive.
"A little of the farmer there. Not all
The *salon*." He is quite aware his men
Say their Executive has no full face:
That he exists in profile only. "Ice,
Though under gas much better ice than fire."
He has the handles, ringing to half speed.
A sudden downdraft hits; the slow ship drops.
"Up elevators! Jerk the ballast!" Von Meien
Leans against the ballast toggles two by two;
The elevator wheel spins three full turns.
In double falls, the vivid ballast water
Hails the fleeing ground crew. Eased, relieved,
L-58 recovers. Lurching forward,
Upward, she attains again her shed's
Roof height, to thrust her way toward open sky.
From vantage in the after gondola,
Her dark Chief Engineer, Rotholz, goes white.
Behind the forward car, too high to see,
Too low to grasp, two human pendula
Swing slowly on the starboard mooring line.
The staring Engineer, the enemy
His own throat rising, puts it down and speaks.
His Maybach engines pound above his voice.
"She almost hit. We fouled two sandbags. Heinz,
Go forward." Forward has, however, felt
That shifting weight. Theiss, looking quickly back,
Detects. *"Who left the sewer-dragging-line out?*
Haul! Haul them in!" But one live counterweight

Releases; one, too much entangled, holds.
Short nose distorted on the isinglass,
Rotholz reports. "The bag smoked when he hit."
Ahead, the Captain has the crash report.
The mooring lines are in; a builder's cable,
Never disconnected, may be culprit.
"Can we reach it?" Doubled on the sill,
Breisgau the Navigator—diaphragm
Protesting—struggles out an answer:
"Not from here. Not even from the keel."
"If thy right hand offend thee," thinks von Meien,
Knowing he has read the Captain's mind . . .
"Cut it off!" Theiss points, however, plainly
Toward the motor. "We cannot go back;
We've got to reach him." As he speaks,
He is again lieutenant, hanging, frail
Archangel of the observation car,
Eight thousand feet above the London docks.
Von Meien, the eternal present tense,
Has found a way. "Old Shatterhand, I think,
Would use a lariat." All engines stopped,
A too thick clock hand in an empty sky,
L-58 turns lazily. Von Meien,
Climbing on the slant control car roof,
All profile, makes his way from strut to strut,
Until, astride the great propellor boss,
He faces aft. One end around his waist,
The other weighted, rope encircles twice
The dangling cable. Hauling in, feet braced
Against the still propellor, he can bring,
Uncertainly, the cable near the car.
Through steady glasses, Rotholz views unmoved.
"If that East Prussian gaucho pushes loose
Our main propellor pins, we're all in trouble."
But the bossing holds; and working free,
The slight ground crewman has begun to climb.
Hand over hand, he nears the lariat.

Von Meien tugs, and, like a trapeze star,
The sandbag legs the undercarriage.

"What is your name, Sailor?"
                                "Nowack, Captain.
Jonas Nowack." Stunned Leo von Meien
Suddenly acquires full face. Although,
Barely, he keeps his peace, he has his thoughts.
"What an omen. Jonah and a Pole."

IN FLIGHT OVER AFRICA

High off the coast of Cirenaica,
Faint sound, a simplified and silver cloud,
L-58 floats south well on her course.
The blue enamel on the middle sea
Is darkened only where her shadow flies;
That silent dome echoes no other storm.
The routine of the watch has settled in;
The outer cover, in the chill dry air,
Stays smooth and taut. New model radios,
And their "Marconi," read the airship's base.
Off-duty, Justin Breisgau, eyes shut tight,
Ascends the open ladder. Linking hull
To the control car, it calls less for climbing
Than for wrestling with its angel. Burned
And windburned, ointment on his nose,
He wrestles. Nose bespeaks his English mother;
Burn the sextant, lookout, and the sun.
He has, from Jambol in Bulgaria,
Their base, the German armies' farthest south,
Set course for Southwest Africa; and, fidget
By profession, checked it every hour.
The slipstream fails, and he is in the keel. [. . .]
In the dim light, an upright fuel tank
Bumps him at shoulder height. From frame to frame

An empty hammock swings. Hose, ballast bags,
Shafts pass as in a dream. Frame twenty, near
The tail, supports a card game. Though the site
Is the traditional, Breisgau's jaw drops.
Executive and Engineer are playing;
Both are smoking. Rotholz draws, and grins.
"Relax, Map Boy. When you've been under gas
As long as we have, you will learn to smell.
We are quite safe."

                        "Well, safe from blowing up.
Dear Master's engines may asphyxiate us."
"Thank them. They may cover your cigar."
Sure touch of the casino in his hands,
Von Meien shuffles. "Shall we deal you in?"
Not certain why, since he came aft to play,
The younger man says no. The dealer frowns,
The deal slows. "Do we have another deck?
There's grease on these." Perhaps too evenly,
Rotholz looks up. "We all can't work the Bridge."
In equal evenness, his knuckles crack.
Chart Room discovers, when the players meld,
What held it back from playing. Their face cards,
Armed, spliced together, self-opposed, are they.
By definition, tertium quid intrudes.
A single counter, neither whole nor half,
They look two ways in self-deforming pride.
"Herr Breisgau, do not stare. If we conceal
Tobacco, you conceal your knife. Not so?"
Von Meien's glance has never left his meld;
To Viktor Rotholz falls the unearned gain:
Herr Breisgau's blush. He, mortified, knows now
That his Executive has read his mail.
I figure, if we crash, I'd have no more
Than thirty seconds to escape the fire.
That means, of course, I'd have to cut my way.
Right through the outer cover. I've a knife
Honed to a razor edge. "I have," he says,

"My family to think of." Red-faced still,
He goes back forward. "You fraud. You know
You cannot censor mail; not officers'.
Have you read mine as well?"
                              "No, nor his either.
My enlisted men are much more gifted.
You are Hamburg at its flattest; he
Is Bremerhaven at its foggiest."
"Then how'd you guess he's carrying a knife?"
"Because I carry one myself. Don't you?"
"No—but you've your family to think of."
The long keel lifts, as though, just out to sea,
A surface liner took the first great swell.
The slack control wires, in their creaking sheaves,
Tighten on cue; the giant cruciforms,
That bear the elevator surfaces,
The balanced rudders, ring out with the strain.
L-58, however, rises by the bow.
"We must have reached the coastline. Who replaced
Lingayen on the elevator wheel?"
"DeKlerk. He may have trouble holding her."
Von Meien gathers up the cards. "Pay off,
And we can have a look."
                              "You have the soul,
Von Meien, of head purser." Ballast bag
For ash tray, he removes his cigarette.
The water hisses. "Do be careful there.
Marconi's raising goldfish in that bag."

STUTTGART AS MIRAGE

The Captain, in the blue Libyan night,
Peers out of crystal. Phosphorescent dials
Diamond the dim-lit gondola;
Its narrow panes have faceted the sky.
A more than crescent, not quite half half-moon

Turns sand to powder, and to powder blue.
The south horizon floats a rich mirage:
Ionic colonnade, the oval lake,
The blank-eyed statuary. Naked trees
Transport the false oasis north; new posters
Localize it, fix it in its time.
It is Theaterplatz, in Stuttgart. Strolling
Feet attest its promenade, the restless swans
A cold and real water. Brilliant tone
In motion on the gray Spring day, themselves
A solar system, sellers of balloons
Assault the strollers of the interval.
Ilona Färber slips a graceful arm
Into her tall fiancé's. "Buy one, Paul.
Have you no sense of camaraderie?"
"A round one or a long one?"

                    "Long, of course.
I am not marrying a free ballooner."
"You are not marrying the gas man—yet."
" 'There is a land where all is chastity.' "
" 'It also has its nomenclature: Death.' "
"Invidious comparisons aside,
Have you enjoyed the opera?"

                    "Enough.
It won't replace *The Count of Luxembourg*."
The straight young woman bends to free her skirt,
Snagged on a partially recessed floodlight.
Her motion sweeps high egrets on her toque
In matching circles. "Beautiful, the swans.
What frightened them?"

                  "Your hat, undoubtedly.
Swans have no sense of camaraderie. [. . .]
Ilona, when I'm gone, what will you do?"
"The classic things: lament and sew."

                     "Sew, yes.
No lamentation. Thread, the folded hands,
The self-absorption . . . it is very nice.

Do I sound foolish?"

        "No, you are correct.
It is a woman's gesture. Years ago,
I spent my Summers with an aunt; in Rome,
In Buenos Aires. She was very . . . how
To say . . . emancipated. Tailored clothes,
Cigars, always a household full of poets.
I had no objection; not to smoking.
Then one day I saw her at her mirror:
She was knotting the cravat she wore.
She always wore it; that is not the point.
It was the gesture: classic, if a man
Is who performs it. When you tie your tie,
Think of me."

        "We have had no home, Ilona."
Edge dissolved from his control car voice,
It suddenly is less assured than hers.
"No hearth, no mirror for the ordinary."
"Spoken like a sailor. Hearth and home
As the extreme exotic."

        "As you know,
My own home *is* exotic; these last weeks,
Downright unreal. Can you visit him?"
"Your father? Oh, Paul; I'm sorry. Of course."
"If there's more rationing, he'll simply starve.
At the best of times he's too impractical
To eat much. Since his cleaning woman left,
He's given up his cocoa."

        "When you fly,
He worries. You are home; he's ceased to care."
"A pretty theory. The fact is, though,
I've never managed to get through his mind
What, actually, an airship is. He has,
However, written three Greek epigrams
In which von Richthofen, that bloody bore,
Is fulsomely compared to Icarus.
I hope the metaphor holds all the way."

Swinging the curved balloon on its long stick
As one might hold a mallet, she replies.
"Whoever the prophet, barons have the honor.
Nonetheless, take heart. When I write verse
You will appear as Sindbad—or the roc."
"Point out that my Executive is Junker,
And is only second in command.
One fancies, though, Leo is déclassé.
The *Nights* I used to read in self-defense.
A little of Olympus goes a long way."
The malleteer, distracted by the bell,
Looks up at the ornate façade, which, gently
Rounded, mirrors in the smooth ellipse.
"The interval is over, Paul. Come on."
"We cannot very well take *that* inside."
He lifts out the balloon stick from her hand.
"Shall we explode it?" she inquires.
                                        "God no.
We'll launch it properly." Untying it,
He sets it free. "Up ship!" he murmurs. [. . .]

IN FLIGHT OVER AFRICA

Flat cheek still further flattened on the stock,
Leo von Meien draws his steady bead.
The rifle cracks; the leaping oryx falls.
"If we could stop the engines," he reflects,
"She'd be the perfect blind." The frightened game,
Below the airship, are like flying-fish
Discharging from the seas of yellow grass.
Erik Lingayen, exiled on the rudder,
Cranes to see. "Fantastic, no? But Sir,
Where do you aim for? We are straight above."
"One goes in, as the matador would say,
Over the horns."
                        "You've seen the diagram

In butcher shops, Lingayen: toward the heart."
Lembecker, from the elevator wheel,
The siege prestigious, can afford the slur.
"Shut up, you fat bellhop." ("A rudder wheel
Is for the oxen drivers.") Leo, flushed
As any adolescent, twice re-loads,
And, when the rippling herd is out of range,
Cannot put down the lush youth in his voice.
"How those would shake the trophy room at home:
Castle von Meien is confined to elk.
My Great Aunt Vicki wanted to remodel;
Her architects discovered right away
They could not disentangle all the antlers.
They had to move the wall in one piece. She
Was dead, but the remodeling went on. [. . .]
Avuncular, he crosses his long legs.
"In those days hunting bored me. Dogs and damp
And servants who mislaid the thermos cups.
This is the way to hunt: up near the sun,
The animals in their world, we in ours.
The little circle in the sights; the great,
Gold circle on the ground. The Good Lord hunts." [. . .]

IN FLIGHT OVER AFRICA

Low walls of cloud, as brilliant on the night
As breaking surf, lie waiting in the sky
Horizon to horizon. On the dark
And concave underside, unceasingly,
Quick necklaces of lightning drop. The ship,
Uneasy in an air still quiet, turns
From left to right, and right to left. "No break,"
Theiss calls aloud. "We'll have to go straight through.
Reel in the main antenna. We're enough
A lightning rod without that added." Slow,
The ship malingers in a last wide circle,

Then the Captain telegraphs full power.
Wave, escarpment, storm—whatever waits,
All engines roaring, flame in five exhausts,
The silver, slender zeppelin attacks.
She goes in low, but on the storm's front edge
A surging updraft takes her by the bow.
Lembecker, facing sideways on his wheel,
Sees, long before the pane goes blind with rain,
The port horizon tilt eighteen degrees.
"Down elevator," drums out the command.
In answer he applies the full five turns:
Hard over. Yet the unchecked rise continues.
Sailmaker, in the steep rake of the keel,
Can hear the gas cells strain to bursting. Brush
In hand, gluepot for his balance rod,
He walks a tightrope in the shrieking dark—
Listening for one sound that means a leak.
The fabric cover slaps against its cord,
Excited like the paper on a kite.
The soaring airship reaches pressure height.
Insistent, the expanding hydrogen,
Like steam, blows off through automatic valves;
And, venting in the tall gas shafts, leaks
On fiery air. Then the great downdraft inside
The storm itself takes hold. More swiftly than she rose,
L-58 is plunging. "Drop all ballast,"
Cries the Captain, while the tropic rain
Sucks in the German springs, the Balkan streams,
And the brunet Marconi's goldfish. Bolt
Continued into bolt, a greenish light
Is focused in the crystal gondola.
Rain pouring down their radiator vents,
The dual engines in the after car
Exhibit silently, below a thunder
Which has drowned them out. The streets of Hamburg,
Imperturbable, the Engineer
Discerns soon how the forward gondola

Is turning on two axes, neither one
That of his own. "The framework," he deduces,
"Must be twisted like a wire wastebasket."
Forward, on the rudders, Jan DeKlerk
Is thrown off balance. Instantly, his wheel
Spins free. "The cable's gone." In sudden calm,
The speaking tube responds: "The fin's hit, Captain;
Lightning hit the upper fin." The gale
Resumes, and what the screaming lookout calls
Is blown back in his mouth. "The air's alive . . .
My fingers . . . I have fire between my fingers."

In sunny silence, engines throttled down,
The battered ship drifts in the morning sky.
Rotholz and Breisgau, plus the two Marconi's,
Surface from the climbing shaft. Upright
Atop the hull, they view their stretched-out planet:
Metal ocean sloping off to blue.
Each on the dorsal girder, single file,
They go aft toward the upper fin. There, torn
From all control, the rudder turns at random. [. . .]
"If we lost much gas in the storm, this job
Will have to be a quick one."
                              "Hurry up,"
Rotholz confirms, and—ritual—the fight
To lash the rudder down begins. Its fabric
Hanging in festoons, its framework swings
As though to gate surrealistic Heaven.
Perceptibly, while they rope-in the frame
Like yachtsmen struggling with a boom,
L-58 is settling: through blue air,
Through golden haze and toward the yellow earth.
A thousand feet; nine hundred. Knots are tied.
Six hundred. She is less than her own length
Above the ground. "He's got to start the engines,"
Breisgau thinks. "She'll scrape down otherwise."
His training profits. It does not occur,

Although he knows it, at another level,
Well, that such a move must threaten him.
It is their mercenary who, for once,
Pays silver sweat in hope his engines stall.
Five-hundred twenty-five. Disjunctively,
Two last propellors labor into action.
Sickle, ax, the rudder lurches free,
And, slashing through a vicious arc,
Folds flush. One man is pinned against the fin;
One lies unconscious. "Tie it where it is!"
Recovering the flailing rope, Rotholz
Is lashing frenziedly. Breisgau restrains him.
"Stop it, Viktor. We can never get him out
If it won't move." The radioman's chin,
Hard over, drops. "He's dead, and we'll be too
Unless we get below. This one's alive.
Help me drag him to the climbing shaft."
"You'll have to cut his line first." Siamese
Attachment ties the living to the dead.
"You are the one who has a knife, Breisgau."
He, seeing sagging lids and pale short hair
Gone dark with drying blood, is for the time
Too sick to take offense. Before he cuts,
He looks along the life-connecting rope.
Upon its other end, the cross of girders
Both before him and behind, the crucified,
Arms swinging slowly as the ship moves off,
Is moving like a clockwork Passion Play.
The blowing strips of fabric wrap him round;
Their silver dope has smeared his windblown hair.

IN FLIGHT OVER AFRICA

It is apparent now the ship is dying.
After six days in the air, her gas
Diminished and her fuel almost gone,

She stays aloft on the dynamic lift
Of two remaining engines. On the bridge,
The officers receive the dark report.
"We're off our course, and by how many miles
There is no knowing. Both the radios
Have died on us, not that it matters, both
The radiomen being dead. I am assured
Both outboard engines are beyond repair,
Not that *that* matters, since we have no fuel.
Both of you, Herr Rotholz, Herr von Meien,
Need a shave, but that we'll overlook."
Theiss smiles. "Let's have some coffee. We have power
For the hot plate, and the twilight of the gods
Would not put off our cook." He hands a thermos.
"If we jettison the cargo—strip
Her down, that is; throw out the radios,
The instruments, the kitchen sink—we can,
Of course, stay up a few days longer. What
I want, though, is to set her down intact.
My guess is that we are not all that far
Off course, and we must think of Namutoni
In addition to ourselves. Our cargo
Means too much to be thrown out piecemeal.
There is, however, that two hundred pounds
We must attend to now. It cannot wait.
Is all prepared?"
                    "Sewed in a hammock, Sir."
"Except for that, there's nothing we can do
Before Herr Breisgau shoots the sun at noon." [. . .]

Two hundred pounds has made a difference,
As has the sun, evaporating weight.
To save on fuel, Theiss has stopped the engines.
Sextant on his waist, the Navigator
Squeezes up the twisted climbing shaft.
Looking like wet, gigantic laundry, cells
Hang loose around him, none completely full.

Facing aft as he climbs, he turns around
As he emerges on the lookout, safe
From that great reliquary on the fin.
He lifts the eyepiece to his eye; he sights.
A shadow flits; involuntarily
He turns behind. His gaze sweeps down the hull,
And then follows, from the arching fin
Into high noon, a black, titanic spiral.
Bird by bird, it narrows toward the base.
"Why aren't they pink?" he wonders. When he knows,
He throws the sextant at them. One arm raised
To fend off shadows, he drops down the shaft.

The Bridge is caught off guard when, from the hull,
A maniac drops on the metal floor.
Before the personnel can drag him back,
He lunges at the gas valves. "Drive them off!
Release the gas. We've got to drive them off."
As though in weariness, the mute ship sinks. [. . .]

THE NAMIB

Like a long gray wing across the moon,
The quiet ship is sinking by the tail.
"Send every spare man forward," orders Theiss.
"We have to get her trimmed." L-58,
Having fought six hours to stay aloft,
Has fought another six to land. The hot,
Strong updrafts off the desert force her back,
Each time more slowly, to her element.
Already, sand is blowing in the keel.
"Put out the mooring lines. This time is certain.
When we hit, Leo, throw off the guns.
The heavy cases first. We'll moor to them.
After that the other cargo. Fast."
"Aye aye, Sir," and, unpocketing his knife,

The only Junker under gas goes aft.
Proceeding forward in their sandy darkness,
Breisgau meets him. Vague since noon, the voice
Has malice: "What a time to pare your nails."
Without momentum, almost gracefully,
The ship scuds off a dune, and, bouncing once,
Then comes to rest along its leeward curve.
Her mooring party drops to earth; amidships,
Crates of ammunition strike the sand.
Only when her cargo is unshipped,
And she is moored, a caliph's folly
In the blue pavilions of the Namib,
Does Theiss call out, quite hoarse, "Abandon ship."

Their faces taut beyond the known aspect
Of weariness, the officers collapse
On packing cases. Faint and far away,
The shade of Viktor: "In the morning, Sir,
I'll cut Marconi down. I tied him there."
"We cannot take the time. This is the desert.
We must reach those hills before the heat."
Some minutes later, moving silhouettes
Along the fin return him to alertness.
"Fool. She's leaking gas from every cell.
Who are the two men with him? Are they shod?
One spark cannot fail to blow them up."
"I'll shoe them. Fast." Leo is on his feet,
The action of the iron boot in his eye.
In hissing quiet, like the snapping strings
Of an immense piano, two struts give.
In colors of a roman candle, twinned
And sure, sparks hang on their trajectory.
The earth is turned to thunder, and the sky
To brilliant yellow. Stiff and small and black,
Like paper cut-outs in a Halloween display,
Three men along the hull take fire and leap.
In its convulsion as of blazing birth,

The framework lurches from its cotton shell.
It is the ember of a molten bird.
The Captain's gaze, however, seeks the bow,
Where, one by one, the sharp call letters burn.
L-58 becomes L-5, then hyphen.
He has shut his eyes. "Farewell, Sultana."
Suddenly he seizes Breisgau. "You,
The maps! Where are they? Did you get them off?"
"Of course, Man," Breisgau answers lucidly.
"They are in here." He hands him, cork awry
And foam erect, the Baron's pink champagne,
That was to celebrate their record voyage.
In Socratic glare, the bearer's face,
Removed of all expression, gives no answer.
Bottle still in hand, Paul Theiss jerks free,
And, sprinting, sees the gondola ignite.
The flaming tail, six hundred feet behind,
Long since has bared the white-hot cruciforms.
Von Meien, flattened in the pounding heat,
Rolls quickly to avoid a fall of fire,
Which, neither slow nor hurried, rises up
And is a faceless human messenger.
Another bright evangel falls; both double,
Straighten, double on the sooty sand.
Von Meien, stumbling forward, trips
And finds himself across another body.
"Viktor. Can you hear me?"
                        "Help me up.
Leo; my leg is broken."
                        "Are you burned?
Your jacket isn't."
                     "Down the back, perhaps.
The leg, however, overtrumps it quite."
As if they parodied a track event,
The two men lurch amidships on three legs.
There, Rotholz stiffens. "Theiss, Leo. Turn loose.
We've got to stop him." Pitching on his face,

He lifts his head in time to see, too late,
The flying tackle fail, and, slower now,
The tackler crawl on toward the wall of flame.

"Now. You are at one with your machine."
Leo admires the splint he has devised
Out of an engine rod.
                        "I like the brace,"
Rotholz replies, "but I don't trust your knots.
Your hand is shaking. Let me tie."
"If I do not tie these, and tie them now,
I'll never tie another. Whole face black
And he said 'Meien, tie my necktie, please.'
I could not look. I had to work by feel,
And it was tying ashes. Then he died."
"How many are we?"
                      "Ten. Lingayen died
Before the Captain did."
                         "You're in command,
Gaucho. Which direction will it be?"
"The hills. We have supplies to be delivered."
"God, Leo. Not the Brave Teutonic Knight.
It is too late for that. We have no maps."
The profile answers what the blood replies.
"I have not said we'll locate Namutoni.
I mean there may be other garrisons."

In the chilly pre-dawn calm, the ten
Strap on their improvised and awkward packs.
Their leader checks each one, and, at the end,
Approves the hammock in which Rotholz lies.
"Very efficient litter. If you die
We'll simply sew you in."
                       "Make certain first
I'm really dead."
                 "I'll poll your litter bearers.
Was the shot enough? How is your leg?"

"If it were better I would mutiny.
I'm sure that we are near the sea. That smell
Is unmistakable."
                          "It isn't sea;
It's waterfront. You smell the unburned oil."
The blackened troop, their unfamiliar boots
The sandal suddenly devoid of wings,
Have lined up by the still warm skeleton.
High, twisted girders hook the flat gray sky.
Von Meien stares. "More tangled than the antlers,"
Muses the inheritor, in pride.
He turns and gives his order: "Toward the East."
And in the swaying hammock, when the drug
Has slowed all motion to a gentle swell,
The opposition falters into sleep:
"Good luck, Leo. Find us charts, and peace,
And chapter houses in the Order Lands."
Unnoticed, Justin Breisgau falls behind.
The short defile winds toward the great rock gates,
And when it vanishes, he squats, alone,
Under the Greek Cross of the rudder posts.
Sunrise lays out their shadow on him, sunset
Lays his own along the burned-out bones.
Intent, he clicks his tongue against his teeth.

EPITAPH

Full throttle low above the high savannah;
Game running into, out of pointed shadow.
Herr, between drummed earth and silent heaven,
We pursue a shade which is ourselves.

III. The Great Crossings

On the third flight, in April 1931, we landed in Cairo. The enthusiasm of the Egyptians knew no bounds and the fire department had to be called out to use their hoses in protecting the airship from the crowds. The Graf Zeppelin *circled the pyramids and the old and new sciences took each other's measure. From Cairo I piloted the airship on a flight over the Holy City of Palestine . . . Over the grave of the Redeemer we reverently sank the prow of the ship.*

—Ernst A. Lehmann

Junius B. Wood

Seeing America from the *Shenandoah*

On the morning of October 7 [1924], the big Navy airship, U.S.S. *Shenandoah*, was starting from Lakehurst, New Jersey, on its record-making cruise of more than 9,000 miles, twice over the Rockies and twice around three sides of the United States.

The autumn sun was peeping over the horizon at 5:35 A.M., as the *Shenandoah* was led out of the big hangar. Every man on the station helped, 300 of them—sailors, marines, Filipino mess boys, and civilians. They came running into the dreary, misty morn like little ants pulling an immense gray worm out of its nest. The run slackened to a walk when she was safely clear of the shed.

Nose to the wind, she was led farther into the field toward the mast, the crew stumbling and slipping in the loose sand. They stopped and waited.

MOORED TO THE MAST, READY FOR THE START

The sun's rays were warming the cells in the big tube and the gas was expanding like a morning-glory. The ship tugged to rise higher. The men braced themselves, held and led her closer to the mast.

A long cable dropped from the ship and was hooked to its mate, trailing on the ground from the mooring mast. A winch rumbled and the big, docile craft was pulled down until the swivel pear on its nose nestled into the cup on the tower. It was moored. That was at 7 A.M., and all hands stopped for breakfast.

At 10 o'clock the ship was ready to cast off. During the three hours, the sun had been warming the helium gas as if it were in a hothouse. With each degree that its temperature rose above that of the surrounding air, the ship was lifting another 300 pounds. More fuel, more supplies, and more officers and men had gone aboard, one by one and each to a particular spot in the long keel tunnel.

While the ship's nose rests on the mast, the delicate balance must be maintained. With a mast only 160 feet high and a big tube 682 feet long, not many degrees' drop is possible before the tail fins scrape the ground.

The earth was beginning to radiate the heat of the sun. The start must be made while the ship held its handicap of superheat. The little elevator in the mast had brought up its last passenger. The fuel was being piped on in driblets, valves opening and shutting, holding her down with a few more pounds every time she strained to go higher.

Lieutenant Commander Zachary Lansdowne, the captain, had gone aboard. Usually he was next to the last to leave the mast. After him came the mooring officer, who closed the gangway after him, making it part of the ship's well-rounded nose. This time the ship's sole civilian passenger was later than the captain.

"Ahoy, control car! Mr. Wood is waiting to come aboard, sir," a chief petty officer on the mast shouted through a megaphone.

"Tell Mr. Wood to stand by," the officer of the deck had megaphoned back.

Each one, as he came to the top of the mast, had asked permission from the "bridge" before he had stepped on to the little gangway. At times the ship was buoyant enough to take him. Others had been ordered to "stand by." In a few minutes the ship would grow lighter, and the order would come for one more to step aboard. That meant only minutes for them, for it was certain that they were going. It meant more for the passenger. Weight in fuel took precedence over passenger cargo. If enough "lift" remained after the required amount of gasoline was aboard, the passenger was going; otherwise, no passenger. [. . .]

THE CRITICAL OPERATION OF CASTING OFF

No one who is not needed is on the "bridge," the forward navigating gondola, during those critical operations. The others are at their designated "landing stations" or being shifted back and forth along the keel, human plummets, to keep the long tube balanced. Water is dropped in spurts of hundreds of pounds when the ship is heavy. In an emergency, even a gasoline tank may go. Men are shifted again to keep the balance. The ship must rise when it casts off, only for a few seconds, until the propellers have caught hold, but enough to clear the mast, which would cut its thin sides like a knife.

Rear Admiral William A. Moffett, chief of the Navy Bureau of Aëronautics, was in the rear of the little cabin as I squeezed down the ladder. I was the only passenger until the mountains had been crossed and San Diego reached. [. . .]

Lieutenant Commander Lansdowne sat in one of the forward windows of the gondola. Lansdowne is one of the type who foresees difficulties and does not get excited, but deftly and quietly avoids them.

Lieutenant Commander Lewis Hancock, Jr., executive officer and navigator, was close by; Lieutenant John B. Lawrence held the steering wheel; Lieutenant A. R. Houghton was officer of the deck, with hands and eyes on the network of handles which empty ballast bags, and Chief Petty Officer L. E. Allenly was at the wheel of the "elevators," or horizontal rudders.

"We must weigh off right away, before we start to lose our superheat," Captain Lansdowne announces.

"Can tell from the mast that we're heavy aft, sir," Allenly reports.

"What water can we drop?" Lansdowne demands.

"We have three emergency bags aft and two forward," Lieutenant Houghton replies.

"You can drop any in the afterpart, sir," says Lieutenant Roland G. Mayer, keel officer.

"What's at frame 40?" Lansdowne asks.

"Four hundred pounds extra at 40, sir," Mayer replies.

"Clear away aft," Lansdowne orders through his little megaphone.

"Are we light?" asks Lieutenant Lawrence. Nobody answers.

"Still putting oil aboard, sir," comes a voice from the mast.

"Idle engines," Lansdowne orders in a sort of resigned voice. The few extra pounds of fuel must be crowded aboard.

"Idle engines, sir," echoes Lieutenant E. W. Sheppard, the engineer officer, holding the signal levers.

The dials are the same as on the bridge of a ship, but there is a lever for each engine in the five separate gondolas. Sheppard swings two handfuls of levers with one motion. The bells ring and repeat as the levers fly back and the men in the gondolas acknowledge the signal.

"Ship at least 300 pounds light," says the mast. "Last fuel coming aboard, sir."

"Very well; shut off fuel," Lansdowne assents. "Secure the water line up there," he adds in a louder voice.

"Aye, aye, sir," the mast replies.

"We're now falling off to the right," says Lieutenant Lawrence, at the steering wheel. Four minutes have been consumed in the jockeying.

"How's the ship?" Lansdowne demands from an officer on the top of the mast.

"Still heavy, sir."

"Let me know when she's light," in a nonchalant voice. Everybody waits quietly; no strain; the ship will rise; only patience is required.

"Elevators neutral, sir," Commander Hancock announces.

"Neutral, sir," Allenly echoes. That means the ship is in equilibrium.

"A cloud is coming over the ship," Houghton announces.

"We'll have the sun again in a few minutes," Lansdowne adds, as if to himself.

"Are all hands on their landing stations?" he suddenly asks.

"On their stations, sir," Command Hancock reports.

"She's coming up now, captain," from the mast.

No more questions; no more conversation. Two more minutes have gone.

"Have an inversion of temperature aloft," the voice from the mast breaks the silence. It is a warning that the ship's buoyance will change as soon as she rises.

"Thank you," replies Lansdowne. "How high?"

"Only up to 2,000 feet."

"How many degrees? Considerable?" Lieutenant Lawrence inquires.

Lansdowne repeats the question. It is not answered. No time. The cloud has passed. The ship is picking up as the sun strikes it again. An opportunity may come in the tick of a second when she can slip away from the mast.

"Is the ship light?" Lansdowne asks.

"Not yet, sir," the mast replies.

"Is her nose secure? Is Rosendahl aboard?" he asks in a single breath.

"Yes, sir; she's just about in equilibrium," Lieutenant C. E. Rosendahl replies, without regard to sequence, as he comes down the ladder.

"Let me know the minute she is light," Lansdowne requests.

"About equilibrium," the mast replies.

"Let go as soon as she will lift out of the cone," he orders.

"Stand by the water for emergency aft," Commander Hancock orders.

Lieutenant Houghton grips two of the handles more firmly. One pull and 550 pounds will be dropped by each.

"Elevators amidships, Allenly," Lansdowne orders.

"Tail's a little down, sir," the mast advises.

"Take your time," Lansdowne replies. "I don't want to get off heavy."

Everybody knows that the clamps, which fit like bent fingers into the rim of the cone, have been released, and that the big ship, gently balancing her length on the still air, will float free from the mast like a feather.

"Five seconds on 110," Lansdowne orders.

Houghton switches handles and pulls. Five seconds spill 300 pounds of water ballast. In the keel 2,200-pound rubber bags hang on each side of frames 40, 100, 110, and 170. Each of them drops 30 pounds a second when a handle in the control car is pulled. Four emergency bags are at frames 30 and 180 and two at 194, each of which drops 550 pounds of water ballast in one splash.

Only 300 pounds lighter, but she starts to rise.

"Free, captain!" comes a shout from the mast.

THE SHIP STARTS TO SETTLE

The ship sways just a little more. Slowly she starts to settle, as she falls away from the supporting mast.

"Water forward!" Lansdowne exclaims, sliding from the window to his feet.

Her nose stops, poised and almost imperceptibly starts upward. Aft she is still dropping.

"Water aft!" he exclaims. Houghton is pulling handles and water is pouring on the ground. She teeters like a swing board.

"Water again, forward, quickly!" Lansdowne says, almost excited.

"Standard speed," he adds. Her nose has drifted back from the mast. The drive ahead can be risked.

"Standard speed, sir," Sheppard echoes. The levers click, bells jangle and repeat, as the levers fly back again. Quicker than it can be told, the men, hands on the throttles in five separate cars, like one machine, have their motors roaring at 1,200 revolutions a minute.

Slowly the ship gathers headway. She seems to hesitate, as if reluctant to leave, holding her nose toward the ground.

"Pull the water in her nose," Landsdowne snaps.

"Pulled, sir," Houghton echoes, as 550 pounds more drop in a single splash, spraying the windows of the forward car.

The nose bobs upward from the released ballast. It is equivalent to dropping three men. One man walking the length of the ship when the engines are not running changes her level 3 degrees, so carefully is she balanced. After she is under way they can move at will, the elevators by their resistance to the air keeping her trim. However, men cannot be dropped overboard to lighten the ship. Men, engines, and a certain amount of fuel and oil are not classed as "disposable" ballast.

"Two more men aft," he adds in the same breath.

"How far, sir?" asks Lieutenant Mayer, as he runs up the ladder.

"All the way."

"A man from 105 and a man from 60, into the tail," is shouted down the long keel tunnel. The vibration of the motors drowns the thud of their feet, as they race uphill along the narrow runway.

The ship is rapidly gathering headway. Her nose is pointing upward at an angle of 10 degrees.

"She's all right," Commander Hancock vouchsafes.

"Watch your rudders," cautions Lieutenant Rosendahl, with an eye on the mast which he has just left and which the ship's tail seems to be clearing by inches.

"Stand by to cut out fuel tanks," Lansdowne orders, and Bauch scampers up the ladder, pulling the cutting pliers from his pocket.

Even fuel must go if necessary. The speeding motors can increase the ship's lift 10 per cent, but that means tipping her nose upward by means of the elevators. After an angle of 13 degrees is reached, the maximum lift is obtained and the only relief is to drop ballast.

The casting off, including the interruptions from clouds and delayed fuel, had taken only 16 minutes. The waiting until the sun generated sufficient heat was of several hours.

"Climb as fast as you can," Lansdowne orders.

"She's climbing, sir," responds Allenly at the wheel.

Patches of mist lie over the bay. The city seems too near for comfort. Automobiles and persons around the mast are becoming specks.

"She's 500 feet above the mast, sir," says Hancock, as we circle upward.

"Keep her climbing," Lansdowne repeats.

"How high, sir?" Houghton asks.

"As high as she'll go, Regg," the skipper replies, as the tension relaxes. "Take her to pressure height."

Pressure height usually is 4,500 feet—that is, if the ship starts with her bags 85 per cent full of helium. As she ascends into more rarefied atmosphere the gas expands, keel officers and riggers pulling and straightening the bags, until at 4,500 feet they are full. Through the keel, in the apex of the triangular tunnel, runs a big rubber pipe, connected with each of the 20 bags. When the twine which closes their mouths is unwrapped, the gas circulates from one to another until the pressure in each is equal.

At 4,500 feet, bags and pipe are swollen almost to bursting. Higher than that, the straining gas escapes through safety valves and the ship's lifting capacity diminishes. The load must be reduced a proportionate amount.

Casting off and mooring are much the same operations, only reversed. In each the ship is headed into the wind; it is balanced along its length, so as to be parallel with the ground, and put out of equilibrium, so as to be light or heavy, according to whether the ship is leaving or landing. In casting off, ballast is dropped to make the ship lighter. In landing, gas is valved to make the craft heavier. The engines are of no assistance in lifting until after the ship is free from the mast, or in landing after its downward drive has stopped.

As the noncombustible helium gas which the Navy uses costs $55 or more per 1,000 cubic feet, valving is frowned on. With the dangerous, but inexpensive, hydrogen, landing can be made almost at will. Similar liberal valving of helium would cost from $5,000 to $20,000 for each landing. Consequently, advantage is taken of Nature's changes. Landings are made at night, when the ship is cool and heavy, and departures well after sunrise, when the gas is superheated and light.

The gas is extremely sensitive to temperature. Frequently, even as late as midnight, when the ship drops within 300 feet of the ground and the engines cannot be used to drive it farther, it bounces up again like a rubber ball, from the heat still in the earth.

Temperature of the ground, in addition to wind velocity and direction, is always ascertained before attempting a landing.

To make a landing, a crew of 200 or 300 men is needed to hold the ship down. To make a mooring at a mast, a dozen men on the ground are sufficient to couple the two cables and start the machinery. To lead a ship out of a hangar requires the same ground crew of several hundred. To cast off from a mast, the only assistance required from outside is to uncouple the gas, fuel, and water pipes and snap back the clamp holding the ship's nose.

The engines help to drive the ship down until it is within a certain distance of the ground. If it is going directly to the mast, a steel cable is dropped, which the men below couple to one from the top of the mast; the ship rises again and a dummy engine pulls its nose down to the mast.

If the ship is going to land on the ground, ropes are dropped, and the ground crew swarms on them like flies as soon as they are within reach. A trained crew is required.

In the fraction of a second that the ship is stationary—the infinitesimal pause between the time engines are driving it down at 45 miles an hour and the buoyant gas starts to shoot it up again—dozens of men must grab the rope and hang on. A second too early would knock them over, as if catching an express train, and an instant too late would skyrocket them heavenward.

An enthusiastic Filipino messboy jumped and grabbed a rope once and rose 30 feet before he could let go. He awoke in the station hospital.

The record of Chief Petty Officer O'Shea is famous in Navy annuals. O'Shea held one rope of a basketless free balloon and some 40 men held the other.

"Let go!" shouted the captain to O'Shea.

"Let go!" echoed the 40 gobs. They did. Like a flash, O'Shea was 100 feet above the ground, at the end of a 40-foot rope. Before it occurred to him to let go, he was several hundred feet higher, and it then was too late. O'Shea started following the rope hand over hand. The balloon was shooting up like a rocket, and if O'Shea's "think tank" was slow, it was determined and unflustered. The last his comrades saw of him before he was a disappearing speck, he had almost reached the bull ring under the bag.

A near-by observatory reported that he was a chilly 14,000 feet high when he gave up trying to reach the flapping valve rope and started to rip the side of the balloon.

It started down in wild circles, O'Shea now on top and again on the bottom. The flapping bag caught in the net, parachuting a few hundred feet, then rolling into a ball and dropping like lead for a thousand, unfolding again into a glide, until finally O'Shea landed, fortunately, in a river. He could not swim, but was fished out, asked for a cigarette, and made no comments.

Later, O'Shea became so excited over an argument with his wife that he piloted a balloon over the family home and dropped the sand ballast, without bothering to take it from the bags, with such accuracy that a hit was made through the kitchen roof at the busiest hour of wash day. O'Shea was retired from the service, but his experience is part of lighter-than-air curriculum, as illustrating the danger of grasping airship guy ropes without holding the motion open for immediate reconsideration.

FLYING OVER NEW JERSEY, PENNSYLVANIA,
AND DELAWARE

As the *Shenandoah* left her home mooring mast at Lakehurst, 10 A.M., October 7, she described a broad circle with a 5-mile radius, until the altimeter on her "bridge" showed 1,300 feet. That was the level above the sea, and in New Jersey it meant practically the same above the ground. A few days later, when the same altimeter registered 7,300 feet, going through the Rocky Mountains, she was only a few hundred feet above the bottom of the canyon and the menacing peaks on either side were above her.

Jersey, with its little lakes and big hotels, patches of fertile farms and smoky cities, miles of stunted pine and cranberry bogs, was left behind when the Delaware River, opposite Chester, Pennsylvania, was reached at 11:25. The *Shenandoah* followed the river, her shadow trailing below like a big fish on its surface, until Wilmington, Delaware, was passed, 20 minutes later. Baltimore was below at 1:37 P.M.

Going 55 miles an hour, the start and finish of a race at Laurel were seen from a safe altitude of 3,000 feet. An escort of airplanes came out from Washington, the ship passed between the Monument and the White House at 2:10, and the District of Columbia was crossed in 10 minutes.

THE EARTH SEEMED COVERED WITH RUGS AND CARPETS

As she sailed along over the low, rolling hills of Virginia, straight into a fire-red sun whose last rays were tinting the tops of the forests in gay autumn hues of red and yellow, the first purple haze of evening had fallen on the streaked brown fields and green pastures in the valleys.

From the skies the undulating earth seemed covered with carpets in drab and green and rugs of bright colors, cut into squares and strange shapes and marked with strings of white, which were highways.

Darkness fell below while the sun still was striking through the windows of the navigating gondola. The ship was over Orange, Virginia, at 3:59 P.M., Charlottesville at 4:35, Esmont at 5, Norwood at 5:30, and Lynchburg at 6:20. Danville, Virginia, was below at 8:10, and a few minutes later the *Shenandoah* was sailing over North Carolina. [. . .]

FEW LIGHTS GLOW ON THE SHIP AT NIGHT

Greensboro was an electric cluster in a black setting at 9:20 P.M., High Point was 1,000 feet below at 9:55, a dozen colored flares burning in a greeting which was easily understood, and Salisbury followed an hour later with a salvo of locomotive whistles from Spencer into town, dimly echoing to the ship. Gastonia, North Carolina, was a fading glow at 12:37 A.M., October 8, and at 1:27 Gaffney, South Carolina, was directly below.

In the navigating gondola the electric light over the chart table was flashed on only to glance at a map or make an entry in the log. A faint glow came from the little bulbs behind the spirit levels and compass.

White running lights were on the forward and aft gondolas, green lights on the two starboard cards, and red on the two on the port side. Within, all was dark, except for a moment on the bridge or for the glow from electric torches in the long tunnel in the keel, as men passed back and forth, changing watch in the engine cars, measuring fuel tanks, inspecting motors and gas bags, and performing other tasks which required constant vigilance.

The ship is not wired for lights. Only those in the navigating room, in the radio shack, and the running lights are on batteries. Each individual carries his own torch. Though helium gas will not burn, no fire is permitted aboard. The only sparks are in the six motors—one runs the radio generator—and in the little two-burner gasoline cookstove in the latter's closet.

In the dark the long keel is eerie with phosphorescent figures and letters, which glow from every latticed frame or piece of emergency generator, with lights which flash in the distance and disappear and lights which suddenly appear from nowhere, while one fur-padded form leans at a danger angle and another passes on the ribbon of a runway.

Day and night the life of the airship is in the keel. It is a triangular tunnel running the length of the ship. Its base is the thin cotton bottom panel of the outer covering of the big tube; its equilateral sides are the gas bags, when they strain full against the wire and twine network which holds them in place.

"THE CAT'S WALK"

In the center, 682 feet long from nose to tail fins, is the runway, 9 inches wide. It is called "the cat's walk," from the skill required to tread it. The thin cotton covering, 12 inches below, gives a false sense of security, but the ground, usually 3,000 feet below, is only two steps removed. A roughly stitched rent in the cotton shows where one man made the first step, and with true sailor veracity the marks of his fingers are shown where he gripped the steel-hard duralumin to save himself from taking the second step.

No admonitions are needed to walk the straight and narrow path. The crew, as nimble as structural steel workers, trot along, pass each other, and even stop to wrestle.

Four lateral runways pierce the sides of the tube to ladders leading into motor gondolas. Though the runway is precarious, negotiating an uninclosed ladder 3,000 feet above the ground while speeding 70 miles an hour requires cooler nerves.

Men skip up and down and even stand on the gondolas to watch the passing scenery. One night in the mountains the chief on his hourly inspections found a door closed at the bottom of one of the ladders. Considerable kicking made him heard above the din of the motor. He inquired why everything was closed.

"You see, we were so close to the mountains, and I saw some goats and was afraid one might jump in here," the man explained.

HOW THE GAS AND WATER BAGS ARE DISTRIBUTED

Every 5 meters in the tunnel, corresponding to the outer circular ribs, is a triangular frame of latticed girders. In the center of the ship the triangular frames are 12 feet across and 9 feet between base and apex. The sides become shorter in the ends, and heads are bumped and cut by the cross-girders. One bump convinces the most skeptical of the rigidity of the *Shenandoah.*

In the upper angle of the triangle is the rubber gas pipe, wilted and loose or puffed to the size of an 18-inch water main, according to altitude. Flanking it are the metal fuel and water pipes. At the sides, distributed so the load will be equalized through the length, are the 724-pound gasoline tanks, the smaller cans of lubricating oil, and the sleeping bunks for officers and men. One habituated youth slept in a hammock, only the cotton between him and space, as comfortable as if his bed were swung between the towering aërials of the Arlington wireless station.

At intervals along the runway are three decks, little 12-foot-square

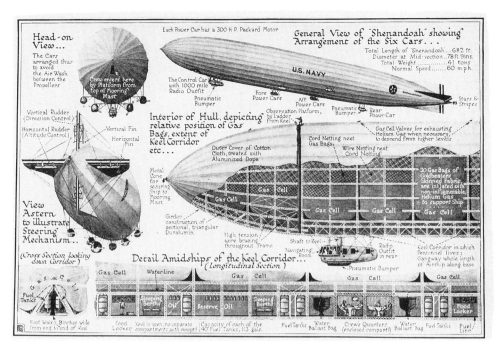

By Charles E. Riddiford. Courtesy of the National Geographic Society.

platforms of thin plywood. One is for the mooring equipment and the other two are euphoniously designated as officers' quarters and crew's quarters. Though discipline does not deteriorate, "side" is lacking on an airship. Instead of a suite of three rooms and private bath and messboy, to which a rear admiral is entitled on a battleship, his private bunk is not different from those of the crew. The same-sized shaving mirrors, the only luxury aboard, hang in both quarters. The rations are the same, the combination cook and messboy is the same, mess hours are whenever anybody has time to eat, and as the food, including the hot soup, is distributed from the crew's quarters, the officers frequently munch their dry sandwiches there.

In daytime the keel is fairly light, through the white cotton flooring, which is not blackened inside, as is the remainder of the outer tube.

At night it is dark and mysterious. The emergency dials glow like ghostly faces with cabalistic words and signs, dots and dashes for levers and buttons. The chill wind whistles against the thin covering, and the motors, which never stop, roar right beneath. Silent muffled figures are huddled on the bunks, some wormed into padded sleeping bags, other bundled in fur suits, fur mittens, and wool boots. Lights always are flashing and moving in the dim distance.

On the crew's deck, lit by a dying electric bulb, will be a group of men who have come off duty—wheelsmen with weary eyes and arms, machinists with ears stuffed with cotton, drinking hot coffee from tiny paper cups—and a chief figuring out his hourly report of the fuel consumed and the gallons of converted water ballast.

While half the ship sleeps, the other half watches and works, day and night, four hours on and four hours off. Other nights were like the first night. The routine never changed any more than did the mad roar of the motors.

Scenery differed with every hour, winds rose and fell, the moon faded from a fat white ball to an emaciated crescent, some nights were foggy and others were clear, but life never varied in that long tunnel, like an uncanny shaft of a mine floating thousands of feet in the air.

Spartanburg, South Carolina, was crossed at 1:57 A.M.

The morning sun was following up over the hilltops, cutting long furrows through the mist hanging in the valleys, before Atlanta was reached. Atlanta was rubbing the sleep out of its eyes at 4:35 A.M. (central time), but, judging by the number on the streets, a large share of the population had left a call, possibly with the fire department, to be awakened when the *Shenandoah* was heard approaching. Carrollton, Georgia, was left behind at 6:32 and the Alabama border crossed a few minutes later.

Long before Birmingham was reached, at 7:15 A.M., the mantle of smoke from her steel mills was visible. Railroads and devious highways wound through the valleys and hills, gullied by freshets of many years, over which the ship was speeding at 55 miles an hour. Three Army airplanes came out to meet her.

Birmingham's whistles could be faintly heard, 2,500 feet below, and nearly every roof on the cluster of skyscrapers in the center of the city was crowded with spectators, their faces white dots in the distance.

From Birmingham to the Black Warrior River the forest seemed without a break.

Motors were running at only two-thirds speed, 1,000 revolutions a minute, but the ship was making time, with a fair wind behind.

OVER THE LAND OF COTTON

The Mississippi border was crossed and Columbus was below at 9 A.M. Greenville and the Mississippi River were crossed at 11:47.

Many of the 24 States sailed over had a Columbus and a Greenville on the route. Columbus may have been an omen for a pathfinding ship and one Greenville was the birthplace of Commander Lansdowne.

Through the second day the *Shenandoah* was over the land of cotton. Baskets of white and scattered groups of darker figures were in the fields, and square bales, dice in the distance, were piled at every railroad station. Clearings around weather-beaten houses with dirt roads faintly visible through the trees would spring out of the forests. Every house seemed to have a family with numerous children. While chickens and cows ran in terrified circles, the children would gaze in awe or wildly wave greetings. [. . .]

The *Shenandoah* was over Bastrop, La., at 2:10 P.M., passed Shreveport and the Red River at 4:15, and was almost to Texas. Night had fallen when the lights of Dallas twinkled below at 7:40 P.M. At 8:30 P.M. she was above the mooring mast, 8 miles outside of Fort Worth. At 9:45 she had cooled sufficiently to approach low enough to drop her cable. The cables were coupled and she rose to be pulled down the mast.

As frequently happens with new machinery, the winch balked and it was 11:05 P.M. before she was wound down by hand and anchored.

Fort Worth is the home of helium gas, of which the United States claims a monopoly. It is extracted from natural gas, and the Navy's helium plant, in charge of Lieutenant Z. W. Wicks, is about a mile from the mast. Other gas deposits contain helium, but none so far discovered has sufficient quantity to be extracted economically.

Fort Worth was enthusiastic, as was all Texas. So many thousands of the well-known make of automobile which will run in all seasons over Texas plains were entangled in the surrounding fields and roads that many of the shirt-sleeved, sombrero-crowned drivers did not get their families home before daylight. [. . .]

FORT WORTH IS LEFT BEHIND

At 9:46 A.M., October 9, the *Shenandoah* left the mast, circled over Forth Worth, followed the main boulevard, over the schoolhouses with their yards filled with children, over the six-story mansion where Dr. Cook has been allotted a 14 years' residence, and was off toward Tolar.

The difficult leg of the voyage—to cross the Rockies—was starting.

Officers and crew had worked through the night and 17,016 pounds of fuel, 850 pounds of oil, and 2,500 pounds of water had been taken aboard. Her gas cells bellied inward, only partially full, along the inside tunnel. As she climbed over the mountains they would be taut, 5,000 cubic feet of gas escaping through the safety valves for every 100 feet of altitude above the pressure height.

Ranger slipped by at 12:45 P.M., Eastland and its oil spindles at 1, Cisco at 1:12, and Putnam at 1:30. In the clear atmosphere which continued through that day and the next to the California border, the horizon was 50 or 75 miles away, and the ship, almost a mile above the surface, could be seen for miles. However, ranchers, accustomed to gazing across the plains, would dash for the nearest windmill and climb its ladder, believing that they could see the ship better. [. . .]

GETTING THE RADIO MESSAGES TO THE AMERICAN PRESS

It seems that all the automobiles in Putnam were on a hill outside the town. Two miles farther the glasses disclosed a dozen cars around a derrick operated by a farm tractor, the drivers watching a freshly struck oil gusher. Five minutes later a railroad train was overtaken in the midst of the plains. It had stopped and crew and passengers were on the ground gazing skyward. School children of Baird, at 1:45, their bright-colored dresses like blowing flower petals, ran along the street after the ship.

Whistles, which echoed faintly 3,000 feet above, announced Abilene at 2:20 P.M. The population was on the roofs or in the center of the streets. In the railroad pens, sheep and longhorns milled around in fright.

The radio operator aboard had been talking with an amateur in town. He stopped suddenly, explaining when he resumed that he was "out looking at the ship."

This was only one of some 200 amateur operators with whom the ship established communication during the cruise. Thousands of others heard the radio either broadcasting talks from the ship or handling messages by Morse code.

Most of the amateurs were members of the American Radio Relay League, and it will be a revelation to many to know that hundreds of these amateurs are communicating across the country day and night, exchanging serious and frivolous messages, but establishing a great, unseen system of communication which might be a national resource in emergency.

These operators stood by through the cruise, ready to send or receive messages. There was seldom an hour, day or night, that one or more could not be raised. Many were boys, one was a bedridden youth, others were retired telegraph operators, and few were former Navy operators.

Messages they received were turned over to the telegraph companies or relayed by their own system across the country. [. . .]

TRYING TO DISTINGUISH BISBEE
FROM DOUGLAS, ARIZONA

In addition to the amateurs, the *Shenandoah* was in communication with fourteen Navy, six Army, and six commercial stations. Not counting messages exchanged by telephone or talks which were broadcast, 45,332 words were sent and received during the 258 hours the *Shenandoah* was in the air. Most of them were weather reports and press messages, the former received and the latter sent.

When the officers are not too busy, talks on the *Shenandoah* and the trip were broadcast at night. These were not announced in advance. Hundreds who picked them up by accident wrote describing their amazement when a voice from the speeding ship sounded over their parlor speaker. Several were in isolated ranch houses or mountain lodges. On account of the clearness of the voice, many inquired whether the messages came from the *Shenandoah* in the air or from a big land station.

The enthusiastic fire chief of Chehalis, Washington, wrote: "It was so foggy when you past over that we couldn't see you, but we rung the fire bell and blowed the siren, and I ran into the house and put on the earpieces and listened to you talking."

When it was uncertain whether the ship was over Bisbee or Douglas, Arizona, the resourceful Lieutenant Palmer asked his auditors, being sure that he had some, to tell the automobilists in the streets to flash their lights on and off—slow in Bisbee and fast in Douglas. He opened the door of the gondola and leaned out. Headlights already were starting to flash below—fast, slow, and assorted speeds. It was Bisbee, as was later ascertained, but no two persons in Bisbee agreed on what was slow. [. . .]

THE GEOGRAPHY OF THE TEXAS PLAINS VIEWED FROM THE AIR

The vast open spaces of Texas were breaking into hills half an hour after Abilene was left, at 45 miles an hour. Part of Sweetwater had trekked out of town and the remainder was on roofs and freight cars at 3:14 P.M. Two women and a little girl in bright sunbonnets had climbed a barren hill.

Roscoe, with its little squares of cotton, was below at 3:28, Colorado at 3:55, and Iatan at 4:20.

A train which had been attempting to keep pace gave up the race at the little town consisting of a railroad station, water tank, three houses, and a cattle corral. The first of the foothills of the Rockies had been reached, and the road would curve and climb while the ship sailed straight ahead.

Railroads and highways are straight for a hundred miles in the corrugated-tin-roof and red-paint belt of Texas and in New Mexico and Arizona as well. From the little cow stations, automobile tracks stretch just as straight across the plains, disappearing in the distance, but showing that life is beyond. Even the cattle paths do not curve as they radiate from the water holes which spot the drab, dry country without regularity or reason. [. . .]

Though the *Shenandoah* was climbing, the ground was coming up faster.

Midland, with the Llano Hotel as a roof garden, was below at 6:47, Odessa 30 minutes later, and at 7:50 the Pecos, both river and town, were crossed at an altitude of 4,500 feet. At 9:50 she was over Van Horn, with an altitude of 6,600 feet and still climbing. Ears stung from the rarefied air.

EVERY MAN ON DUTY AS THE SHIP SPED TOWARD
THE MOUNTAIN PASS

The ship was lighter, from the fuel which had been consumed in the 12 hours from Fort Worth, and the gas was cooled both by the chill night and by the 74-miles-an-hour speed; but the bags were swollen and straining against the nets, and gas flowed in a steady stream through the safety valves into the wicker chimneys to the ventilators above.

Water ballast had been dropped until only fuel could be jettisoned to lighten her further.

The *Shenandoah* was rushing toward the first of the mountain passes, with cross-winds whipping around the peaks and eddying into the valleys below. Every man was on duty.

Half of the officers were in the navigating car. Others patrolled the keel, watching the gas cells or ready to cut out more ballast.

Two men were on duty in each of the motor gondolas. Time was figured in split seconds; each man was ready, so close might be the difference between safety and destruction. Commander Lansdowne was on the "bridge."

The ship was now going through the passes, keeping as low as possible to save gas, but an unforeseen emergency might force her to rise suddenly and go over the ridge.

The clear night with a full moon was almost as bright as day. In the bottom of the valley thin lines of black and white under the moonlight were the railroad and highway on either side. Open fire boxes of passing locomotives sent up a red glow and automobile headlights made long flashes on the road. Red and green pin points of switch lights and the white clusters of tank stations came and vanished, as the ship followed its winding course.

The black peaks were above the ship and the brown, furrowed shoulders of the mountains seemed to reach out in the pale light to rub the fragile side of the graceful intruder. They came close, but always fell back.

The eddying wind blew in fierce gusts, which if they had swerved the 682-foot tube, would have dashed it to pieces in the narrow pass.

The lights of Sierra Blanca were below at 10:15 P.M., and the giant ship was speeding through the tortuous channel at 60 miles an hour. Her motors were roaring at full speed, 1,400 revolutions a minute. She responded to her rudders without a quiver, riding as smoothly as a ship on a calm sea.

The line of white road disappeared through the mountains and the black ribbon of steel vanished into a tunnel. The *Shenandoah* climbed and passed over the top. Ahead could be seen the valley of the Rio Grande. The first ridge of the Rockies had been crossed. Fort Hancock, on the river, was below at 10:45, and the course was headed northwest, toward El Paso, skirting the loops of the winding stream and Mexico, lying darkly beyond.

TEXAS IS LEFT BEHIND

El Paso gave a welcome of whistles, flashing flares, and a searchlight, which played on the sides of the ship when she sailed over, at 11:30 P.M., and left Texas behind. Strong winds followed up the valley. She sped across New Mexico at 79 miles an hour, over Deming at 12:10 A.M., October 10, and Lordsburg at 1:32.

When the Arizona line was crossed, at 2:10, the winds changed. The *Shenandoah* fought them until she reached her hangar at Lakehurst, two weeks later.

Bowie, Arizona, was below at 3:07 A.M. The ship's nose was pointed toward the canyon beyond; Dos Cabezos, 7,300 feet high, guarding it on the south, and the Pinaleno Range, more than 10,000 feet high, on the north.

A 25-miles-an-hour wind was whistling out of the mountain pass. The moon had slipped behind a cloud, and the dim line of railroad which we had been following was no longer visible. The headlight of a locomotive flashed into view far ahead in the pass and the *Shenandoah* drove toward it into the wind. The current caught her broadside.

She drifted for a breathless second. The rudders held and she slowly slid forward between the towering peaks, which rose out of the gloom, and into another valley.

"THE WORST OF THE ROCKIES CROSSED"

Cochise was passed at 4:12 A.M., and the even narrower Dragoon Pass was ahead. The lights of the little cattle station of Manzoro were below at 4:30, and the *Shenandoah* was driving into the pass. In the dim starlight it seemed that the mountain walls were within a few feet on either side, and that the long ship could not even turn in the narrow defile. A freight train showed the way into the inky tunnel and the ship worked slowly through. Benson, near the summit of the divide, sparkled ahead at 5:19, the east was faintly pink, and the worst of the Rockies had been crossed. Commander Lansdowne climbed the ladder and threw himself on his bunk.

Tucson, thousands of feet below, looked like gaudy stage scenery with its red roofs, green streets, and white walls on a background of brown desert, under the clear morning sun, at 6:30 A.M. If any inhabitants were awake, they were not visible. No life marred the picture. Maricopa at 8:20, Estrella at 9:40, and Gila Bend, with the Gila River a dark-green line through the clouds of dust far to the north. Irrigated farms were green squares on the prevailing brown. From the air, the new Southwest seems to be growing in squares—towns, blocks, houses; farms, fields, and barns—as life is irrigated into the desert. [. . .]

Mohawk Pass, with a few green-roofed houses and black mountains, straight as a wall, went by at 11:42. Just as little breezes toss the dust into patterns, the winds and waters of years had traced giant figures over this dry country, their lines measured in miles. The broad outlines are disclosed only when viewed from the clouds. From the height at which the *Shenandoah* was sailing, the panorama was unbroken for 50 miles in any direction.

The brown ribbon of the Colorado River, with a fringe of green on its east bank, was crossed at 1:55 P.M. Yuma lay across the river to the south.

Dust dimmed the sunlight, even at the ship's altitude, as it entered California and turned northward along the east shore of the Salton Sea.

The Imperial Valley was another irrigated checkerboard of green, its borders fighting against the shifting sands of the desert as tropical clearings do against an ever-encroaching jungle. Indio was reached at 5:15. Darkness fell suddenly.

Rain and snow were driving against the ship when she reached Banning, at 7:05. Sunny California's greeting, which swept in from the San Jacinto Valley, was frigid. The temperature in the forward car dropped to 35 degrees and the ship started to drop from the chill and weight of snow. This quickly melted, and at 8:10 the course turned westward over San Bernardino, reaching the Pacific off Seal Beach at 9:15.

The *Shenandoah* was over the North Island naval air station mast at San Diego at 10:48 P.M., Pacific time. Thirty minutes later she landed on the field, but was not moored at the mast until 1 A.M.

THE ONLY ACCIDENT OF THE CRUISE

The only accident of the cruise occurred in this landing. The guy ropes were dropped and the ground crew pulled the big ship slowly down. It was the crew's first experience with such a job. Urged by the officers inside the forward gondola, they caught and eased it gently to the ground. The rest of the crew, a city block away, seeing a shape as large as a battleship slowly settling toward them, stood back, and the rear gondola met the ground with a sharp bump. The jolt was transmitted through the struts, which anchor gondola and tube, to the framework inside the latter, buckling one of the vertical girders in the triangular runway.

The ship, when on the ground, rests on the rattan and pneumatic cushions under the forward and rear gondolas. The ship, 682 feet ¾ inch long, is 97 feet 1 inch high from the bottom bumper to top. The tube is 78 feet 9 inches in diameter at its eight widest frames.

HOW THE "SHENANDOAH" IS BUILT

The crumpled girder was replaced while the ship was at the mast, 150 feet from the ground. All the parts were hauled up by hand. Only two men could work in the cramped quarters at the same time. Five days were necessary, but it showed that major repairs could be made at a mooring mast.

The silvery covering of the tube is stretched over a skeleton of triangular-shaped, latticed girders of duralumin, which is one-third the weight of steel.

The *Shenandoah* was built on the plans of the Zeppelin L-49, which came down in the American area in France. Her structural strength was increased, which adds to the weight, but which stood in good stead through the Rockies. An additional frame was added in the center, increasing her length and making possible an increasing lift by another gas cell, but not improving her stream line or speed.

The five engines which carried the *Shenandoah* through the mountains are each of 300 horsepower, the two forward, close under the tube, with direct-drive, 11-foot propellers, and the remaining three with propellers 18½ feet in diameter. Two of these are reversible and water-recovery condensers are on three of the motors. They recover from 110 to 122 pounds of water ballast from every 100 pounds of gasoline consumed.

The *Shenandoah*'s gas cells have a displacement of 2,148,070 cubic feet. Under certain barometric conditions, if filled with hydrogen, they would lift 150,365 pounds, and with helium 85 per cent of that, or 128,884 pounds. As the gas starts to expand as soon as the ship rises, it seldom is more than 85 percent filled. Under such conditions, the lift of the helium-inflated *Shenandoah* is 109,551 pounds.

The dead weight of the ship, when dry and without water, gasoline, or oil, is 82,000 pounds. This cannot be changed, and the ship must be lightened from the "disposable," in distinction from the "useful," load. The 15 per cent reduction in inflation means a 40 per cent reduction in the entire load, as well as 40 per cent less than what an 85-per-cent-full hydrogen ship could lift.

Helium is safe and the *Shenandoah* has demonstrated that it is practicable. Its cost is the principal argument against its use. A single minute's valving to descend may lose from $2,000 to $3,500 worth of the precious gas.

THE START UP THE PACIFIC COAST

The weather was raw and hazy, with head winds down the coast, when the *Shenandoah* cast off from the San Diego mast at 9:15 A.M., October 16. Fifteen minutes later she had rounded Point Loma and was headed northward, over the Pacific Ocean, and 5 miles offshore. The battle fleet was at target practice, shots ricocheting across the surface with splashes a mile apart, in San Pedro Channel, off Catalina Island, at 12:15 P.M.

Greetings were exchanged between Admiral S. S. Robison, commanding the fleet, and Rear Admiral Moffett, the first of such high rank to make a cruise by air.

The *Shenandoah* circled inland over Los Angeles, skirted Hollywood at 1:10, passed over Santa Monica five minutes later, and was again out over the Pacific.

Picturesque Santa Barbara, white surf breaking below, mountains in the distance, and a string of automobiles on the winding road, was on the starboard side at 3:40. Dusk was falling over the lighthouse and white-fringed rocks of Point Conception at 6:07 P.M. Point Arguello was off the bow at 7 P.M. and the course laid out to sea, straight for Point Piedras Blancas, which was turned at 10:55. Point Sur Light was sighted at 1:17 A.M., October 17, and Point Cypress at 1:55.

Farallon Light was to port at 6:15, but San Francisco, 30 miles away, was invisible in the fog. Point Reyes was turned at 7 o'clock, the town of Mendocino at 11:34, and Fort Bragg, with its peaked-roof redwood lumber mills, at 11:55 A.M.

Point Delgada was reached at 1:04 P.M., and Cape Mendocino, a graveyard of ships of the sea, with its bobbing lightship, at 2:50.

When Admiral Moffett had charge of lighthouses a sleepy skipper told his Scandinavian wheelsman to steer straight for that lightship. He obeyed, and the captain was awakened by the crash, as his craft cut the lightship in two.

Thousands of seals, basking on Sugar Loaf Rock, off Cape Mendocino, flopped into the water as we passed.

Dogs, whales, and pelicans seemed the only denizens of earth, water, or air which were not terrified by the ship. Dogs barked, while other live stock ran; a pelican followed the ship's shadow on the surface as if it were a possible fish, while the whales played with it for miles.

Eureka and the Eel River valley were near at 4 o'clock, and at 7:35 P.M. Brookings, Oregon, was opposite and the California coast had been left behind. The rising moon was silvering the sky back of the mountains and lights were flashing at the black mouth of the Rogue River at 9:10 P.M., and at 12:30 A.M., October 18, the ship turned inland over Florence, Oregon, up the Siuslaw River valley, turning northward again in the Willamette Valley, about 15 miles north of Eugene, at 1:58 A.M. It passed between Corvallis and Albany at 2:25, over Salem and the lights of the capital at 3:10, Silverton, with two red flares, at 3:15, and was invisible in the fog when the lights of Portland glowed below, at 4:16.

CRUISING TEN HOURS TO SAVE HELIUM

The radio telephone told the ship that it was over the mooring mast at American Lake, a part of Camp Lewis and about 10 miles south of Tacoma, at 8:15 A.M. As far as the eye could see, there was a solid floor of fog, the peaks of Hood, Rainier, and Glacier, of the Cascade Range, like sentries on a 200-mile front, to the east, and the tip of a single smokestack, the second tallest in the world, to the west.

The mooring mast was invisible, and in the sunshine, over the fog, the ship was two tons light. It cruised at 40 miles an hour to keep down, but did not moor to the mast until 6:30 P.M., October 18.

With the enforced time-killing to avoid valving helium, the voyage north against the head winds had taken more than 57 hours. It was the most monotonous leg of the entire cruise. Smoking is tabu on the ship. A dry smoke, plug, or chewing gum is the only consolation. Smoking one cigar for 57 hours, with an inch unconsumed at the end of the trip, is almost a record.

The Sunday sun was late in rising in Tacoma, and it was 12:05 P.M., October 19, before the *Shenandoah* cast off from the Camp Lewis mast on its return voyage. Tacoma was crossed at 12:25 and the ship circled over Seattle from 1:00 to 1:20. Green Lake, at 1:05 P.M., was the farthest north of the voyage or for any airship on this continent. Admiral Moffett was on the hill of the Bremerton navy yard, with the *Mississippi*, which he once commanded, below and the *Shenandoah* above, at 1:35. The fish traps in the tip of the Hood Canal were on the right at 2:20.

For the next hour the *Shenandoah* was sailing over the drear Skokomish Indian Reservation, with its virgin forests, its cleared circles furrowed like big chrysanthemums by the fallen pines, little homes springing up and prosperous farms along the streams—a pictorial story of growing civilization from the forest and the chase to industry and the farm.

Hoquiam was passed, at 3:25 P.M., and we turned southward over the Pacific at 3:47. [. . .]

Cape Lookout was passed at 6:12 and Cape Arago, in a thick fog, at 9:10 P.M. Cape Mendocino Light was sighted at 1:55 A.M., October 20; Punta Gorda at 2:30, Fort Bragg at 4, and after that everything disappeared in the fog. Beneath it could be heard the sirens of steamers, and through the chasms in the solid mantle of white came glimpses of white-capped waves, surf breaking on rocks, and once of a ship rocked by the storm.

SAN DIEGO MAST LOST IN A FOG BANK 1,000 FEET DEEP

At 8:15 the fog had disappeared and the *Shenandoah* was facing a 50-miles-an-hour gale off Point Arena. For an hour the rocks of the point stuck by her side. Bodega Head was reached at 12:30 P.M., and Point Reyes at 1:55. Only 68 miles had been covered in 5 hours and 40 minutes.

With another struggle she rounded the last rocky head, changed course at Duxbury Point at 2:30, crossed Drakes Bay, where Sir Francis refitted his ships, but failed to discover San Francisco harbor, and sailed over the Golden Gate at 3 o'clock. She swung across San Francisco and was out by San Mateo and over the Pacific again at 3:30.

Monterey was passed at 3:58, Point Sur at 7:41, Point Piedras Blancas at 8:50, Point Arguello, where the skeletons of seven destroyers lie, at 10:32, Santa Barbara at 11:45, the fleet anchored off San Pedro at 2 A.M., October 21, and the San Diego mooring mast at 4.

The mast was unseen and unheard under the fog bank, 1,000 feet deep. When the first pink flush of dawn showed the black peaks of Mexico over a snow-white world, the *Shenandoah* was 20 miles south of the border. She doubled back until Table Mountain, in Mexico, was sighted, at 7:30 A.M. [. . .]

At 9:03 the fog started to burn off. Point Loma suddenly jumped into view, seemingly only a few feet under the bridge, at 10 o'clock. The ship landed on the field at 10:55 A.M. and was moored to the mast at 11:40.

Rear Admiral Moffett had left the ship at Camp Lewis. Captain Stanford E. Moses, commander of the air squadron of the battle fleet, and Lieutenant Commander R. D. Kirkpatrick, battle fleet aviation officer, had made the voyages between San Diego and Tacoma. Joe Johnson, the movie operator, made the northbound voyage.

Captain Thomas T. Craven, commander of the San Diego station, came aboard at San Diego. No more passengers could be risked for the trying trip over the mountains.

The *Shenandoah* cast off from San Diego at 11:07 A.M., October 22, headed south toward Tia Juana, circled between the Otay reservoir and the city to warm up and increase her buoyancy, to get an altitude of 6,000 feet before crossing the first cordillera of the Rockies. She was going south of the Salton Sea. [. . .]

Sailing was bumpy, and the heavy ship was gliding on the swirling air waves in dips which the altimeter showed were nearly 1,000 feet between trough and crest. It was the same during the next day over Ohio—no roll, but a pronounced tip to decks and runway.

"She's 5,000 pounds heavy and tipped all she can stand, and the engines going full speed," Halliburton insisted.

"Do you want to spill fuel?" Commander Lansdowne asked. [. . .]

"Not just yet," Lansdowne decided.

GASOLINE TANKS EMPTIED TO KEEP AFLOAT

Cottonwood was below at 12:25 P.M.; Campo, 12:50; Jacumba, where the last emergency water ballast was dropped on the corrugated tin roofs, at 1:00; Coyote, the first city in the Imperial Valley, 1:40; El Centro, with Calexico and Mexicali, in Mexico, seeming only a few feet away, 2:01; Yuma, Arizona, three miles to the south, 3:10; Mohawk, 5:20; Aztec, 5:46; and Gila Bend, 6:55.

More than a mile above sea-level, the gas was cooling rapidly in the heavily loaded ship. Two gasoline tanks were jettisoned of their contents and another was dropped outright farther on.

The night was cool, and even with a ton of ballast gone, the motors were forced to drive her at an angle to maintain the altitude. Enid was recognized at 7:30; Maricopa, 7:50; Casa Grande, 8:15; Tucson, 10:00, and the course was changed to the southeast west of Benson at 10:41.

Near Naco, along the border, the faint moon disappeared. The ship slipped over a mountain, picked up the railroad track, and a few minutes later was over a brilliant city nestling in a bowl of the Mule Mountains, with black peaks on three sides. It was Bisbee, and railroad and valley ended.

"She's tilted to 13 degrees and can't do any more," Halliburton declared, as he clattered through the metal door and down the ladder.

The motors were straining to the limit. If one had missed, she would have dropped on the mountain side, rapidly coming nearer. Another tank of gasoline was dropped and she rose to 7,300 feet, turned over Bisbee and its mountain walls at 12:40 A.M., October 23, and was going so fast when Naco was sighted ten minutes later, that she was in Mexico before she was able to swing around again to the eastward.

RADIO WHISPERS OF TRAGEDY

The danger was passed. Clear sailing was ahead. Hunched over his key and dials in the radio shack, "Mr. Sparks" resumed his interminable experiments; testing, picking up messages here and there and trying to get stations thousands of miles away. Suddenly his heart jumped as his headpieces, clamped to his ears, ticked out the fragment, "——in the explosion automobile burned. Both dead."

That the 724-pound gasoline tank had hit an automobile when it crashed to the ground and burst into flames flashed through his mind. The catastrophe had happened. No need to alarm the other officers. Frantically he worked at his key to locate the station which had sent the message. It was gone. No answer came. Other stations came in but knew nothing. He persisted, groping through the air. Then out of the clear, after what seemed an age, came another message, "Man arrested here confesses automobile accident."

This time he located the station. It was several hundred miles from the course of the ship. He took off the headpieces and realized he was perspiring. Even up in the chill clouds the cabin seemed stuffy. He opened the door and looked out. Aft the motors were roaring as if alive, 3,000 feet below the earth slept under the moonlight. It seemed like a nightmare from another world.

Douglas was passed at 1:27 A.M.; Rodeo, New Mexico, 2:30; Hachita, 3:47; Hermanas, 4:40; Columbus, of Villa infamy, 5:21; El Paso, Texas, 9:00 (central time); Fabens, 10; Fort Hancock, 10:45; Sierra Blanca, 11:40; Van Horn, 12:45 P.M.; Pecos, 3:14; Odessa, 5:05; Midland, 5:34; Big Spring, 6:26; Colorado, 7:27; Sweetwater, 8:06; Abilene, 8:57; Fort Worth, 1:30 A.M., October 24, and moored to the mast at 2:27.

The fuel ballast lost in the mountains had killed hopes of a nonstop flight across the continent. If the first night had been less cool or the winds more favorable, it might easily have been made, so much influence do heat and wind have to the sailing time of an airship. However, the return was by the rougher northern route.

The Fort Worth mast was left at 10:33 A.M., October 24, with 16,296 pounds of fuel aboard. Dallas was passed at 11:30; Rowlett at noon; Greenville, 12:48 P.M.; Clarksville, 2:55; Morris Ferry, Arkansas, 4:17; Lockesburg, 4:45; Hot Springs, 6:57; Little Rock, 8:17; Newport and the White River, 10:25; Jonesboro, 11:55; the Mississippi at New Madrid, Missouri, 1:46 A.M., October 25; Paducah, Kentucky, 3:39; Evansville, Indiana, 5:17; Columbus, 8:00; Richmond, 9:30; Greenville, Ohio, 9:55; Dayton, 10:38; Springfield, 11:15; Columbus, noon; Zanesville, 1:06 P.M.; Moundsville, West Virginia, 2:30; Waynesburg, Pennsylvania, 4:10; Chambersburg, 6:28; York, 7:25; Chester, 9:00; Philadelphia, 9:40, and Lakehurst, New Jersey, 11:00, landing on the ground facing the hangar at 11:55.

THE "*SHENANDOAH*" COMES TO REST BESIDE THE "*ZR-3*"

An hour later the $2,000,000 *Shenandoah* was berthed in the $3,600,000 hangar, at the side of the fat ZR-3, a sailing palace compared to the strictly utilitarian American-built airship.

America's first venture in rigid airship building with its American crew had made the longest cruise of any dirigible from a home base, was the first to see the Pacific or the Northwest of the United States, and had proved that mountains are not a barrier to the big ships, and that helium and mooring masts, which the Zeppelin-seasoned builders and navigators scorn, are practicable. [. . .]

The cruise of the *Shenandoah* was over an uncharted world. Beacons by sea and signs by land have been built through the ages for those who voyage on the surface. A new era of transportation is coming nearer, in which the airship will have a place as a conveyance of peace as well as an instrument of war. Many lessons were learned on the *Shenandoah*'s cruise.

The American-built and American-manned airship in that cruise showed that mountains and distances are easily negotiable. It also tested the practicability of the American innovations which have been added to the plans Count von Zeppelin laid down.

The voyage to the North Pole and the exploration of the vast unknown polar regions have been made nearer realization by the *Shenandoah*'s venture in the face of a blustering autumn. With the springtime, polar flights may come and the world's most inaccessible region will be within easy reach of man.

The United States now has two great airships, small when compared to those of 5,000,000 and 6,000,000 cubic feet displacement, which are planned, but which have already demonstrated their airworthiness and capability for the rigors of polar exploration.

The WRECK of the SHENANDOAH

Words and Music by MAGGIE ANDREWS

The Wreck Of The Shenandoah

Words and Music by
MAGGIE ANDREWS

Shen - an - do - ah_____ The pride of all this
brave - ly strug - gled_____ They worked with all their
crew lay sleep - ing_____ Her last great flight was

land_____ Her crew was of the bra - vest_____
might_____ But the storm could not be con - quered_____
o'er_____ They'd gone to meet their Ma - ker_____

___ With a he - ro in com - mand._____
___ And the ship gave up the fight._____
___ Their ship will fly no more._____

The gi - ant mo - tors thun - der'd_____ She proud - ly
Her sides were torn a - sun - der_____ Her ca - bin
Their lov - ing wives and child - ren_____ And friends with

sailed a - long___ Each man was at his sta - tion___ Each
was torn down___ The cap - tain and his brave men___ Went
brok - en heart___ Are mourn-ing for their loved ones___ Since the

heart was true and strong___ They start - ed for St.
crash - ing to the ground___ And four - teen lives were
storm tore them a - part___ But their faith will not be

Louis___ As day turned in - to night___ With not a
taken___ But they've not died in vain___ Their names will
shaken___ They'll see them bye and bye___ For they're wait - ing

thought of dan - ger___ On that sad and fa - tal flight.___
live for - ev - er___ With - in the Hall of Fame.___
up in Heav - en___ Where the brave go when they die.___

Arthur Rebner
Lyrics translated from the German by
Friederike von Schwerin-High and Jeffrey L. High

The Zeppelin March: "Los Angeles" U.S.A.

Respectfully dedicated to Dr. Hugo Eckener, the famous commander of
our Z R III

Till recently people would snear
"cleverly" at the idea
that anyone would wish to fly to God's domain.
The modern Icarus,
and all his followers,
paid no attention to their critics' disdain!

Though he worked relentlessly
he still did not live to see
the day when the heart soared in everyone's chest.
Friedrichshafen's favorite son,
now you rest, your work is done.
You helped us build the bridge from East to West.

Each town square, corner, alleyway
is filled with masses of people today
gazing into the sky as if hypnotized.
In cellars low, on rooftops high,
people gather to watch the sky.
Berlin, Berlin, can it be? You've been mesmerized!

Then from the fog there streaks
an airship with pointed beaks,
soars over gigantic in the bright sunshine.
The thund'ring propellers roar
while hundred thousands and more
sing Zeppelin, Child of German land.

Zeppelin, they join the joyous refrain,
Zeppelin, Zeppelin, Zeppelin.
Symbol that one day peace will reign,
across the oceans to and fro you shall glide.
One fine day all men will be brothers,
war, discord, hatred and envy subside,
again on that day we will see each other
Zeppelin, Zeppelin, Zeppelin.

ON THE Z·R·3

Uke arr. by *Jeanne Gravelle*
Words by
SAM M. LEWIS
and **JOE YOUNG**

Music by
WALTER DONALDSON

Was-n't I in a hur-ry,
An-y-time that I'm lone-some,

To leave my
I wish I

hap-py lit-tle home, and roam a-way?
had a pair of wings, so I could fly.

Am I in a hur-ry,
I feel mighty lone-some,

To see that same old lit-tle home?
But I'm an an-gel with-out wings,

Well, I should say!
so I must sigh.

But the fast-est go-in' train would be too
Oh! I'd give the world to see my folks to-

slow,_____ If I had my way, Here's the way I'll love to go._____
day,_____ And I al-ways dream that I'm go - ing back this way._____

Chorus

On _____ the Z. R. 3. _____ I wan-na go back, I wan-na go back to

Ten-nes-see. _____ While I'm fly-ing high, You'll hear me

cry; "Look up, folks,__ no more you're gon - na look down on me."_____

And when I see, _____ those Dix - ie farms _____

Car - o - lin - a, You look fin - er, Ev - en bet - ter than you did be - fore.

Hear that hum - min', Ban - jos strum - min', Bet two bits it's the Swan - ee Shore.

Oh! boy smell those frit - ters Ain't smelled frit - ters since the Lord knows when,

Oh! boy smell that chick - en, Some - thin' tells me that I'm home a - gain.

Tie this blimp of mine __ To the Mas - on Dix - on line. Oh! can't you

rit

D.S. al Fine

Phenomena

Great-enough both accepts and subdues; the great frame takes
    all creatures;
From the greatness of their element they all take beauty.
Gulls; and the dingy freightship lurching south in the eye of a
    rain-wind;
The airplane dipping over the hill; hawks hovering
The white grass of the headland; cormorants roosting upon the
    guano-
Whitened skerries; pelicans awind; sea-slime
Shining at night in the wave-stir like drowned men's lanterns;
    smugglers signaling
A cargo to land; or the old Point Pinos lighthouse
Lawfully winking over dark water; the flight of the twilight
    herons,
Lonely wings and a cry; or with motor-vibrations
That hum in the rock like a new storm-tone of the ocean's to
    turn eyes westward
The navy's new-bought Zeppelin going by in the twilight,
Far out seaward; relative only to the evening star and the ocean
It slides into a cloud over Point Lobos.

The ZR 3 *Los Angeles*. Courtesy of the National Air and Space Museum.

from Beyond Horizons

The *Norge,* a semirigid type, was simply a skeleton of three-quarter-inch steel tubing encased in an envelope of strong rubberized fabric. She was 348 feet long. Her inner hydrogen cells had a capacity of 672,000 cubic feet of lifting gas—about one third that of the British R 34, which had recently crossed the Atlantic. To accommodate the cabin, the lower keel was broken, well forward, and the cabin was roofless and integrated with the envelope. Thus, one in the cabin could look up into the rigging beneath the gas cells, or could stand and see up and down the whole length of the keel. A light duck walk rested on the bottom tube of the keel, and forward there was a duralumin ladder leading up to the air valves in the space between the envelope and the gas cells. [. . .]

The cabin of the *Norge,* a basket framework floored and covered with canvas, was but thirty feet long and six feet wide. Canvas partitions divided it into three compartments—the pilothouse forward, a central room for the navigator-captain, observers, and weather service, and a radio room aft. These partitions, however, were little more than suggestions, wide arched doorways cut in them giving a view from one end of the car to the other. A corner of the radio cubicle was curtained off as a toilet.

On the walls hung portraits of King Haakon and Queen Maud which [Roald] Amundsen had had on the *Fram* in Antarctica. There was also a picture of the Virgin, which the Italians installed. The Pope gave the Italian members of the crew a special audience in Rome before their departure and blessed for them medallion pictures of the Madonna, which they wore on chains around their necks. Most of them also wore bracelets with gold identification tags. For a good-luck piece, on the wall hung, pressed between panes of glass, a four-leaf clover given to the expedition by Major Scott, the British dirigible pilot.

We had all been coached in advance in the safety rules for the flight, and a copy of these rules was pinned up in the cabin. Nothing was ever to be thrown overboard. The propellers were all aft of the car and, when spinning, might be shattered by even a small object hitting them. No one could walk on the keel gangway except on rubber soles, for fear of striking sparks in an atmosphere of gasoline vapor and escaping hydrogen. No smoking, of course. For hot food we must rely entirely on the coffee and soup in the thermos bottles. We carried primus stoves, but they were in the rigging, to be used only if we were forced down.

To spare every ounce of weight we could for the fuel, we all agreed in advance not to carry any extra clothing or personal effects beyond what could be put into an ordinary rucksack. Our riggers, for instance, dressed in overalls and canvas sneakers, though they had warm flying clothes over them. I wore only slacks, flannel shirt, and sweater, but over them I had on Byrd's polar-bear trousers and my own reindeer parka. Most of us in the cabin had on ordinary town shoes, but in the cabin were big canvas overshoes filled with senna grass into which we could thrust our feet. Nevertheless, the temperature remaining low during the entire flight, we all suffered more or less from cold, especially when in fog. When the sun shone it warmed the canvas sides of the car a little.

Having made such sacrifices, taking with us not even an extra pair of socks apiece, we were rather startled to see General [Umberto] Nobile climb aboard, carrying his little terrier Titina done up in a dog sweater. Titina was the only female being aboard on the flight. She stayed most of the time under her master's sleeping bag in the folding armchair in the pilothouse—the one chair in the cabin. But Titina really behaved very well—as well as you could expect of a dog cooped up in a tiny crowded space for three days and nights.

After Nobile boarded the *Norge*, the rest of us came on. Though we had succeeded in raising the useful-load capacity of the ship up to almost eleven tons, with all weights being estimated we knew we were figuring very closely. The original plan was to carry nineteen men, including five Italian riggers; but since the principal service of the riggers was to assist in a landing, they were not indispensable. After ten of us were in the cabin, the engineers in their nacelles and Omdal aboard, the lines in the hands of the ground crew began to sag a little.

Alessandrini and Arduino, the riggers, climbed in, and the ropes went limp in the groundmen's hands. The airship was in exact equilibrium. We therefore closed the cabin door, leaving behind three riggers who had flown up from Rome.

Every man now took the place assigned to him. Nobile's seat was in the bow at the port side of the pilothouse. Behind him was a control board with signal wires to the engines and cords running to the hydrogen exhaust valves and ballonets. Across from Nobile was Horgen at the wheel of the lateral rudder, controlling direction. Behind Horgan sat Wisting at the elevator helm, in control of climbing or descent.

Riiser-Larsen's place was on the starboard side of the middle compartment, where he had a little table for his maps and calculations. On the floor at his feet were his sextant and other navigational instruments. A slot cut in the middle of the floor accommodated the drift indicator. Malmgren was at the back end of this compartment, his blackboard weather map on the partition behind him. Amundsen, Ramm and I sat in the other three places here, changing about as we pleased. I say sat, but actually there were only three or four folding camp stools in the car. We stood up, squatted on our heels or cross-legged, sat on rucksacks, or even sprawled on the floor, when we could find leg room. There was little comfort. The two wireless men in their booth aft, however, had stools and narrow shelves for tables.

The morning had advanced so far that the sun began to warm the balloon, and the hydrogen cells, pumped full at night temperature, became overinflated. Nobile released gas, and the ship lost lift. A pull at some cords dumped the contents of several sandbags suspended under the cabin, and the handlers' ropes once more tautened. Everything was ready. The idling engines were shut down completely; and at 8:55 A.M. [May 11, 1926] Nobile shouted in Italian from his window: "Let go the ropes!" An instant later Riiser-Larsen repeated the order from his side in Scandinavian, and slowly and without a sound the great airship began to rise.

The morning had brought a flat calm, and our ascent was almost perpendicular. Nobile dumped more sand, and the movement accelerated. It was so smooth, so even, as to suggest planetary motion. We were not rising; we were poised, and the world was falling away from us as if lowered by hydraulic power. The walls of the fjord leisurely went downward past us. Familiar faces, uplifted toward us, grew indistinct and then unrecognizable. From behind the fjord mountains rose up, glaciers and infinite snow fields glittering in the sun. Kings Bay became a toy town set in an immense white plain.

Then came a phenomenon for which we were not prepared. Swarms of gulls and other polar birds flew out from their rookeries in the cliffs to inspect this huge new cousin of the air. The air vibrated with thousands of flashing wings and shrill, excited cries. In the stillness of our cabin we could hear the roaring of the Josephine Ford far below, as Byrd and Floyd Bennett took off to bear us company during the first stage of our journey.

We rose above the fjord, and once more the North spread out under our eyes. The Byrd plane climbed up to us, its engines scaring away our feathered escort. Signal bells rang, and the engines started. With the dignity of an ocean liner, the ship came around, headed for the mouth of the bay. There we turned northward to maneuver for the meridian of the Kings Bay wireless station, which we were to follow to the North Pole.

For half an hour the *Norge* moved at its calm fifty miles an hour up the Spitzbergen coast, past a majestic procession of glaciers and snowy peaks. The Byrd plane, much faster, literally flew rings around us. The *Norge*'s motors were far enough back to allow easy conversation in our canvas gondola, even over the length of the car. The temperature at Kings Bay had been about ten degrees below freezing, but the upper air was colder. Thin clouds scarcely obstructed the sun at all. [. . .]

We worked eastward and adjusted the ship along the Kings Bay meridian, then set the sun compass for the North Pole. Let me note that our flight proved to be the longest meridional voyage—that is, travel on a due north and south line—ever recorded. After a final swing around us, Byrd and Bennett waved farewell and turned back. Below us lay the crinkled water of the Arctic Ocean; but far ahead on the horizon a "blink"—that shining band which ice reflects into the sky—showed that the polar pack was still there.

Two hours after leaving the hangar we reached the fringe of the pack, and then the pack itself. It was just as it had been, piled and broken, a vast sweep of white desolation, silent, mysterious. Our practiced eyes told us that the few narrow crooked leads were studded with ice blocks and newly frozen over. At first we saw a few seals, a few polar-bear tracks, an occasional little auk, but after Lat. 84° N. there was no more life. [. . .]

The sun was almost due north, and we kept watching the chronometers for midnight. The moment came, and I started a new day in my diary—May 12. May 12? In the bustle and absorption of getting away on our flight, I had forgotten the significance to me of May 12. My birthday—I was forty-six years old! Ramm, the news hawk, heard my exclamation and sent a dispatch about it. A little later I received a radiogram of congratulation signed "Your friends in Kings Bay."

About this time another personal dispatch came aboard the *Norge*. It was for Gottwaldt, informing him that the king had that day decorated him with the Golden Medal of Merit. Gottwaldt was the Norwegian navy's chief wireless expert.

But the fog began to thin out at last, and at 1 A.M. we had it behind us. After Lat. 88° N. there had been several holes in it through which we saw that the Arctic was still an ice-locked sea. At about 1:15 A.M. Riiser-Larsen knelt at his window with his sextant, and we knew that the North Pole was close at hand. The sun had come around to the east, on our navigator's side of the car.

To the layman I think I can explain the simple method by which we determined that we had reached the Pole. From radio bearings, sextant observations, the sun and magnetic compasses, and drift corrections, we knew that we were exactly on the meridian of our course. The ship's true speed had been determined by frequent sextant observations for latitude. Riiser-Larsen knew that we should be at the Pole approximately at 1:30 A.M., May 12, Kings Bay meridian time. He knew the height the sun should have at the Pole at that moment. He set his sexton for that height and held it to his eye, ready, the bubble level keeping the instrument horizontal. If all these calculations were correct, the instant the image of the sun covered the bubble in the sextant we would be on the exact top of the world.

When Riiser-Larsen knelt down at his window, a silence fell over the cabin, broken only once when Riiser-Larsen admonished Horgen to hold the ship very true and steady to its course. Minutes dragged. Then Riiser-Larsen, with his sextant to his eye, announced calmly: "Here we are!"

At once Nobile rang the engine bells, and the motors shut down. A dirigible having little momentum, the *Norge* stopped almost immediately. I saw Oscar Wisting in the pilothouse turn around and look at Amundsen. Amundsen returned his stare, and neither said a word. They were now the only men ever to reach both poles. [. . .]

We now took care of the little ceremony of planting flags at the Pole. The riggers and engineers were summoned to the gondola to watch. We bared our heads, Amundsen dropped the flag of Norway, then I the Stars and Stripes, and finally Nobile the Italian ensign and some Italian societies' flags. The staffs of these flags were provided with vanes to make them drop straight and stick their steel points into the ice. They all stood upright on the pack, the light breeze we had come to know so well barely lifting the banners.

The engines were started at half speed, and for an hour or more we circled over the Pole at a low altitude, three hundred feet. There was really nothing to see—ice, ridged by pressure, fewer leads in it perhaps, but no doubt drifting and eddying like all the rest of the pack. Since all directions now were south, the setting of a course to Alaska was a matter of angles—twelve degrees to the left of the meridian that brought us up from Europe. We set the sun compass for this track and at 2:30 A.M. started full speed south.

And now Amundsen had his little joke with me. He said I had celebrated my birthday prematurely. The moment we left the North Pole on the Point Barrow meridian, we were in Alaska time. It was no longer 2:30 A.M., May 12, but 3:30 P.M., May 11. We had the afternoon and evening of May 11 to live over again. The sun, which an hour before had been in the northeast, starting its southern swing that brought official day, was now in the west, beginning its night phase in the north. Though I had already celebrated two hours and a half of my forty-sixth birthday, I still had to wait nearly nine hours for it to begin. [. . .]

For Amundsen and me, the real interest of the voyage began at the

North Pole. We then entered the largest unexplored area left on earth. That journey of fifteen hundred miles began with perfect visibility. The ship flew at an average altitude of 1,200 feet, giving us a view of fifty miles or more in every direction. We kept watch always for land, but there was always the same ice under us.

After leaving the Pole, most of us tried to sleep, but we found sleep almost impossible during the entire voyage. The noise, the cold, the uncomfortable positions, and the fact that men were always moving about and stepping over one drove sleep away. The best we could do was nod a little when sitting or sprawling on the floor.

At 7 A.M.—for convenience we continued to use Norway time—we came to a hypothetical spot on the map hitherto unseen by man, the so-called Ice Pole. The Ice Pole, at Lat. 88° N. and Long. 157° W., is the geographical center of the Arctic ice mass, the edges of which are all explored and known. Looking down upon it, we could also believe that it was actually the physical center of pressure, the pivot around which the whole polar pack was drifting. It was nothing but a chaos of barricades and ridges, without ever an open lead among them. We agreed that surface travel of any sort would be impossible here.

Two hours later, when we were twenty-four hours out of Kings Bay, we reached Lat. 86° N. and were halfway to Point Barrow. We had used less than one third of our gasoline. For this entire distance we had had almost perfect visibility. Since Sverdrup had already established the nonexistence of land masses between Siberia and the North Pole, we could say with assurance that the eighty-sixth north parallel embraces no land at all. If our mode of travel had permitted us to make a sounding of the ocean at this point, the scientific results of our expedition thus far would have been complete.

But at this point our troubles began. At the Pole itself we had looked forward with some confidence to a perfect voyage to America, but it was not to be. Between 88° and 86° N. Lat. a few scattered pools of fog lay on the ice, but at 86° fog began in earnest and continued during the rest of the flight.

At first we flew above it in clear sunshine, since the bank only reached up to an altitude of a thousand feet; but after a while, as the fog continued to thicken, this became impossible. With the radio working well, however, and the accuracy of the Arctic isogonics already established, the ship could still be navigated truly. Our chief concern was over the fact that we could no longer see the surface of the earth. I would not give the impression, though, that this whole fog area was solid. There were numerous breaks in it, some of them big ones, so that we were able to make an adequate observation of the sea all the way to the Alaskan coast.

After about an hour of blind flying, our radio reception grew fainter and finally ceased altogether. The aerial had iced up. This antenna was a wire 450 feet long trailing from the after end of the gondola, under the radio room. Fog particles froze to it in the form of milky ice, until, when the radio failed, it resembled a long flexible rod of porcelain. The air propeller, providing power for the wireless, iced over, too, and finally locked, leaving only the storage battery for the radio. Gottwaldt and Strom-Johnson wound up the aerial and cleaned it several times, but in vain. As soon as it was dropped it iced over again. Increasing static added to the difficulty of reception. As a matter of fact, we received no more wireless messages south of 80° N. Lat., and later we learned that our own signals failed at about that point.

There was no more nodding or drowsing for anyone now. The situation was too anxious. All afternoon of May 12 (Norway time) the *Norge* drove southward, often flying between clouds and fog. Through breaks we frequently observed the polar ice and found its character much the same as the ice of these latitudes on the European side—floes massed together, leads running east and west. By evening (morning, Alaska time) clouds and fog began to merge in one woolen mass. At 8 P.M. May 12 (9 A.M. in Alaska) we came out into an open area, and there was sunshine long enough for Riiser-Larsen to use his sextant. We were only 350 miles off the American continent.

Fog made our cabin miserably cold, and it was especially hard for Riiser-Larsen, Malmgren, and the two radiomen, who had to work with their bare hands. A new note of peril sounded. One of the riggers dropped down into the cabin with the news that the engine propellers were detaching fragments of ice from the outside braces and wires of the nacelles and blowing them as projectiles through the envelope under the keel, making holes which the men above were patching.

We all knew now we were in the critical stage of the flight. If ice plates or large splinters went into the propellers, smashing them, the flying blades would most certainly be shot up through the balloon, tearing open the hydrogen bags and forcing an immediate landing. Or, even if this extreme disaster did not occur, with disabled engines the ship would be powerless and impossible to navigate in the grip of an Arctic cyclone. As if sensing the peril, the terrier Titina, who had slept most of the way from Spitzbergen, now jumped from her chair to the floor, where she cowered and whimpered. She did this several times during the last part of the flight.

The bombardment of the envelope by ice particles continued. By standing up in the cabin, we could hear the pieces hit the taut fabric. Once a big piece ripped through and made a hole so large that the dirigible had to be throttled down while the riggers repaired the break. Thus hour after hour the *Norge* battled on. Malmgren kept giving us the safest levels. The weight of ice on the bow could still be balanced by shifting the gasoline ballast. Most of the time the ship limped along on two engines while the riggers and engineer chipped ice from the propeller blades of the third. [. . .]

When Riiser-Larsen got his four-o'clock shot at the sun on the morning of May 13 (Norway time), we discovered that the ship was holding a true south course practically on the meridian we had chosen at the North Pole—twenty-one miles west of it. This was magnificent navigation—blind flying for hours, having only the oscillating magnetic compass for direction and only yesterday's weather map on which to base estimates of drift. Moreover, Riiser-Larsen was making no particular effort to keep on the meridian. We were now aiming not at a particular point, such as the Pole, but at a coast line 700 miles long. Yet, though we did not know it until later, our navigator brought the *Norge* in so close to Point Barrow that we were actually sighted from that town, and the government telegraph there sent out the first news that our expedition had crossed the Arctic.

At the time he made that observation Riiser-Larsen, after averaging our speed during the last eight hours, announced that we could expect to see land soon after 6 A.M., ship's time. The wind, which had started to blow from the southeast, was backing to the northeast. Fog conditions had improved. As we approached the coast we had several miles of visibility, the ship no longer gathered rime, and the fusillade of ice against the keel had ceased. At 6:50 A.M. Riiser-Larsen, who for some time had been studying the southern horizon through his binoculars, sang out: "Land off the port bow!" He had been observing it for several minutes but wanted to make sure before he spoke.

We all got out field glasses and scanned the distance ahead. The ship was now running above packed shore ice, and all that was to be seen, thirty miles or more away, was a faint black line in the solid sheet of white. The course was altered to the southeast, giving us a rough, quartering headwind, and it was an hour before we came in. The black line proved to be a string of immense boulders on the beach itself. Behind them the snow-laden coastal plain, flat and almost as low as the shore ice, lost itself in fog.

We came over the beach at 7:50 A.M., Norway time, having made the voyage from Spitzbergen, 2,000 miles, in a little less than forty-seven hours, including two hours spent at the North Pole. Scientifically speaking, the expedition was ended. We could conservatively claim to have looked down upon a hundred thousand square miles of unexplored territory. We could tell geographers that there is no Keenan's Land north of Point Barrow, no land at all between Alaska and the Pole. We had established the scientific fact that the North Polar Region is a vast, deep, ice-covered sea. The white patch on the top of the globe could now be tinted blue.

Hugo Eckener
Translated from the German by Douglas Robinson

On the *Graf Zeppelin*

I have always felt that such effects as were produced by the Zeppelin airship were traceable to a large degree to aesthetic feelings. The mass of the mighty airship hull, which seemed matched by its lightness and grace, and whose beauty of form was modulated in delicate shades of color, never failed to make a strong impression on people's minds. It was not, as generally described, 'a silver bird soaring in majestic flight,' but rather a fabulous silvery fish, floating quietly in the ocean of air and captivating the eye just like a fantastic, exotic fish seen in an aquarium. And this fairy-like apparition, which seemed to melt into the silvery blue background of sky, when it appeared far away, lighted by the sun, seemed to be coming from another world and to be returned there like a dream . . .

The LZ 127 *Graf Zeppelin* on the ground at Lakehurst, New Jersey.
Courtesy of Hepburn Walker.

Hugo Eckener
Translated from the German by Douglas Robinson

A Sentimental Journey to Egypt

The great success, beyond all expectations, which had been achieved by the flight of the *Graf Zeppelin* could at first glance have led to the agreeable conviction that we had been delivered from all troubles and difficulties, and could now count on the Zeppelin Company being generously supported by public officials. But we promptly found that nothing of the kind was happening. What we needed was to raise the capital to build a better ship with improved performance, and we also needed operating funds to continue with the flights of the *Graf,* as the world called the ship. Compliments are very fine, but then cannot be eaten, and popular enthusiasm is elevating and bestows on effort and hard work a moral uplift and exaltation, but these cannot take the place of lifting gas, with which the airship's cells have to be filled. At that time, in the winter of 1928−29, I had not yet comprehended the degree to which the interest of great newspaper enterprises and of stamp collectors could be exploited to supplement the receipts from carrying passengers.

We had to raise operating funds somehow. Where were they to be found? Theoretically, we could imagine a capitalistic enterprise seeking to develop a business out of commercial Zeppelin transportation. But at this time they seemed to lack courage and confidence. There must still be eager groups in the population, enthusiastic about the Zeppelin, who would contribute to a subscription. But how could I dare to direct another appeal to the German people? And so there remained only the State, the Government itself, to help us out of our difficulties with subsidies. Yet the agencies most important in this respect, in spite of taking an unmistakably more friendly attitude, were still very noncommittal, since there were yet more important tasks, in their opinion.

Finally I struck on the idea of inviting a number of important Government officials and influential party politicians on a fairly long flight, to give them an opportunity to learn from their own experience the safety and comfort of voyaging in a Zeppelin, which they only knew in theory. This flight would naturally have to be a specially attractive one, and I decided, for three reasons, to plan one to the Eastern Mediterranean with a landing in Egypt. Firstly, such a voyage would provide an easy opportunity to solve a number of navigational problems which would also be interesting to our passengers; secondly, it would lead through a region which scenically, as well as being the site of many historical events from antiquity to most modern times, would be extraordinary and rich in associations; and, thirdly, it would be an effective publicity flight, both for the people whose cities we would fly over, as well as for the German politicians who would observe from on board the extraordinary impression which the Zeppelin airship aroused in the world generally.

I had intended to prepare for our very influential guests, who perhaps would be the ones to decide whether a Zeppelin air line was to be or not to be, a beautiful journey in an even greater sense than that mentioned above. It was the severe winter of 1928–29, and in Germany since the beginning of January we had had temperatures hovering around zero. I had planned the take-off for February 24, in order to meet early spring on the Riviera and full spring in the Eastern Mediterranean. But on February 20 we registered 11 below zero in Friedrichshafen, and the masses of snow covering the whole of Western Europe and Russia made it seem certain that we would have to wait weeks longer for milder weather.

So I postponed the journey a full four weeks, and set it for the 21st of March, the beginning of spring, according to the calendar. And even then it was still so cold over Central and Southern Germany that the passengers in our cabins, which were then unheated, did not take off their winter coats until we reached Crete. Most of the palm trees along the Riviera had frozen in this, the severest winter for the past fifty years. It was a wonderful experience, therefore, for our passengers, after a rather chilly midnight take-off from Friedrichshafen and a night journey across France, to find warm sunshine beaming down on them at Marseilles, on the first morning of spring.

In the next hour and a half we flew along the Riviera to San Remo at such a low and comfortable altitude that all the beauties of this attractive stretch of coast could be taken in at our ease. We then turned off to the south, and soon saw to our right the imposing mass of the mountains of Corsica, where Napoleon was born, and to our left little Elba, where he spent some months as a prisoner, a potent reminder of the changes of fate which even the great experience.

We swung over ancient Ostia, rich in memories, on our way to Rome, the "eternal city," which for so many centuries determined the fate and course of the world for good or evil. We looked down on the ruins of antiquity, on the gardens of the Vatican, the ruler of the Middle Ages, and on the teeming streets and squares of modern Italy. And we decided it would be a good idea to send Mussolini a telegram of greetings. It read: "Filled with admiration as we look down on Eternal Rome with its timeless remembrance of a glorious past, and its lively activity as a flourishing modern metropolis, we respectfully offer our greetings and our good wishes to the genius of this splendid city." As I handed this message to the radio operator, I remarked rather maliciously, "I can't help wondering whether Mussolini will assume that he himself is the genius of the city." Mussolini's answer read, "Many thanks for your friendly greeting! I wish you a happy journey. Mussolini." I don't dare to guess what Mussolini really meant.

We continued our journey along the coast and entered the Bay of Naples, where the city itself, Vesuvius, Capri, Sorrento, and Amalfi competed for the prize of beauty. "See Naples and die!" "Yes indeed!" we thought, "but from on board a Zeppelin!" With approaching darkness we came to the toe of the Italian boot, left behind on our right hand the already-darkened Straits of Messina, and went up over the toe from the Tyrrhenian to the Ionian Sea. For the first time there was nothing to see outside, and our guests seated themselves around "the candle's friendly flame" at the attractively decorated tables. We had: Turtle soup, ham with asparagus, roast beef with vegetables and salad, celery with Roquefort cheese, and an excellent nut cake from Friedrichshafen, together with wine in abundance. The passengers, who were able to enjoy this meal in completely steady flight across the dark sea, were, we liked to think, pleased with our offering.

On the following morning they looked out on the coast of Crete as they sat down to breakfast. During the night I had deviated somewhat to the north from our flight course on account of a very strong south-east wind, which had greatly retarded our progress, hoping that this south-east wind would not prevail on the northern side of the long island that was traversed by high mountains. And such was the case. In calm and peaceful flight we ran along the north coast, giving our classical scholars on board much to see and to remember. Similarly we quickly passed the island of Cyprus, lying somewhat to the north of our course, where so many Romans, Turks, Venetians, and Crusaders had contended for its strategically important territory.

We now steered for Haifa, and crossed this busy harbour in its beautiful, protected bay. Then we flew along the coast and over Tel Aviv towards Jerusalem. Below us was the stage on which so many acts of world history had been played, as ancient and legendary as that of Crete, but how different in the emotions aroused! There antiquity and ancient Greek culture, here Biblical and Christian associations, but both fundamental for our still-valid spiritual standards.

I now had the idea of offering the guests on our publicity flight a sensation of a quite extraordinary kind. The surface of the Dead Sea lies almost 1,300 feet below sea level. We were irresistibly tempted by the opportunity to fly our Zeppelin at an altitude well below sea level. Jerusalem lies at an altitude of about 2,600 feet, and within a quarter of an hour we were at the edge of the high plateau from which there is a sheer drop into the gorge at the bottom of which lies the Dead Sea. It was evening, and the barely risen full moon shone still with little power, so that the great lake lay reflected in semi-darkness, as mysterious as the nether world. We slowly sank down, carefully feeling our way lower and lower, until we hovered a few hundred feet over the surface of the water. We looked up to the heights towering around us as if from a cellar. It was a strange sensation to be in a ship which ordinarily soars high above the sea level, now flying some 1,000 feet below it. We opened a couple of bottles of Rhine wine and celebrated the occasion, which each of us found unique, with a gay round of drinks. Later I had a chance to use it in playing a simple but astonishing joke.

I had been invited by a young friend, a U-boat commander, to a celebration of the commission in his new boat. I was supposed to say a few words to the crew at the dinner, and remarked, "You know that my calling usually has me flying *over* the surface of the sea, and often we have also floated with the gondolas of our ship *on* the surface of the sea. But it will be news to you that we, just like you, have journeyed *below* the sea's surface. And I believe that we have hung up a record in our ship that you cannot equal in your U-boat. On one occasion we went down 1,000 feet below the surface of the sea." Great astonishment and disbelief were reflected on the faces of the young U-boat crew, but this vanished in loud laughter as they heard the subsequent explanation.

After a short sojourn in our defile we slowly rose again and flew low over the fissured precipices which rise on the west side of the sea towards the plateau of Jerusalem. The full moon meanwhile had risen higher, flooding the cleft and rocky landscape with a ghostly light, and disclosed to us an intricate, confused labyrinth of crevices and hiding-places in which robber bands of all kinds could conceal themselves. Was some such game being played there now? We paid a short farewell visit to Jerusalem and then faced the question: "What now?"

The pyramids of Egypt lay only three hours by air to the south of us, and a visit to them should have been the high point of the journey. But the Foreign Office had forbidden us to fly over Egypt! Yet we were not forbidden to fly along the coast of the Land of the Pharaohs. And I decided to do this, as we wished to arrive in daylight, not earlier than the following morning, in Greece, and had considerable time to spare. We therefore took our departure from Jerusalem on a southward course. Under us lay, in bright full moonlight, the broad caravan route which, since ancient times, has communicated with the Land of the Pyramids. There, almost 3,000 years before, had traded the sons of the Patriarch Jacob, to buy grain from their brother Joseph, the greatest and luckiest grain speculator of all time. In that period there were apparently no boundary difficulties, as in our enlightened age.

As we approached the border we turned out to sea, on a direct course for the lighthouse of Port Said. From there we would travel at the prescribed six-mile distance from the coast towards the site of the famed ancient lighthouse of Pharos, which had provided illumination for Antony and Cleopatra.

From here we continued our flight, which had already provided us in such an agreeable way with a geographical object lesson on significant sites of importance in the history of European culture, in a happy and expectant frame of mind. The impressions which the day just past had brought were overwhelming. We were completely satisfied at being able to sleep quietly and comfortably for a few hours, while the ship flew, vibrating gently, across the waters of the Levant, gleaming like a mirror in the silvery rays of the full moon, with her bow turned north towards Athens; for we could expect that the next day would bring us many scenes and experiences in the region of the ancient Greek world, for which we should have to be properly rested.

At 6 A.M. we aroused the Athenians from their morning slumbers with the thunder of our motors as we flew over the city and circled the Acropolis, and we were already far on our way by the time they had wrapped themselves in their togas and collected in the streets and squares. Soon we came to high Olympus, where dwelt the gods of ancient Greece. Its slopes were still covered with snow, but the summit, where the gods were wont to seat themselves, was unfortunately hidden by a black cloud. Here we turned back. Our intention had been to fly over the famous monastery of Athos and Homer's ancient Troy to Constantinople, and then return in the general direction of home by way of the Rumanian oil-fields and Vienna. But the incoming weather reports informed us that the whole Balkan area was covered in deep clouds. We could not therefore expect much on this route. And so we turned, in order to fly by way of the Gulf of Corinth to the Adriatic, whose islands and coasts promised a rich and interesting feast for our eyes all the way up to Trieste. Athens, which we reached again at 9 o'clock, had meanwhile awakened, and here we were enthusiastically received, particularly, I suspect, by those who had slept through our first visit and had been teased about it by their neighbours.

We traversed the Isthmus of Corinth and from a low altitude looked down on the canal, which is particularly significant, in my opinion, as the ancient Greeks lacked the means and the energy to dig it. Now it has filled up so as to be hardly wide enough for small craft, and it looked from 500 feet like a passage for rowboats. We flew along the north coast of the Gulf of Corinth at about 1,000 feet, and could see far into the land of fantasy and legend.

Ithaca, a small island which we, from on board our ship, could encompass in a glance, was set miraculously in a cobalt-blue sea, through which its chalk foundations shimmered like silver. We left this poetic spot of land only after some delay, to fly along the Adriatic coast. We gazed on the beauty of Corfu and many other picturesque islands, looked on quaint little towns like Ragusa and Sebenico, and everywhere encountered reminders of the eventful history of these shores.

The sun set at last as we reached the most northerly point of our Adriatic journey at Spalato. Our philosophical pleasure flight in light and sunshine, which we had offered for three days to our rigorous Board of Examiners—if I may so describe them—was practically ended. The remainder was a trial of the navigational capacities and the airworthiness of the Zeppelin; for the weather north of the Alps, according to the forecast, was still foul and wintry in this severe winter which seemed to have no end. We were trapped, so to speak, in the giant horseshoe of the Alps, which we had to surmount if we were to reach Friedrichshafen.

There were three routes we could follow: we could cross the Brenner Pass, following the valley of the Adige; we could traverse Lombardy to the Riviera and the mouth of the Rhone and thence retrace our outward route; thirdly, we could fly over the outer ranges of the Dinaric Alps to Pressburg and Vienna. The first route was impossible, for it presupposed daylight and completely clear, fine weather to find our way between the towering Alpine ranges. The second way was not very attractive, for it was very long. There remained the third. But this was not so desirable either, for we also needed clear weather for it if we were not to get into unpleasant, not to say dangerous, situations. We would in fact have to rise to an altitude of 4,600 feet to fly over a high plateau, and then would have to go through a narrow pass between two mountains, which were almost 6,500 feet high. If this pass should be hidden in cloud, we should have no choice but to climb to 6,500 feet in order to be safe. But that would be very undesirable, for we would have to blow off a great deal of gas while climbing, and the ship as a result would be about 11 tons heavier. If we should later, with our heavy ship, have to fly through rain or even snow-squalls, we would not only have to drop the last of our slender supply of ballast water, but would probably have to drop several tanks of fuel also, in order to keep the ship in the air.

In a considerable state of excitement we started our flight over the high passes. At first it was all we could wish for. It was clear with good visibility, although the moon had not yet risen. We came to the highest pass, and could see the two mountains which flanked the passage looming up ahead of us. Within ten or fifteen minutes more we would have them on our right and left, and it seemed almost dead calm, so that we then would be able to steer by compass out of the maze of peaks. But suddenly we noticed that clouds were gathering on the sides of the peaks. There were only a few wisps; but we knew how quickly everything can be hidden in the mountains. We later found that a stiff east wind was blowing on the windward side of the whole mountain chain, causing the usual cloud-formation on that side, while we on the lee side had had up till then the prevailing gentle south wind. The tension in these last few minutes was absolutely unbearable, and every minute I was sure I would have to give the order to climb to 6,500 feet. But our luck held: we still had sufficient visibility on reaching the point where the mountain walls soared upward to right and left. A great load was removed from my mind as the ground began to fall away below us and we were "through." The passengers had been watching anxiously while the ship ran past the dark walls in the narrow passage, which looked like a ravine. Apparently they were feeling more tense than I did; for the pilot naturally knows a lot more about the situation and realizes, if he is a prudent person, what has to be done to meet the threatening danger. But the Minister of Commerce, who was on board, came afterwards into the control car and said, "Thank God we got out of that hole!" And I was glad that we had succeeded without having to climb.

Next we entered some really bad weather. Above the Plattensee the wind was blowing so violently out of the pass, where the Danube debauches between Vienna and Pressburg, that we advanced very slowly over the ground and did not reach Vienna till midnight, in a beginning blizzard.

In Vienna they had been waiting for the ship since 11 P.M., and the radio audience had been promised a speech from on board her while she cruised over the city; for the people of Vienna had also given their mite to build the ship and had a right to a show of gratitude. I had volunteered to give this speech myself. But when the time came I was busy with navigational problems. After the tensions of the preceding day, and particularly of the last few hours, I had so little inclination to say anything that the good Viennese might have wanted to hear that I did not care to keep my promise. So I asked the President of the Reichstag, Herr Loebe, who was on board, to speak in my place. He was kind enough to take over for me, and certainly did it much better than I could have done. I heard later that the people of Vienna were very well satisfied with his speech, and I believe that he was too.

The blizzard had meanwhile increased greatly, and it was quite like winter. Not only were there "delicate grains of ice brushed across the green plain," as Goethe describes it in *Faust*, but it was genuine winter, which would not let up. The passengers who were still out of bed had once more wrapped themselves in their heavy coats, and even the staunchest patriots agreed that the German climate was nothing to boast about. The wet snow froze the panes of the windows of the control car and formed an ice layer a quarter of an inch thick, through which we could not see. Navigation on a dark night was hazardous in such circumstances. It was difficult to hold the ship on her course over the Danube valley, between the great heights on both sides. But I was privately not nearly so angry over this situation as I pretended to be, as we could show our Board of Examiners how safely the airship could find her way even under such unfavourable conditions. In case of need we might have turned off to the north at greater altitudes. But we were quite happy when we got out of the Danube valley at Passau, and had ahead of us only the final stretch, which posed no difficulties.

The weather had cleared when we reached Ulm, and towards 8 o'clock our shed came in sight, and half an hour later we had landed, after a flight of eighty-one hours. We were sure, and we heard it from our passengers in words of enthusiastic thanks, that this flight—perhaps the most splendid that one could make in Europe—had created a great impression on every one of them. We were sure that henceforth they would be true friends of the Zeppelin airship. And so it proved.

Out of the Blue

In 1929 Germany announced that the mighty new dirigible *Graf Zeppelin* would fly around the world. This stirred a great deal of excitement in the United States, not only because such gigantic airships were thought to be the future of aviation but also because the newspaper publisher William Randolph Hearst had put up two hundred thousand dollars to finance part of the Zeppelin's flight and was promoting it aggressively.

Hearst had insisted that the journey begin not in Germany but in America, with the Statue of Liberty as the starting point. The Germans agreed, and on August 7, 1929, the *Graf Zeppelin* left Lakehurst, New Jersey, passed over the Statue of Liberty, and headed east—across the Atlantic and on to Poland, Russia, and Japan. Finally, on August 25, it was spotted just west of San Francisco approaching the Golden Gate.

By now the trip had become a major event. People all over the United States hoped to catch a glimpse of the great dirigible as it crossed the country to New York. The Hearst papers published an itinerary: The *Graf Zeppelin* would attempt to fly over as many towns and cities as possible.

There had not been so much excitement around the country since the news of Charles Lindbergh's landing in France. I was eight years old and already an avid reader. I followed all the accounts of the *Graf Zeppelin* and did my best to build a model out of small branches covered with newspaper.

For some time my father had wanted to own a radio. Now, inspired by the Zeppelin, he went out and bought one on credit. It didn't have a speaker. We listened to it, one at a time, through earphones, as stations in Chicago trumpeted news of the Zeppelin's progress. The nine inhabitants of our little farmhouse five miles from Tampico and fifteen miles south of Sterling, Illinois, had never before experienced such a high level of sustained excitement.

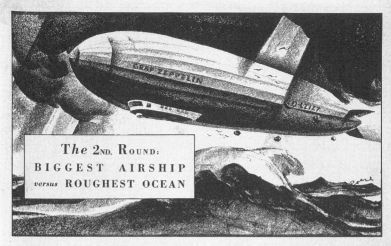

Courtesy of the National Archives.

I listened to my father and Henie Schauff, our hired man, discuss the ship's dimensions. "It's nearly eight hundred feet long," my father said. "That's almost a sixth of a mile."

"Almost as long as the pasture is wide," said Henie.

"A hundred feet in diameter," Father said. "That's two windmills stacked on top of each other." It was hard to imagine that anything so large could get off the ground.

The phone rang. Only a few people in the neighborhood had a telephone, but since my father was chairman of the board of directors for our one-room school, he had reasoned that the expensive device was necessary.

The caller was Uncle John. He had just returned from Sterling, where he'd heard that at ten the next morning the *Graf Zeppelin* would fly directly over. The town was wild with excitement, and the word was spreading. Everyone from town, township, and county for miles around would be heading to Sterling. It was harvest time in northern Illinois, time for wheat and oats to be cut and shocked, but no one dreamed of working on that red-letter day.

"We'll all get up at five, get the milking done, and head for town," my father said. "We want to get there at no later than nine. We can stand near the bridge along the riverbank and get a great view."

"I'll stay home," Grandma said. She was seventy-eight years old, and although she was healthy and spry, she no longer liked to leave home.

"You don't want to stay here alone," Aunt Kee said.

"I do," Grandma said.

"You'll miss all the excitement," my father said.

"I'll manage," she said.

"I'll stay," I volunteered.

The words were a reflex. My grandmother and I were the best of pals. The family said that I was her favorite, and often, when the others went off to town, I stayed at home to keep her company. When we were alone, she would tell me stories of growing up on a prairie farm in the Midwest, of the great celebration at the end of the Civil War, of Indians—she thought they were Illini—looking in the windows of their house one winter night. And when she and I were home together, she always served the same main dish: bread and milk and afterward apple dumplings and strawberry pie.

But this time I really did want to go with the others. I had committed myself to stay before I had stopped to think. My heart sank.

"I don't want to see the Zeppelin anyway," I said. There was nothing in the world I wanted more to see.

And so we remained behind next morning while the whole neighborhood left for Sterling. Father and Mother, Aunt Kee and Henie, my older sister, Maxine, my younger brother, Howard, and baby Margie drove off in the Model T right after morning chores. A little later Grandma and I waved at the McGraths as they went by—and the Christensens, who lived just half a mile down the road. And last, always last, Homer Burns and his wife, arguing furiously, sped by on the dirt road at twenty miles an hour.

After the Burnses had driven by and there was no more activity to expect on the narrow road, Grandma went into the kitchen to prepare our double dessert.

I stayed in the yard for an hour or so, building sand castles and trying to forget about the Zeppelin. Time drifted slowly by. In addition to my disappointment, I was a little uneasy. Something wasn't quite right. Suddenly I realized why. We were alone, absolutely alone, and surrounded by a profound silence. That whole land, usually so full of sound and action, was empty and still. Even the animals were quiet. There was no wind, not the slightest breeze.

Into that remarkable silence there came from far away the smallest possible purring, strange and repetitive, gradually approaching, becoming louder—the unmistakable beating of powerful engines. I looked to the west and at first saw nothing. Then it was there, nosing down out of the clouds a half-mile away, a gigantic, wondrous apparition moving slowly through the sky.

"Grandma!" I screamed.

She was out the kitchen door in an instant. I pointed to the sky. The great dirigible was very low, perhaps because the captain was trying to find some landmark.

There is a wonderful opening scene in the movie *Star Wars*. A great starship is passing very low and directly overhead so that one sees only the underside. That underside moves deliberately and interminably on and on and on until at last it is gone. The *Graf Zeppelin*, moving ever so slowly above us, was like that. We saw every crease and contour from nose to fins. It was so low that we could see, or imagined we could see, people waving at us from the slanted windows of its passenger gondola.

We stood entranced. Slowly, slowly the ship moved over us, beyond us, and at last was gone.

We looked at each other, my grandmother and I, then silently walked to the front porch and let ourselves down on the steps. And we gazed at each other in triumph.

Now we were suddenly aware that barnyard, pasture, and field were filled with alarm. The dogs were barking madly, the horses galloped in the pasture, cows mooed, pigs squealed, guineas screamed, chickens cackled, flocks of birds swept wildly by.

"They'll settle down soon," Grandma said.

I was speechless with excitement, but I was already constructing the triumphant tale I would tell anyone who would listen. Grandma rose, went into the kitchen, and came back with two glasses of milk and two chunks of strawberry pie. I could neither eat nor drink. Seeing the Zeppelin was wonderful. Telling the world would be wonderful times ten.

My grandmother stirred a little beside me.

"John," she said. I looked up. Just for a second she was a young, smiling woman, filled with excitement and anticipation. Then she sighed and was Grandma again. "We have to keep it a secret. We mustn't tell the others what we saw."

I was astonished. "But why not tell?"

"Because they'll be disappointed enough that they missed it. We don't want to hurt them more."

"But, Grandma."

She shook her head. "It will be much more fun if we keep it a secret, just you and I. No one else will ever know. We'll just keep the Zeppelin to ourselves forever and a day. We'll never tell."

I loved her. "I'll never tell," I promised, and I never have until now.

IV. When Heaven Rained Down Fire

Due to its light construction and the vulnerability inherent in its large size, [the Hindenburg *] can thrive and exist only in an atmosphere of unclouded peace. . . . It is like one of those opalescent butterflies, which fascinate as they flutter in the summer sunshine, but seek a sheltered corner whenever a storm blows up. Often, when people greet it so enthusiastically as it appears in the heavens, I have felt as if they believed they were seeing in it a sign and symbol of lasting peace, or at least a symbol of the universal dream of lasting peace among peoples.*

—Hugo Eckener

After lunch we went to the Zeppelin works. Dr. Eckener was away. We went first to the museum, then to the hangar which sheltered the new Graf Zeppelin *(the sister ship to the* Hindenburg*). [. . .] The great ship, shining new and clean, floated stilly at her cables. I felt depressed looking at her. [. . .] This airship represented the result of all the years of development of lighter-than-air. She seemed to me like a last member of a once proud and influential family. [. . .]*

—Charles A. Lindbergh

from The Millionth Chance:
The Story of the R 101

Even in death the R 101 was impressive. From a quarter of a mile away her great frame of girders towered above the trees, and at the tip of the enormous tail fin the Royal Air Force ensign still flew, the only piece of fabric the fire had spared.

It was difficult to believe that this smoke-blackened skeleton, like the bones of some giant fish, was actually the frame of the airship that had left Cardington only the previous day, and not the girders for some great new building among the trees. [. . .]

All the gas-bags and the outer fabric had been completely burned away, but still the gas-bag harnesses remained, a fine and elaborate tracing of thin wires looking in the afternoon light as though giant spiders had been weaving some strange web in the midst of the ruined vessel. Towards the centre of the airship such fittings as water-tanks, the great gas-valves, even parts of a staircase, were plainly recognizable. A row of gilded pillars, the last remnants of the lounge, glittered grotesquely.

The nose of the airship ran into a thin wood of hazel and oak trees, and the tail, as large as the latticed entrance of Paddington Station, lay out in an open field. The giant rudder rocked slowly to and fro in the afternoon breeze. The oil that experts had said could never burn had soaked into the earth all round and then the sodden ground had blazed like a wick, roaring in a fearful frying-pan of heat and light, in the midst of which villagers and local firemen had staggered, searching for survivors and dragging body after body out from the blaze. As the experts arrived on the scene, flames were still licking parts of the airship and burning the trodden earth.

The bodies had been carried a little way into the wood of stunted trees and laid out in a row under sheets willingly provided by local people. Some peasants had placed posies of flowers near them, and others, mostly old women with black shawls over their heads, had brought candles and knelt in prayer until daylight in the churned mud by the blackened shell of the airship. The survivors were already being cared for by nuns in the local hospital with every kindness, but conditions were a little primitive; this particular hospital had been built by Napoleon as a barracks, and was rather lacking in modern amenities. As soon as the survivors were fit to be moved, arrangements were made for them to be flown back to England for further treatment.

The concert room of the town hall had been converted into a mortuary, and so that no one's susceptibilities should be offended, all religious emblems were forbidden. The walls had been draped with black cloth. The potted palms that had graced the stage for concerts were stacked to the ceiling at one end; at the other hung the tricolour of France, and each coffin, resting on trestles, was covered by a small Union Jack.

Throughout Monday, French army lorries and carts drove from the wreckage to the town, three miles away, carrying the new coffins. Crowds had gathered from miles around, so that by mid-day the lorries were driving through lanes of silent watchers, many of whom made the sign of the cross as the coffins passed by. Never had so many people collected in Beauvais; it was the centre of the world's attention. The French Cabinet ordered a day of mourning in France and throughout the colonies. As the coffins were carried into the town hall—called, for the time being, "The Chapel of Repose for the Sons of Britain"—a sudden storm started unexpectedly in the warm morning, with a flash of lightning and the rattle of hailstones on the cobbles round the lorries.

Most of the dead were unidentifiable. Each of the coffins was numbered, however, and the same number was also on a small box in which were placed any articles retrieved from the body—a steel pencil, a cigarette case, the shell of a watch—that had survived the fire. Afterwards, attempts were made to identify these sad relics.

The feeling of immense tragedy that silenced the crowds at Beauvais was shared by the rest of the world. King George V, who only a few weeks before had watched the great airship drone over Sandringham, sent a message of condolence to the Prime Minister: "I am horrified to hear of this national disaster."

Ramsay MacDonald announced that he was "grieved beyond words at the loss of so many splendid men, whose sacrifice has been added to that glorious list of Englishmen who, on uncharted seas and unexplored lands, have gone into the unknown as pioneers and pathfinders, and have met death. . . ."

The Kings of Belgium, Denmark, Egypt, Italy, Sweden, Norway, the ex-King of Portugal, and the Regent of Hungary all sent messages of sympathy. So did Mussolini, and the Presidents of France, Switzerland, Lithuania and Portugal. The American Secretary of State and the Governors-General and Prime Ministers of the Dominions also expressed deep regret, and thousands of letters and telegrams came from lesser people who had wished a safe journey for the R 101's crew. John Masefield, the Poet Laureate, wrote: "The sudden loss of so many of our best must touch every feeling heart with the thought that these men died while advancing man's mastery over the elements, increasing his knowledge, and breaking down his boundaries. The men of this race have ever been pioneers, content to spend themselves thus. May a sense of the immortality of all high endeavour comfort those grieving for them."

If in life the designers and crew had been rushed, in death their fame was international, and now that time had no meaning for them, it was ironic that nothing was to be hurried or too good for their memory.

In Shortstown, Royal Air Force dispatch riders delivered notes to the next of kin of all the crew, and after them came the reporters; it is hard to say which were the more unwelcome. Other people, doubtless meaning well, arrived in cars at the little houses in Shortstown and invited themselves inside to console the widows and their families. Not all had kindly motives. One widow discovered, after the initial flood of callers, most of whom she had never seen before, that not only was her husband's gold watch missing, but also his set of tools—and even his bicycle. She was not the only widow to discover, too late, that some people came with condolences and left with more than they brought. [. . .]

In Bedford, on the Sunday and throughout the following week, blinds were drawn in nearly every house, and the Salvation Army band marched through the streets playing the Dead March from *Saul* over and over again. Everyone wanted news, for almost everyone was concerned, but the *Sunday Express* was the only newspaper circulating locally to print news of the airship that Sunday morning. This was due to the initiative of the night executive on duty, Arthur Christiansen, a young man from Wallasey, who on his own authority stopped the presses in the early morning, roused out his staff from their beds, and completely "remade" the front page—a prodigious feat of journalism for which he was very soon rewarded by being made editor of the *Daily Express*—a position he was to hold with brilliance and distinction for many years.

Not every house in Shortstown and Bedford had wireless sets to receive the broadcast news, and by evening, after a day of fearful rumours, crowds besieged the offices in the High Street for copies of the *Bedford and District Circular*, a local paper printed every Sunday. Police formed them into a queue and then someone started to cry that they should go instead to the printing works in Howard Street, and so hundreds rushed there and papers were sold as fast as they left the machines. The demand for copies went on long after the presses stopped at ten o'clock that night.

All Monday and until Tuesday morning the coffins lay in state in Beauvais town hall, guarded by soldiers, gendarmes and four Red Cross nurses. On the Tuesday they were moved to Boulogne, and a great procession, with full service honours, mustered in the main square of Beauvais. More than a hundred thousand people gathered to watch them go. Two battalions of the French 51st Infantry Regiment, in their pale-blue uniforms, with steel helmets and polished bayonets, faced the Town Hall, with two mounted squadrons of Spahi Cavalry in their magnificent robes. There was a detachment from the French naval airship base at Orly, and, in places of honour, stood the three R 101 survivors who were well enough to attend: Joe Binks, Arthur Bell and Harry Leech, all still wearing the clothes they had on when the airship crashed.

A hundred and one guns fired the salute shortly before eleven o'clock, bands played "God Save the King" and the "Marseillaise," and then the long line of twenty-three army carts, each drawn by four horses, and each containing two coffins, set off for the station. They headed a procession of Beauvais firemen who had gallantly tried to fight the fire, with long columns of infantry, gendarmes, marines, ex-Service associations, nuns and Girl Guides. Overhead, Nieuport-Delagè fighters and Breguet XIX reconnaissance aeroplanes flew in formation. Beauvais station had been decorated with hundreds of Union Jacks and French flags hung with crape. At Boulogne, where the train was unloaded, the coffins were carried aboard two British destroyers, H.M.S. *Tempest* and H.M.S. *Tribune.* Thousands had lined the railway line through northern France, and at Etaples, the largest British war cemetery in France, the Union Jack flew at half-mast.

The tide was low, and the tips of the destroyers' funnels were level with the side of the quay. As the doors of the railway vans opened massed bands again played first the "Marseillaise" and then "God Save the King." Squads of firemen toiled back and forth with the coffins, which were swung by a crane aboard the nearer destroyer. Even then things were not going perfectly for the men of the ill-fated airship. One destroyer had developed propeller trouble on the crossing from England, and at the last moment, in case she broke down, it was decided that all the coffins were to be carried in one ship instead of two.

Wreaths and bunches of flowers were heaped on the coffins, and sailors stood round them with heads bowed and arms reversed. As the last order was given, rain began to fall, and with searchlights playing ceaselessly on the flags and the flowers, the ships drew slowly out into the darkness.

From Dover searchlights reached out to meet them while they were still at sea, and a special train bore the coffins to Victoria, still under Union Jacks and in newly painted vans lit by dim blue bulbs. Even the engine carried a wreath.

They arrived at Victoria on the stroke of midnight, and the entire station had been cleared for the occasion. A small party waited to unload the coffins on to Service lorries and take them first to a mortuary and then, for a further lying-in-state, to Westminster Hall. All officers who had travelled back to England with them had been cautioned not to speak to anyone at Victoria lest the inquirer should be connected with the Press, for much Service indignation had been aroused by a British newspaper report of certain statements which an officer was alleged to have made about fragments of wreckage found some distance away from the scene of the disaster. This was officially denied, but the denial did not alter the fact that some wreckage *had* been found miles from the crash — possibly blown there by the force of the explosion.

After lying in state at Westminster Hall, there was a Memorial Service at St. Paul's, where the King was represented by the Prince of Wales. Representatives of every foreign power with an embassy or legation in Britain were also present. At the same time a requiem mass was said at Westminster Cathedral for the four Roman Catholics who had died in the disaster. The officiating priest was Father Harry Rope, brother of Squadron Leader Rope.

Then, on the Saturday, exactly a week after the airship had set out, the bodies of the passengers and crew were brought back to Cardington to demonstrations of national grief that had previously only been associated with the deaths of Kings. More than half a million people turned out to watch the funeral procession from Westminster Hall to Euston Station. It was two miles long and took an hour to pass. During the afternoon there was a two minutes' silence at Brooklands in the middle of a meeting of the British Motor-Cycle Racing Club. All clubs affiliated to the Football Association observed a similar silence, the teams standing drawn up on the field; and even the bookmakers and racegoers at Kempton Park stood bareheaded for two minutes' tribute.

Immediately the funeral procession had passed along Whitehall, scores of young men hurried into the Air Ministry to enlist for the Air Force. The R.A.F. reported that since the disaster its recruiting department had been working at full pressure and waiting lists were longer than had ever been known before.

At Euston the crowd was the biggest ever remembered. Over the last half-mile of the route only the people who had arrived very early in the morning had any chance of seeing the procession at all. Thousands who later poured out of the Underground at Euston were diverted into back streets behind the station and so saw nothing whatever, so dense were the throngs between them and the cortege. The vast whispering throng spread to the station roof, the tops of buildings and to every balcony within sight.

So many wreaths arrived that there was no room for them all on the coffins and they had to be loaded on to other R.A.F. tenders. Their scent filled the autumn air with a cloying sweetness. Two engines, the "Arabic" and the "Persia," drew the train, the former bearing a huge wreath of red, white and blue flowers under a glass case, the gift of the London, Midland and Scottish Railway.

Windows overlooking the railway lines were packed with people; platelayers on the line and the drivers of other locomotives stopped work and removed their hats as the funeral train passed by. Even in the suburbs the crowds were out; at Willesden hundreds stood in the road overlooking the railway, and there were silent crowds at every station on the way. Saturday afternoon gardeners ceased digging their allotments; motorists stopped their cars and stood beside them at attention; flags flew at half-mast on church-towers, and from poles rigged up in the back gardens of small houses all along the route.

Finally, at a quarter to two, the train steamed into Bedford station, where waiting bearers walked up to the carriages, and in a deep silence lifted down the first coffin. At that precise moment the quiet was dramatically broken as two flights of bombers flew overhead in spearhead formation.

An R.A.F. firing party with reversed arms led the procession at Cardington; then came the grey lorries with pipeclayed tyres, each lorry laden with two coffins, still with their Union Jacks half hidden under the flowers. Of the forty-eight coffins only fourteen bore the names of the dead on aluminum plates. On all the rest the inscription was simply: "To the memory of the unknown airman who died on October 5." The plates had been made from metal used in the airship.

Bedford observed a day of mourning; all shops were shuttered and there was no traffic on the streets. Blinds were drawn in the houses as the crowd of thousands poured out all morning towards Cardington, and then massed on the path overlooking the station. Most were wearing black, and many carried flowers. At Cardington the police threw a cordon round the village, and allowed no wheeled traffic to enter.

In the churchyard labourers had worked all night by the light of flares to dig the enormous grave for the burial, tidying the sandy soil where it sloped into the grave and covering it with bronze and white chrysanthemums and fresh green turf, which also lined the bottom of the grave. A boarded ramp led down from the top, ready for the coffins.

So great were the crowds here that by early afternoon 500 police and special constables, with 100 ambulance men, lined the streets; so long was the funeral procession that when the last tender was on the outskirts of Bedford, the head was halfway to the churchyard. The sound of the escorting aeroplanes, and the howling of a dog, were the only things to break the silence, save for the tolling of the church bell, which was rung for half an hour before the procession arrived.

It was nearly four o'clock when the Air Force lorries appeared in the early October dusk and the service began. The Anglican Bishop of St. Albans, tall in his silk gown and crimson hood, with the Roman Catholic Bishop, robed in crimson and attended by his acolytes carrying incense, conducted the service, with the Vicar of Cardington, the Rev. Sydney Seccombe, the Senior Chaplain of the R.A.F. with two staff chaplains, and two non-conformist ministers. The band played "Abide with Me," as the coffins were slowly brought in, one by one, from the road, and carried down the slope to the T-shaped grave, where they were laid in rows, still covered with their flags.

It took half an hour to lay out all the dead from R 101 in their common grave among the flowers. As the Vicar intoned the first sentences of the burial service, "I am the Resurrection and the Life. . . . The Lord gave, and the Lord hath taken away. Blessed be the name of the Lord. . . . Yea, though I walk through the valley of the shadow of death, I will fear no evil, for thou art with me . . .," the only sound was the crunch of boots on the ground as the bearers bore in coffin after coffin.

The Chaplain read the Lesson and the Bishop of St. Albans took the main part of the service, while the aircraft in the darkening sky flew and dipped in salute. Then came the Last Post and Reveille from the trumpeters, and a peal of muffled bells. Slowly the crowds began to drift away, and the deepening dusk shrouded the outline of the two great airship sheds and the mooring mast.

Rita Dove

The Zeppelin Factory

The zeppelin factory
needed workers, all right—
but, standing in the cage
of the whale's belly, sparks
flying off the joints
and noise thundering,
Thomas wanted to sit
right down and cry.

That spring the third
largest airship was dubbed
the biggest joke
in town, though they all
turned out for the launch.
Wind caught,
"The Akron" floated
out of control,

three men in tow—
one dropped
to safety, one
hung on but the third,
muscles and adrenaline
failing, fell
clawing
six hundred feet.

Thomas at night
in the vacant lot:
    Here I am, intact
    and faint-hearted.

Interior view of the hull of the U.S.S. *Akron* under construction at the Goodyear-Zeppelin Airdock, 1930–31, Akron. Courtesy of the University of Akron Library.

Thomas hiding
his heart with his hat
at the football game, eyeing
the Goodyear blimp overhead:
　　Big boy I know
　　you're in there.

THE future needs of the national defense and of transoceanic commerce by air find Goodyear prepared. Already Goodyear has built 1,051 passenger carrying balloons, 123 airships of all types, and now has under construction for the United States Navy the two largest airships the world has ever seen, each of these two aerial leviathans being nearly twice as large as the famous Graf Zeppelin and nearly 3 times as large as the Los Angeles.

Courtesy of Goodyear Tire and Rubber Co.

from Even the Birds: U.S.S. *Akron*

Out of the softening sunset came the airship; and the manner of its moving was beautiful. Few inanimate objects attain beauty in the pursuance of their courses, and yet, to me, at least, the flight of this ship was far lovelier than the swooping of a bird or the jumping of a horse. For it seemed to carry with it a calm dignity and consciousness of destiny which ranked it among the wonders of time itself.

That night, at my first sight of her, she overawed me as nothing else has ever done. She was so huge and strong, so inspiring of emotion and at the same time so remote of it herself. But perhaps the strongest magic which she exerted came from the fact that her hues, and hence her moods, were ever changing. She never looked the same, for no two days are even quite alike; and her silvery hull took to itself the color and feeling of every time of day or night in which she flew.

On she came toward us with a motion as smooth as a glide, though by the steady droning music of her engines I knew her to be a powerful creature going calmly about her business. Lower and lower she slid as she circled wide above the lake. And so still was the water that the ship's reflection seemed more clearly formed than was she herself. The whole life of the evening was attuned to her rhythm.

Looking On

By Paton Edwards for the *Akron Times Press*, August 8, 1931.

Courtesy of the *Akron Beacon Journal*.

The U.S.S. *Akron* seen through the columns of the Lincoln Memorial, Washington, D.C.
Courtesy of the Theodor Horydczak Collection, Library of Congress.

AKRON
Queen of the Skies
MARCH

ANNE BERRODIN, B.S.M.

James Tate

Images of Little Compton, Rhode Island

Here the tendons in the swans' wings stretch,
feel the tautness of their futuristic necks,
imagine their brains' keyhole accuracy,
envy their infinitely precise desires.

A red-nosed Goodyear zeppelin emerges from the mist
like an ethereal albino whale on drugs.

One wanders around a credible hushed town.

Mosquito hammering through the air
with a horse's power: there will be no cameramen.
We will swap bodies maybe
giving the old one a shove.

That's an awful lot of work for you I said
and besides look at your hands,
there are small fires in the palms,
there is smoke squirting from every pore.

O when all is lost,
when we have thrown our shoes in the sea,
when our watches have crawled off into weeds,
our typewriters have finally spelled perhaps
accidentally the unthinkable word,

when the rocks loosen and the sea anemones
welcome us home with their gossamer arms
dropping like a ship from the stars,

what on earth shall we speak or think of,
and who do you think you are?

The Violent Death of America's Last Dirigible

By any yardstick, the U.S.S. *Macon* was colossal, the biggest man-made thing that, up to then, ever had flown. Germany's *Hindenburg*, bigger and equally ill-fated, was yet to come. The *Macon* was almost as long as three football fields and as high as an eleven-story building. Her skeleton was a maze of aluminum forming rings, longitudinal girders, and taut steel stabilizing cables. Twelve great balloons, captive within her framework, lifted her. Fully expanded at altitude, they contained enough gas to run an ordinary kitchen stove for a thousand years—6,500,000 cubic feet of it—except that the *Macon*'s gas was nonflammable helium. Eight engines of five hundred and sixty horsepower each drove her at three to four times the speed of a surface ship. Wrapped around it all were more than a dozen acres of thin, aluminum-painted fabric skin.

Two horizontal and two vertical stabilizing fins at the stem were equally gargantuan. The two main surfaces of the dorsal fin alone contained enough area for three tennis courts. Where it attached to the airship's main framework the fin was eleven feet thick. The lower fin was sufficiently capacious to house an emergency steering and watch station.

Aloft, the normal complement of ninety-nine officers and men lived snugly in the *Macon*, mostly in her belly. They steered and navigated her from a spacious control car—a bridge—clipped to her underside two hundred feet from her bow. Partitioned, the control car also was a smoking and off-duty room. Machinist mates kept watch in eight separate engine compartments. The crew ate steaks from an electric kitchen and slept in fabric-walled bays strung along two ventral keels. There was a third, a dorsal, keel. Each keel had a narrow walkway. The crew's inspection tours were made on a half-mile of these and other catwalks and ladders, snaked bow to stern, top to bottom, among the rustling gas cells.

Incredibly, this motorized Leviathan gasbag was an aircraft car-

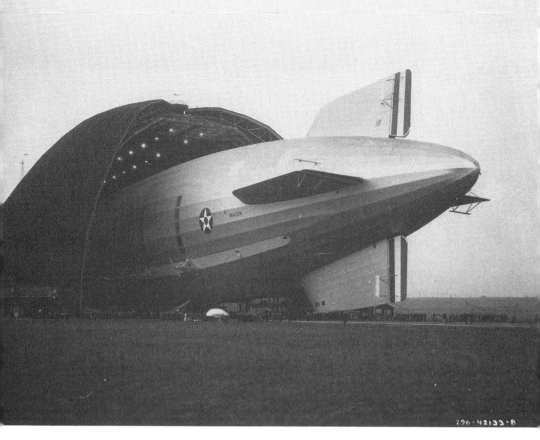

The U.S.S. *Macon* at the Goodyear-Zeppelin Airdock, Akron.
Courtesy of the National Air and Space Museum.

rier, with launching and recovery gear and even a hatch that swallowed airplanes for stowage in an internal hangar. The *Macon*'s planes always flew aboard her after she was aloft. That was to save her the burden of lifting almost fifteen thousand extra pounds at the command, "Up-ship!"

All this the *Macon* was and more. To those of us assigned to her, she was a haven. She was home. She was elegant. She was a queen of the air.

It was February 12, and the *Macon* had just completed two days of maneuvers with the Pacific Fleet. We had only eighty-three crewmen, sixteen under complement. Lt. (jg) Jerry Huff and I, returning from patrol in our scout fighters, swung into tandem formation off the *Macon*'s beam. Rain stung our faces. A squall, which was tattered at its base, sat athwart in *Macon*'s course.

Huff was first on the trapeze. As officer in charge of the airship's heavier-than-air unit, I always went aboard last. With a technique learned in hundreds of airship landings, Huff jockeyed stick, rudder, and throttle until a hook atop a pylon on his upper wing closed on the *Macon*'s trapeze bar and locked in place. An electric motor hoisted the plane into the hangar bay. There, on its hook, it was shifted to an overhead rail and spotted in a corner of the fabric hangar.

When I had completed my own landing, I headed for the bridge and reported the squall to Lt. George Campbell, officer of the deck.

He nodded. "I've got it spotted," he said.

In the smoking room the world's oldest airborne acey-deucey game was in progress. I lighted a cigarette and accepted a cup of coffee from Edquiba, a diminutive Filipino mess attendant. He and his fellow messboy, Cariaso, were close friends, hailing from the same part of the Philippines.

The *Macon* was at twelve hundred feet, doing a standard sixty knots. To starboard, murky under the cloudy sky, were the spires of the Santa Lucia Range. Waves were laying a ruff on the shore. Ahead, on Point Sur, a lighthouse winked. It was gusty. Now and then the airship wallowed.

In an hour and a half we would be moored at the Naval Air Station in Sunnyvale, our base thirty-five miles south of the Golden Gate. At the forward end of the smoking room an open door looked out on the bridge. Fog whipped by the windows. Lieutenant Commander Wiley, the *Macon*'s skipper, altered course slightly to move us farther out to sea. In this soupy weather, he was taking no chances on drifting off course and colliding with a mountain.

Everyone aboard the *Macon* was weather-conscious. There was good cause. The Navy airship *Shenandoah* had broken up in a storm over Ohio in 1925. The *Akron*, the *Macon*'s sister ship, had fallen prey to weather off Barnegat Light, New Jersey, less than two years earlier. On the previous April 21, the *Macon* herself had been damaged in violent thermal currents near Van Horn, Texas, in the course of a flight from Sunnyvale to Opa-Locka, Florida. Some stern girders had broken. Others had buckled.

The Naval Bureau of Aeronautics had authorized a beefing-up of the *Macon*'s stern structure in the Sunnyvale shops, but stipulated that the work was not to interfere with the airship's operating schedule. Only a third of the projected repairs had been completed when she took off for her last exercise with the fleet.

In the control car on this bleak February day, the first dog watch was on. Lt. Calvin Bolster, the *Macon*'s construction, repair and trim officer, had just finished prowling the top catwalk and made his report. The rain had bothered him. Rain tended to ease the tautness of the outer fabric. Lt. Cdr. Scott Peck, the navigator, was taking a drift sight. All was shipshape.

Captain Wiley and his executive officer, Lt. Cdr. Jess Kenworthy, stood spread-legged peering out the forward windows. Prudent, terse on duty, Wiley knew every webbed girder in his airship. In lighter-than-air for ten years, he had been one of only three survivors out of a complement of seventy-six in the *Akron* disaster. That, too, had been his command.

Knappy Kivette, another of our scout pilots, and I, had been pilots aboard the *Akron*. But it was foggy that night when the *Akron* left Lakehurst Naval Air Station for her rendezvous with fortune, and we were unable to take off to join her.

The *Macon* hit the outlying fringes of the squall. The ship creaked. Rain hung a gray curtain around us. In a couple of minutes we were through it. We relaxed.

Off the starboard bow the skipper saw more rain. "Left rudder," he ordered. It was 1705 hours—5:05 P.M.

At that moment the *Macon* lurched. Captain Wiley later described it as a "jar." Bolster and Kenworthy said it felt like a sharp side gust; so did Campbell. To Clark Thurman, assistant engineer, and himself an alumnus of the Navy airship *Los Angeles*, it was the most severe bump he had ever experienced. To me personally, it felt as though a giant hand had swatted us.

The airship's nose dropped. Then it swerved wildly to starboard. In the smoking room we grabbed for support.

The quartermaster, Brandes, just completing an inspection, felt the lurch and heard a snap, as though something had hit the outer cover. Coxswain Connolly, the *Macon*'s rigger, who was in the stern, also heard the snap. Seaman Conover, on the elevators, turned his wheel to overcome the dive. The bow recovered. Then the wheel jerked from his hands. Four spokes struck his left hand before he could check it. Now the bow swept upward sharply. Bolster and Boatswain's Mate Shellberg, who was in charge of the bridge watch, helped Conover apply down-elevator.

The rudderman, Clarke, also lost his wheel. Captain Wiley grabbed and held it until Clarke could get his hands on it again.

As the bow rose, Lieutenant Commander Peck strode in back of Clarke. "Left rudder," he told the helmsman. That would steer the *Macon* away from the mountains.

In the lower fin two seamen, Freas and Gallatian, had been standing watch. They felt the sickening plunge of the stern as the bow went up. Chief Boatswain Davis, the leading chief petty officer, had been under the top fin. He had just put his hand between it and the airship envelope to determine the "breathing" clearance when he heard a crash. He started aft. Helium enveloped him, and he staggered forward out of the gas.

Five miles over the darkling waters to the west, Signalman C. F. Wilkie, on the cruiser *Houston*, looked with only faint curiosity at the *Macon*. The upper fin seemed to have disappeared. He thought little of it. He knew nothing about airships.

Three miles to the east, Thomas Henderson, lighthouse keeper on Point Sur, had been watching the *Macon* through binoculars. She was broadside to him under a cloud rack. Suddenly, the top fin seemed to explode. Material from it blew back and draped over the upper rudder. He could see a hole in the top of the hull just below where the fin had been.

Aboard the *Macon*, Coxswain Connolly stared unbelievingly at the pieces of metal bouncing off the walkway. Two turnbuckles near the steering clutch box were whirling and hitting each other. He rang the bridge telephone. Campbell answered.

"The controls are carried away starboard, sir," reported Connolly. He looked up. "Cells Zero, One, and Two are deflating."

Recovering from his gassing, Boatswain Davis discovered that brace wires on the top fin had pulled loose from the ship structure, and the fin—or most of it—was gone. He tried to telephone the bridge. The line was busy.

Campbell reported Connolly's report to Kenworthy and Captain

Wiley. The *Macon* obviously had sustained a major wound. The bow now had assumed an upward angle of twenty-five degrees. Spinning on his heel, Kenworthy raced to the stern.

"Twenty knots," snapped Wiley. The ship had to be slowed down. With the bow high, the engines were driving the airship upward. Throttling back also would decrease the aerodynamic strain on the ship's tortured tail.

Davis finally raised the bridge on the phone. Campbell relayed the message to the captain: "The top of the ship under the fin is wide open."

In the smoking room we had heard a crackling sound in the stern. I glanced at the faces around me. Nobody looked scared. We were just incredulous. Lt. (jg) John Reppy, assistant hangar officer, had shrugged off the initial lurch, even as it had thrown him against the starboard side of the room. He started to go topside, only to encounter Kenworthy hurrying aft.

"Emergency," Kenworthy shouted over his shoulder. Reppy responded. He ran aft along the walkway. He could see that cell. One was almost deflated. The top rudder controls were slack. As he ran to unclutch the rudder controls he noticed that Cell Two was collapsing.

Midway of his mission, Kenworthy bumped into a seaman. "The tail's breaking up, sir," said the seaman. Leaving the rest of the probe to Reppy, Kenworthy raced back to the bridge for orders from Wiley. As he reached the bridge, the telephone rang. Kenworthy snatched it up, listened, then said to the captain, "Cells One and Two are gone, sir."

"Drop ballast aft," Wiley ordered.

Bolster pulled the toggles on the water ballast tanks. Great dollops of water plunged from the ship.

"Drop slip tanks aft," ordered Wiley. The fuel tanks were in groups of threes. The center tank in each cluster, the slip tank, could be jettisoned. Each slip tank held seven hundred pounds of fuel.

Freas and Gallatian, in the lower fin, looked up and saw the gas cells deflating. They clambered up their ladder to inform the rigger. Connolly on the walkway was hanging up the phone.

"You know about it, Joe?" asked Freas.

"Yes," said Connolly calmly, "the controls carried away."

Connolly and Freas helped Quartermaster Brandes release the slip tanks from their restraining wires. Four tanks ripped through the *Macon*'s fabric skin and spun downward. Freas could hear the sounds of girders breaking, and wires thrumming in the wind.

All ballast now had been dropped aft of frame 102.5 which was amidship. With the engines at one-third, the *Macon*'s climb had been arrested momentarily. But after a moment the ship began to gain altitude again. The stern refused to come up even with hard down-elevator. We had traded ballast for altitude.

"Left rudder," ordered Wiley. That would take us farther to sea, nearer the fleet. But the ship refused to respond to the wheel.

"Permission to shift rudder control to the lower fin, sir?" Bolster asked the captain.

"Immediately," said Wiley.

Halfway down the slanting walkway Bolster found Coxswain Hammond. "Shift control to the lower fin," he said. Hammond climbed into the fin to synchronize the emergency rudder wheel with the clutch box. He tried the wheel, but the ship did not respond.

In the smoking room, as we stood riveted to the sharply sloping deck, we felt the ship rising.

On Point Sur, Lighthouse Keeper Henderson watched the *Macon* describe a lazy, drifting half-circle and—nose high and aimed south—disappear into the clouds.

"Ahead port engines," ordered the skipper. "Idle starboard." Then: "Ahead all engines." In the last hour winds had decreased from twenty-five to thirty knots to fifteen to eighteen, but had backed from north to westerly. If we could steer by the engines, they might take us out to sea.

On the bridge the altimeter registered two thousand, then three thousand, then forty-five hundred feet. For seconds Captain Wiley stood watching the instrument wind up.

"SOS the fleet," he instructed Campbell. Less than five minutes had elapsed since that first, sickening swing of the *Macon*'s bow.

Captain Wiley was having trouble getting response from the engine room telegraphs. Now he discovered why. Tilted up by the bow inclination, the engines were being robbed of the cooling water in their jackets and they were overheating. They ran, but only sporadically.

The senses of those of us in the smoking room were being filed to a needle point. We had no duties to perform. Now and then cracking sounds issued from the stern. The potentialities were becoming obvious. If more girders broke and ripped more cells, the ship would stand on her tail. Then the remaining cells, crowding their restraints, might burst.

"Every available man to the bow!" called Campbell through the door. He clipped off his words.

Up the canted catwalks, around the gas cells fattened by altitude, we climbed. At the bow we huddled, twenty-seven of us, behind a five-foot-wide door. The door was opened only for mooring and take-off. Just inside it was an array of lines full-hitched to the nose cone. We opened the mooring door. We might need quick access to the outside of the cone.

Now the overhead engines quit for good. The *Macon* teetered at forty-six hundred feet, a giant, slanting obelisk, a great panatella cigar buoyed in space by a bubble of gas. On the bridge the captain's dilemma in aerostatics was acute. To save his crew, he needed a keel level enough to launch life rafts along the entire length of the airship. That meant valving gas forward. But how much lift would that cost? How many more stern cells were going to rupture before we reached the water? He risked plummeting his ship into the ocean—a terrifying choice.

"Valve Cells Eight and Nine," ordered Wiley.

The gas hissed out, vented through holes in the airship's top. The nose began to ease down. The *Macon* began losing altitude, but too fast. Bridge instruments indicated a drop of three hundred feet a minute. For an airplane that would be nothing. For the airship, this rate of descent would crush the keels at impact. Wiley had to jettison some heavy equipment fast.

"Plane-handling crews lay down to the hangar!"

Five seamen among those of us hanging to the framework, crowded on to two small platforms, slithered down toward the hangar bay.

At the hangar, the plane handlers under Reppy's direction struggled with one of my precious planes. They wrestled the machine to the hatch, shoving desperately. But it sprawled and jammed—half in and half out.

The *Macon*, in her agonies of self-destruction, sank toward the ocean. Eighty-three men, silent and waiting, clung to perches in her cathedral interior. As the altimeter unwound on the bridge a conversation in low monosyllables was punctuated by the distant cry of anguished metal framework.

Now it was time to dump the last of the water for as much cushion as that weight decrease would provide. At fourteen hundred feet Campbell began toggling. In the control room anything that had weight went out the windows. An officer winced as he pitched expensive instruments overboard. Another threw out drawers from the chart lockers.

Our rate of descent was slowing. From the bow we could see the murk begin to lighten. We had broken through the cloud ceiling.

"Stand by to abandon ship," Captain Wiley said to Peck, "and make it a personal order. Never mind the communication tubes." The skipper wanted to be sure that every man got the word.

Peck raced along the catwalks. "All hands," he called, "stand by to abandon ship!"

Wiley sent a final radio message to the fleet: "Will abandon ship as soon as we land on water somewhere within twenty miles of Point Sur about ten miles at sea."

"Everyone to a window," Wiley told the men on the bridge. Clarke, the helmsman, clung to his wheel, hypnotized by the disorder. Wiley snapped, "Get ready to jump!"

Edquiba and Cariaso, the messboys, had raft stations on opposite sides of the ship.

"Adios, Florentino," said Cariaso.

"Adios, Max. Good luck."

They shook hands.

In the lower fin Coxswain Hammond was at his post. Brandes, on the port walkway, yelled, "Hammond, for Christ's sake, get out of the fin!" Hammond scrambled up the ladder.

Methodically, Brandes secured a raft to a girder with a line, inflated it and passed it outside through a hatch. Men who could not swim could slide down the line.

The helmsman, shaken from his trance, climbed from the control car and ran to frame 170 on the port side. In a moment Dailey, a radio-man, joined him. Together they shinnied up the frame so as not to be under the curvature of the *Macon*'s envelope when she landed. Clarke kicked a hole in the outer cover.

In the bow we could hear someone calling out altitudes as though taking soundings with a lead line: "Four hundred, three hundred, two hundred, one hundred, here she goes!"

The *Macon* was almost on an even keel. We braced ourselves. From far aft came a dull rumble, a crunching. But there was no jolt. The airship touched almost gently. A ripple went through her as the bow settled to the water.

It was 5:40 P.M.

In the lower keels men launched rafts and jumped through holes kicked in the airship fabric. Some slid down lines.

On the port walkway Hammond took a long, agonizing look around, and leaped outward into the water. As he swam aft, the port fin kept squashing him, pushing him below the surface. Farther forward on the crumbling airship, Clarke and Dailey were preparing to jump. "It looks too far," said Clarke. Without warning, Dailey jumped feet first. As in a dream, Clarke watched him turn over slowly several times as he fell. He landed on his back. Clarke climbed down to a safer exit point.

McDonald, a coxswain, found himself with Edquiba on the port side. Before he jumped, McDonald saw the little Filipino, in an inflated life jacket, start to climb toward the bow. Edquiba was terrified of the sea. He could not swim.

On the bridge Captain Wiley satisfied himself that everyone in the control room had left. He turned to follow. Then he heard voices in the keel. He stepped toward the ladder. The top of the control car cracked. He dived out a window.

In the water he heard Campbell call, "I'm in trouble." The deck officer had struck his head in getting out. Wiley grabbed his collar and towed him toward a raft.

In the bow, some of the men around me began seizing the mooring lines. They crawled through the mooring doorway in the nose of the ship, and lowered themselves into the water. One seaman caught his leg in a bight. Another, above, slid into him, knocking his grip loose. Dangling by one knee, the man kicked and squirmed free, tumbling into the water.

Eight of us were still in the bow. It had begun to rise.

At the stern, the last remaining bits of life were being crunched from the *Macon*. Calcium flares, bobbing on the water, silhouetted her broken ribs. Gas whooshed from more punctured cells. Men paddled for their lives. What remained of 400,000 pounds of airship could smash them in another minute.

The bow rose more, tugged upward by the forward gas cells. Those of us still clinging there, inside the envelope, found ourselves not a comfortable dropping distance from the water but one hundred and twenty-five feet in the air. I felt a strange puff of pressure.

"What's that?" I exclaimed. My voice squeaked. Then it dawned on me—the uptilted hull formed a chimney, and we were in its throat. "We're being gassed!" I croaked.

We clambered outside on the hull, grabbing the lines for support on the rain-slick fabric, gulping great draughts of fresh air. Faint flashlight beams played on us from the water. A seaman had found a Very pistol in the rigging. The bright shells arched into the leaden drizzling sky. It was nearly dark now.

One of the seamen near me was verging onto panic. "I'm going to jump!" he yelled. It would have meant certain death. Captain Wiley, far below in a life raft, saw the man and shouted: "Don't jump! Wait till the bow comes down!"

We waited, clinging to our ropes like school girls around a Maypole. Far at sea, the fingers of searchlights were probing the dark night. That was the fleet, racing to our rescue.

Beneath, in the hull, more girders were breaking. Closer to us now, they sounded like muffled shotgun blasts. We could feel the shaking of the tortured hull far below the surface as an engine would pull loose from its bed and go plunging to the bottom, tearing aluminum frames as it went, and—fortunately for those of us still on board— also tearing open another gas cell, thus lowering the bow closer to the water. Another and another engine let go until finally all that was left of the once mighty *Macon* above the water was a bubble the size of a barn. It was time to get clear.

One by one, we lowered ourselves on the wet lines and dropped into the water. There was a strong swell but no waves. The lights of the calcium flares wanly dappled the bow of the *Macon*, towering above us. A life raft floated by; three crewmen climbed into it, and the rest of us clung to its sides—swimming, pulling, to enlarge the distance between ourselves and the wreck. Suddenly a fire bloomed. Gasoline on the water had been ignited by the flares.

"Pull!" I yelled at the oarsmen. The massive star insignia painted on the underside of the bow was reflected by the glare, even as it was consumed. Then the fire died and the last skeletal remnant of what had been the world's greatest airship slipped beneath the surface.

One by one, the bobbing flares snuffed out. An hour later, cruisers of the fleet found us, a cluster of rafts in the pitch blackness. Up over the side we went, pausing, each of us, at the top of the gangway to give our names and rank or rating.

One jacketed, but trouserless officer, his legs blue with cold, saluted smartly. "Permission to come aboard, sir?" he said to the officer of the deck. That was the Navy; observe the niceties even at time of disaster.

In all, three cruisers, the *Richmond*, *Concord*, and *Cincinnati*, found eighty-one survivors. Only two out of the ship's company had failed to make it—the radioman, Dailey, and the cheerful little Filipino mess attendant, Edquiba.

Yvor Winters

An Elegy

For the U.S.N. Dirigible, Macon

The noon is beautiful: the perfect wheel
Now glides on perfect surface with a sound
Earth has not heard before; the polished ground
Trembles and whispers under rushing steel.

The polished ground, and prehistoric air!
Metal now plummets upward and there sways,
A loosened pendulum for summer days,
Fixing the eyeball in a limpid stare.

There was one symbol in especial, one
Great form of thoughtless beauty that arose
Above the mountains, to foretell the close
Of this deception, at meridian.

Steel-gray the shadow, than a storm more vast!
Its crowding engines, rapid, disciplined,
Shook the great valley like a rising wind.
This image, now, is conjured from the past.

Wind in the wind! O form more light than cloud!
Storm amid storms! And by the storms dispersed!
The brain-drawn metal rose until accursed
By its extension and the sky was loud!

Who will believe this thing in time to come?
I was a witness. I beheld the age
That seized upon a planet's heritage
Of steel and oil, the mind's viaticum:

A Sad Home Coming!

Courtesy of the *San Francisco Chronicle*, February 14, 1935.

Crowded the world with strong ingenious things,
Used the provision it could not replace,
To leave but Cretan myths, a sandy trace
Through the last stone age, for the pastoral kings.

Janet Lewis

The Hangar at Sunnyvale: 1937

Above the marsh, a hollow monument,
Ribbed with aluminum, enormous tent
Sheeted with silver, set to face the gale
Of the steady wind that filled the clipper sail,
The hangar stands. With doors now buckled close
Against the summer wind, the empty house
Reserves a space shaped to the foundered dream.
The MACON, lost, moves with the ocean stream.

Level the marshes, far and low the hills.
The useless structure, firm on the ample sills,
Rises incredible to state again:
Thus massive was the vessel, built in vain.
For this one purpose the long sides were planned
To lines like those of downward pouring sand,
Time-sifting sand; but Time immobile, stayed,
In substance bound, in these bright walls delayed.

This housed the shape that plunged through stormy air.
Empty cocoon! Yet was the vision fair
That like a firm bright cloud moved from the arch,
Leaving this roof to try a heavenly march;
Impermanent, impractical, designed
To frame a paradox and strongly bind
The weight, the weightless in a living shape
To cruise the sky and round the cloudy Cape.

Less substance than a mathematic dream
Locked in the hollow keel and webbed beam!
Of the ingenious mind the expensive pride,

The highest hope, the last invention tried!
And now the silver tent alone remains.
Slowly the memory of disaster wanes.
Still in the summer sun the bastions burn
Until the inordinate dream again return.

Jay Meek

The Week the Dirigible Came

After the third day it began to be familiar,
an analogue by which one could find
himself in finding it, so whenever it came
outside the window what came to mind was how
marvellous and common the day was, and how expert
I'd become at dirigibles. And when
it stayed, one felt the agreeable confidence
that comes with having a goldfish
live four days. So I began to watch its shadow
passing through back yards, only once
looked at the tie-line swinging from its nose.
How much it seemed to want an effigy, a fish,
something that might save it from being simply a theory
about itself, and on the fifth day
old ladies came stomping out in their gardens
as the shadow passed under them,
and in the woods hunters
fired at the ground. The sixth day rained,
but morning broke clear and the air seemed grand
and empty as a palace, and I went out,
looked up, and the sun crossing my nose
cast such shadows as sun-dials make,
and I knew whatever time
had come was our time and it was like nothing else.

The Incorrigible Dirigible

Never in any circumstances think you can tell the men from
  the boys. (Or the sheep from the goats.)
Nevertheless unavoidably and interminably—up to a point!—
  one observes tendencies, the calculus
Of discriminative factors in human affairs. Alcoholism, for in-
  stance, is the "occupational disease of writers"
(And a good fat multitone in the vox populi too, that sad song),
  and I cannot but approve
My friends Ray Carver and John Cheever, who conquered it in
  themselves;
I cannot help, for that matter and to the extent I am friendly
  with myself at all,
Approving my own reformation, which began 30 years ago to-
  day, the 3rd September 1953.
Well, your genuine lush never forgets the date of his last one,
  believe me, whether yesterday or yesteryear,
And one time I asked John, who had quit at 65, why he both-
  ered. "At your age I think I'd have gone on out loaded,"
  I said.
"Puking all over someone else's furniture?" he answered, and
  much can be derived
From his typical compression of judgment. We were men as
  men go, drinking coffee and squinting through cigarette
  smoke
Where we sat at a zinc-topped table at 7 o'clock in the
  morning.
We were men buoyant in cynicism.
Now I remember Lucinda de Ciella who drank a pony of
  Strega every morning before breakfast
And was sober and beautiful for ninety years, I remember her
  saying how peaceful

Were the Atlantic crossings by dirigible in the 1930's when her
husband was Ecuadorian ambassador to Brussels.
Such a magnificent, polychronogeneous idea, flight by craft
that are lighter than air!
I am sure it will be revived.

Charles Edward Eaton

The Luck of the Zeppelin

The dirigible was like a floating nude,
The cloud-tufted blue sky her great divan—
In the light, from silver to damascene,
Sliding tints on a woman's sleek thighs.

So love looks tethered there for a moment,
The fabulous, elongate, opaque bubble
Scanning the mountain's puncturing purple peak,
The sea's decuman lifting its lavish tongue.

Thus do we dream to start the lover's day,
Immense, moored, still but pregnant with journeys.
Can we not at least indulge ourselves at dawn
With life's loveliest, elated languor?

Ah, comes the scented wind, the slightest puff
That questions our control as if, after all,
No virgin but a demimondaine stirs,
Welcoming many from those foreign lands.

Jazz blares from the pendent cabin—One thinks
Of the necklaced women, the spatted men
Uncluttered by commitment or belief
As if always high and tuned for evening.

The skin of the balloon now sweats champagne—
You can imagine the monocled captain
With a side interest in the white slave trade
Stumped in his puzzle by the one word Love.

If we do not yell the answer from below,
He will give command to sail without us,
And the woman we did not know was ruined
Will not even leave a short goodbye note.

Over the Atlantic in deepest night
One turns to the girl beside one
As if she wore waterwings forever,
The safe, soft breasts of the born stowaway.

Cocooned in the corrupt oval, one floats—
Jazz in the saloon, the diddling captain,
Free of the mountain's finger, the lush mouth
Of the sea. Nothing but us is moving.

This is what we tell ourselves about sex:
Metaphysics stopped by inflated walls,
Magic lanterns surrounding us with lights,
Intense, exquisite, stationary pictures.

I recall blowing bubbles as a child,
How they lit like exploded butterflies—
One lives with wiped, iridescent fingers,
Launching every morning with another ship.

Two 27-Hour Days

Late in April, 1936, I sailed on the *Bremen* to Germany to make the first transatlantic flight in the Zeppelin *Hindenburg*, inaugurating the first regular passenger service by air across the North Atlantic.

Although I had traveled about 150,000 miles by airplane in America, Europe, Africa, and Asia, this was to be my first experience aboard a lighter-than-air craft. The United Press insured my life at Lloyd's in London; the one-per-cent premium was comparatively low; they had paid seven per cent for my flight to India five years before.

The little town of Friedrichshafen, beside the placid Lake of Constance, close to where Austria, Switzerland, and Germany meet, seethed with excitement. The German nation regarded the inauguration of air service to the United States with justifiable national pride, for it had definitely gained supremacy in passenger, mail, and freight service to both North and South America by air. Only seventeen years before, the Treaty of Versailles had virtually swept Germany's shipping from the seas when the Allied Powers had seized her merchant marine and also crippled her air development by the treaty. Now the German flag had returned to the seven seas; the *Bremen* and *Europa* were two of the fastest and largest liners in the world, and the airship *Graf Zeppelin* was making her 107th crossing of the South Atlantic to South America. She had safely carried more than 12,000 passengers in her career and traveled nearly a million miles. The first flight of the *Hindenburg* would clinch German predominance in transoceanic air traffic, and a sister ship for the Atlantic services was under construction. Germany rejoiced.

As darkness fell on May 6 buses took the fifty-one passengers and about a ton of baggage to the vast Zeppelin hangar. Fifty pounds of baggage could be carried free; excess weight cost about seventy-five cents a pound.

After we passed through the customs and passport control and were warned against carrying matches aboard, we mounted into the

By Hungerford for the *Pittsburgh Post-Gazette*, September 9, 1936.

bottom of the craft by a retractable stairway. A band played, hundreds scurried around under the ship shouting farewells, the passengers craned out of the open windows, Herr Arthur Voigt, a Danzig millionaire, unbuckled his wrist watch and tossed it out as a farewell present to a relative. There was as much tension and excitement as at the sailing of an ocean liner.

About a quarter past eight the two hundred men of the ground crew hauled at cables and briskly walked the craft, which was attached to a movable mooring mast, out into the field.

At a word from Commander Ernst Lehmann, the cables were thrown off. The huge ship, nearly one-sixth of a mile long and as high as a thirteen-story building, weighing 236 tons with its load of fuel, mail, freight, foodstuffs, water, passengers, and crew, lifted gently as thistledown. One hundred and six persons were aboard, the largest number ever to embark on a transoceanic flight.

As the huge bulk drifted upward silently and slowly we looked down into the upturned faces of thousands of frantically cheering townsfolk, spotlighted by the downward beams of two searchlights in the belly of the ship. The waving forest of arms gradually receded. Signal bells jangled in the engine gondolas and the four 1,100-horse-power motors roared. It was 8:27 P.M.; we were off on the 4,300-mile flight to America, suspended in air by 6,710,000 cubic feet of inflammable hydrogen gas.

From the slanting windows of the passengers' promenade deck, we glimpsed the snow-covered mountains of Switzerland and Austria and the gleaming surface of the Lake of Constance beneath. The *Hindenburg* headed down the Rhine toward the English Channel—a detour of hundreds of miles because France refused to permit the ship to cross her territory. Stewards with wireless telegrams paged the passengers and distributed a passenger list like that of an ocean liner. They announced that smoking was prohibited until an hour after sailing, and then it must be done in the hermetically sealed smoking room.

After the excitement of the take-off subsided, passengers inspected their accommodations, which comprised about 4,500 square feet entirely enclosed within the belly of the craft. On each side of the twenty-five two-bedded cabins ran a promenade forty-six feet in length flanked by slanting windows permitting a view outward and downward. Alongside the starboard promenade were a salon and a writing room furnished with duralumin chairs, writing desks, and piano. The dining room, forty-six feet long, with two tables seating fifty persons, adjoined the port promenade. The rooms were tastefully decorated. Each small, comfortable cabin had a wash basin with hot and cold water, a tiny desk, a clothes closet, and an electric light.

The deck below the cabins housed the shower baths, the kitchens with electric cooking apparatus and refrigeration, the toilets, and the smoking room. Inasmuch as the hydrogen gas in the sixteen bags that supported the craft was highly inflammable, extraordinary precautions had to be taken with the smoking room. You passed through a special entrance constructed like two leaves of a revolving door, and this locked the air in the room. Air pressure was maintained higher inside than outside in order to prevent gas from entering even if leaks should accidentally develop. The ash receivers automatically closed airtight to extinguish the lighted butts. Drinks were served from a small bar adjoining.

Within an hour after the take-off the passengers settled down to a routine of life similar to that on shipboard, playing cards, writing postcards, drinking beer, and eating sandwiches. Professor Franz Wagner, a celebrated European musician, played the piano; Pauline Charteris, wife of the British novelist, and Lady Wilkins, wife of Sir Hubert Wilkins, danced with several of the passengers. Others strolled to the promenade and hung out of the open windows to see the Rhine gleaming in the moonlight a thousand feet below.

I had difficulty convincing myself that we were actually making a historic flight, the first regular passenger service to North America. We slipped through the air with velvety smoothness and almost no vibration. The ship did not sway or buck, the motors hummed but faintly. It was only when you thrust a hand out of the open window into the eighty-miles-an-hour wind that you had any idea of our speed.

At 10:20 P.M. the lights of Mannheim slipped beneath us, and at 11:15 we slid over the millions of lights of the great city of Cologne. Except for the initial take-off, that provided about the only thrill of the evening. After passing Cologne most of the passengers adjourned to the smoking room and toasted Commander Eckener and Captain Lehmann. Others went to bed, leaving their shoes out in the corridor as on shipboard. Newspaper correspondents aboard set up their type-writers in the salon and typed occasional bulletins, which were wire-lessed direct to the United States.

Before daylight we reached the mouth of the Rhine, coasted down the English Channel, and caught a glimpse of the white cliffs at Dover. As the British objected to the *Hindenburg's* flying over England, it kept about a dozen miles out at sea.

As we slipped along the south coast of England at eighty miles an hour the rising sun silhouetted the South Downs like a relief map. The sea was calm and the passengers all slept, except the newspaper correspondents. Shortly after six I leaned out the promenade windows and watched the last land we were to see for 3,000 miles slowly slide away from us—or so it seemed. That was the jutting point of Lands End, the southwesterly tip of England; its white houses, red cliffs, and fresh green fields glistened in the early morning sun.

As the rocky finger of Lands End faded from sight and we started across 3,000 miles of rolling water, the full realization of the romance and adventure of the flight came home to me. During the forenoon we flew for hours a few hundred feet above a vast sea of dense, cottony clouds so white that it was almost impossible to look at them in the blindingly brilliant sunlight. The sharp black cigar-shaped outline of the *Hindenburg* flashed along across the snow-white floor, sometimes surrounded by three concentric circles of brilliantly glowing rainbows.

At 8:30 A.M. the passengers assembled for a breakfast of fruit, sausages, jam, toast, and coffee. The tables bore vases of fresh flowers and exquisite blue-and-white china. Presently we sighted the liner *Staatendam*, which saluted us with blasts of her siren; passengers crowded the decks waving handkerchiefs. Throughout our crossing we saw only half a dozen vessels although we were on the regular steamship track part of the time. [. . .]

Captain Ernst Lehmann conducted me through the interior of the craft. I reminded him that nineteen years before he had commanded a Zeppelin which bombed London. "I was two miles below you dodging your bombs," I said. He laughed: "Well, that was a long time ago."

On a foot-wide catwalk a few inches above the fabric of the belly of the ship, we threaded our way from the stem down into the immense tail fin of the *Hindenburg*. Sixteen great hydrogen bags filled most of the interior. They contained nearly seven million cubic feet of gas ten times as light as air and so inflammable that one spark would explode the craft in an instant. The huge rings of aluminum alloy which formed the Zeppelin's outline were braced by an intricate system of strong "Swiss cheese" girders and finger-thick wires. On either side of the catwalk lay great tanks carrying 143,000 pounds of Diesel oil, water tanks, bays for food supplies, freight, and mail, and officers' and crew's quarters.

As I trod the narrow runway I clutched nervously at struts and girders, fearing that a misstep would plunge me through the thin fabric into the ocean half a mile below. "You needn't be so concerned," Lehmann said, noticing my expression. "That fabric is strong enough to bear the weight of a man. You wouldn't go through if you slipped off on it." He perceived my incredulous look. "Here, I'll show you." He jumped off the catwalk on to the fabric, only a fraction of an inch thick. It bore him easily, although it was not attached to the body structure anywhere within eight feet. He explained that the fabric was unbelievably strong, having been manufactured at great expense for this particular duty.

Lehmann took me down into the control cabin, suspended under the belly of the ship, whence the Zeppelin was navigated. From there we viewed a marvelous panorama of ocean in every direction, with the immense bulk of the *Hindenburg* above and behind us. Dials, gauges, meteorological and navigating instruments filled the cabin. He showed me the operation of devices which valved out gas or water ballast to lower or raise the ship, a duplicate steering apparatus, and signal telegraph and telephone to every vital part of the ship. He explained the weather charts, which were revised every few hours on the basis of wireless reports from ships at sea.

With Fritz Sturm, chief engineer, I visited one of the engine gondolas, suspended on struts fifteen feet in space outside the envelope of the craft. That was an experience I do not want to repeat, and when I asked Lehmann's permission I did not know what it entailed.

To reach the gondola I climbed out over empty space on a collapsible ladder a foot wide slanting down from an opening in the envelope into the egg-shaped gondola. Before starting Sturm tied a helmet to my head, told me to leave my overcoat behind, and then showed me how to clutch the frail ladder on two sides, crooking my elbow around it to the windward and clutching the other edge with my fingers. This precaution was necessary to prevent the eighty-miles-an-hour wind from tearing me bodily off the ladder. I found it a ticklish, frightening business; each time I raised a foot the wind wrenched it away from the ladder rung and flung it back toward the stern of the ship. Nothing in the world could save you if the hurricanelike wind tore you off the ladder. Nothing but yawning space spread out on either side, and the ocean lay half a mile below. After a few steps down the slanting ladder I wished I hadn't conceived the foolhardy idea of visiting the gondola.

Inside the gondola a narrow passage ran alongside the 1,100-horse-power Diesel engine, which drove a huge nineteen-foot propeller that deafened me with its thunder in spite of my padded helmet. Only a few struts the size of an ankle fastened this power plant to the craft, which loomed gigantically beside us. Once inside the gondola, Sturm closed the collapsible ladder. Empty space surrounded us on every side; we felt as if we were being shot through the air inside a huge artillery shell with open windows. An engineer remained continually on duty inside each of the four gondolas, shifts being changed every few hours.

Next morning, from an altitude of about three-quarters of a mile, I actually detected the curvature of the globe with the naked eye. From that height we could see scores of miles; the atmosphere was remarkably clear and the horizon sharp as a knife. By following the horizon closely I perceived, or thought I did, the slight bend of the earth's surface. That provided one of the greatest thrills of the trip; I had always known that the earth was round, but it was deeply stirring actually to see an infinitesimal section of its rotundity. Once before I had felt that same awesome sensation—when I stood one night on the edge of the chasm of the Grand Canyon and watched the opposite lip of the abyss wheel up toward the stars. I saw the turning of the earth as the rim of the Canyon rose, covering star after star; I imagined I even felt the world whirling under my feet.

About one o'clock Friday morning, in mid-Atlantic, the *Hindenburg* ran head on into a severe storm. In inky darkness as black as the inside of a black cat, the vast bulk of the *Hindenburg* swayed and bucked; hail and torrents of rain lashed at the windows of the promenade decks. With a few passengers I gazed down at the fascinating spectacle of the heaving ocean 2,000 feet below, one round area in the blackness illuminated by the spotlight in the belly of the craft. The downpour of rain and gale-force wind buffeted the craft about half an hour. This was the first time we had felt any deviation from the velvety motion of the ship.

So far as I could tell, none of us watching the storm felt any trepidation or appreciable sense of danger. The passengers already asleep were not awakened, vases of sweet peas and carnations on the writing and dining tables did not turn over. In my cabin not a drop spilled from a full glass of water. But at last you realized you were flying the Atlantic and were out here alone and helpless, 1,500 miles from land, fighting the elements and beating them.

Dr. Hugo Eckener, his deeply lined, weather-beaten face calm and composed, lumbered up from the control car. "This is really a severe storm," he said, "but I am pleased by the behavior of the ship. As you see, the motion is gentle. We have collected in special tanks five tons of water from the storm to replace many tons of weight lost by consumption of fuel oil. That will be useful to us in landing. With that additional weight we shall not have to valve out so much gas to get her down at Lakehurst. Sometimes when we sight a rain storm on the horizon we go over and run through it for the purpose of collecting water ballast. Unless we collect water from rain storms during a flight, we sometimes have to valve out as much as one-third of our gas. That is expensive; it has to be replaced before we commence another flight. We collect in tanks all of the water used by the passengers for toilet and bathing purposes during the trip and use it for ballast."

In the morning I saw a lone white bird 900 miles from land; he tried to follow us for awhile but gave it up, and we left him out there alone. I'll wager he doesn't go home to roost very often. Some 500 miles off Sable Island we passed over several glittering icebergs, one about an acre in extent, and watched three whales spouting.

Father Paul Schulte, of Aix-la-Chapelle, known as the "flying padre," celebrated the first mass in the air, for which the Pope had granted special permission. Schulte erected an altar in the salon, where all the passengers gathered. The candles were not lighted because of danger of explosion.

That night stewards served a five-course gala dinner, including fresh trout from the Black Forest. Many of the passengers wore evening clothes for the occasion. After dinner we made a broadcast to the United States including a piano recital by Professor Wagner, songs by Lady Wilkins, and speeches by Dr. Eckener and several of the passengers, including myself. After the broadcast, passengers gathered in the smoking room and bar to celebrate with many toasts and songs our approach to the American continent. Pauline Charteris introduced a song she had picked up in Nassau which ran: "Mamma don't want no gin, because it makes her sin." We discussed a suitable name for the first child conceived in mid-air aboard a Zeppelin—a possibility nowadays. I suggested Helium, if it were a boy, and Shelium, if a girl. That idea was adopted. The hilarious party continued most of the night.

In the morning before dawn we caught the first glimpse of the American continent. At 4:12 A.M. we sighted on our right a necklace-like string of lights miles long—the coast of Long Island. Passengers crowded to the promenade windows. At 4:35 we came over Long Island and cruised toward Brooklyn while passengers gathered in the dining salon for a light breakfast of sliced sausages, coffee, toast, and jam. The sleeping millions a thousand feet below seemed unaware of our passage.

At exactly five A.M. the *Hindenburg* slid over the Battery. Dawn was just breaking. Suddenly a great pandemonium of hundreds of whistles from steamers and liners rose to greet us. We saw white jets of steam from the whistles of boats in the Hudson and East rivers.

Passengers craned from the windows in excitement, chattering in several languages. Lights in the promenades were turned out to afford a better view.

We cruised up past the Empire State Building at reduced speed, passing only a few hundred feet above it. The sight brought exclamations of wonder from Europeans aboard who had never seen New York.

About the center of Central Park the *Hindenburg* swerved toward the Hudson and flew over Germany's other symbol of re-emergence in world commerce—the liner *Bremen*, which directed two powerful searchlights upon us. Her deep-throated whistle bellowed. Our German passengers waved handkerchiefs from the windows in a fever of patriotic excitement.

The continued shrieking and bellowing of steamship whistles awakened thousands below. We saw people running from buildings and pointing and staring upward. Then, as the sun rose the airship turned down the Hudson and flew directly over the Statue of Liberty toward Lakehurst. I hastily wrote a description of our passage over New York and dropped it out of the window to one of our men when we hovered over the Lakehurst field.

The gigantic bulk of the craft settled gently at Lakehurst sixty-one hours and thirty-eight minutes after leaving middle Europe, a flight of 4,381 miles. We had eaten only two luncheons, two dinners, and three breakfasts aboard. We had spanned the ocean so rapidly that we had difficulty keeping track of the time on board because our days were twenty-seven hours long. This led to constant confusion between Greenwich time, Central European time, ship's time,—which roughly corresponded with our position on the globe,—Eastern Standard time, and Eastern Daylight time; and a prankster who frequently set back the clock in the bar so he could celebrate longer introduced still another factor. Even the airship officers sometimes seemed a little uncertain about Eastern Standard and Eastern Daylight time and their relation to ship's time and Greenwich time.

This rapid translation from continent to continent across 3,000 miles of ocean left in me an uncanny sense of confusion. The mind had not been able to keep pace with the body. Less than sixty-two hours before I had been in middle Europe. In that time 106 of us had been transported across one-fourth of the globe and my body, so it seemed, had left my mind behind. It took another day before I became orientated and fully grasped the idea that I was back in America.

I Will Not Follow the *Hindenburg*

In September or October of 1936, I was six years old, at school in Ridgefield, Connecticut, in those days a small, exceedingly rural town. I was a shy little girl, always trailing along behind my 10-year-old brother Blair. One day we were outside during the lunch recess, when a shadow crossed the schoolyard. We all looked up; something huge was floating by. Blair said excitedly, "Hey, that's the *Hindenburg*! Let's follow it!" I hadn't the faintest idea what he was talking about or what a *Hindenburg* was, but whenever Blair said "follow," I followed; so I ran behind him and his friends, trying hard to keep up. We ran across fields and brooks and over stone walls, trying to keep the airship in sight. Blair finally admitted defeat — the *Hindenburg* was faster than we were — and we made our way back to the school, very late and very dirty, to face angry teachers. I don't remember what Blair's punishment was, but I was made to stand at the blackboard and write "I will not follow the *Hindenburg*"100 times.

The LZ 129 *Hindenburg* in flight over Lakehurst, New Jersey, 1936.
Courtesy of Hepburn Walker.

Kay Boyle

from A Complaint for Mary and Marcel

I believe in the
scenic railways
that have not
run yet because
the scaffolding
is still unsafe
and in the
buildings they
have not had
time to finish
I believe this
year and this
time of the
year there is
never the time
to finish only
the time left to
begin again.
If it is wiser
to say too
little than
too much there
being less to
take back in
anguish later
then it is
easier to say
too much for it
leaves that
much less to

You did not come to the Paris
   exposition of 1937 on the
   opening night when I
   asked you.
You did not see the fountains fresh
   as lilacs spraying along the
   river in the dark
Or the fans they had bought for the
   occasion made of blue lace and
   used instead of illumination.
You did not wait behind the scenes
   in the wings for the actors to
   come and the curtain to rise
Or the cues to be given. You were
   not there when the searchlights
   poured the milk of avalanches
Into the obliterated alley of the
   Seine.
Where you were you could not hear
   the roman candles breaking the
   way glass breaks under a fist
Or say with a thousand other people
   who were there "Ah-h-h-h"
   with the voice of one person
Awed when the tour Eiffel was
   transformed to burning wire,
   nor could you see
The fireworks climb like larks in
   spring to those explosions of
   indecipherable mystery

carry about in That liberate metal or song more valuable
the veins than money is. The savagery
seeking to say Of serpents and birds imported from
it or not to Japan pursued their own
say it or not to incalculable wealth
remember to In emeralds, diamonds, rubies, and
say it or to topaz, writhing and spiraling
forget it is not through the firmament,
things like this Crashing in thirst and frenzy through
that can be the tropic underbrush that
said. leafed in conflagrated satin
  Trunked in seething palm and cocoa hair
  the sky's wild blistering jungle.

You did not You had people to dinner. You could
visit the Belgian not come. You did not see the
or the Russian small thick hooded candles
or the Italian They set out like gondolas on the
or the German current, drifting in slow
pavilions or ride flickering formation like folded
up in the lift with gulls
the smell of roses With hearts ignited moving a-light
thick as smoke upon the river's on the tide's
but sweeter in declining.
your eyes. You They were extinguished one by one
were expecting by breath or wind or by their
Man Ray or own defatigation
Nancy Perry or (As the complaints I set out lighted
Dali or Brancusi in the dark for you expire in
to come and sit in their passage
the garden with the Because of the long way through
tiger lilies with you. silence they must go).

THE STORY I WANTED TO TELL YOU

Well, when I got up to the top of the German pavilion I thought
I'd die laughing, for there was a man I'd seen dead at least twice in

his life. He was wearing a waiter's white jacket, the kind he'd worn when he was an Austrian barman and he was carrying the steins of beer people had ordered, three in each hand by the handles. There was just one difference in him: he'd broken his leg at the ankle ski-jumping since I'd seen him last and he was limping. It was so hot there was a string of priceless beads bound to his forehead; he was so pale that when I gave him the rose the color from its petals was reflected an instant on his face. He put down the steins of beer on the stone rail instead of on the tables and he said My God you look awful, and I said Hubert you look simply terrible. We'd been waiting two years to say things to each other and these were the words that came the quickest. The fireworks had begun outside like war on the river, giving the people a taste of what they wanted and the perfect aspect of the night a lust to civilize it for consumption, and Hubert and I did not sit down and did not stand up but watched the foam perish on the beer he had forgotten. What month did you die in, Hubert, I said, and he said, It must have been May. You know you look very badly, he said. You look very thin. It was that afternoon we were going up too late in the year and the side of the Grossglockner gave up what snow was left. Over the thunder of the tons of it falling I could still hear his voice like the cry of a marten, the last breaths he drew the plucked strings of a harp humming still. There was no more life in his face then than now except for the eyes bleached golden as his hair and sightless as a cameo's. The whole south side avalanched that month, he said, it must have been in May. However it was, I said, you were alive and kicking next October. We went to Vienna for the newborn wine, we were in at the birth, we danced ourselves sick. I began laughing again, look-ing at Hubert and laughing until my cheeks ached from laughing out loud and I said I remember the place they buried you was standing wide open Christmas eve in the churchyard. I went there with a little tree for you with the candles lighted on it and silk ribbons tied in its branches. I fooled them, said Hubert, and I said, Hubert your English is beautiful and your French is music and your German makes the edelweiss grow colder sharper purer in my heart.

Well, the upshot of it all was that he broke his shoulder skiing ahead of me on the Fleck Alp. Blood poisoning set in right away and in twenty-four hours he was dead to the world. You paid your debt to nature once too often, Hubert my love, I said, you crossed the Stygian ferry without me, you shuffled off this mortal coil. You went out like the snuff of a candle, passed in your chips, you launched into eternity without my arm in your arm. Hubert held up his hand against the convulsions of the aerial display and I could count the bones in it and see the illuminations shining through it as if through mist and he said Look the blood is gone from it, not flowed away put parched the way a spring will dry.

When they let you into the room at the hospital that night it was all over, Hubert said. I'd died half an hour before. Listen, Hubert, I said, I didn't take a drink all day that day so as to be able to walk straight past the other beds to you. You kneeled down but you didn't cry, Hubert said, but anyway I kept all the things you said to me. I said them out loud to myself all night and all during the funeral service the priest was saying for me laying me away in death. What was it I said to you, I asked him, and Hubert answered: Whenever they put a shovelful of earth slap down on my face I kept saying what you'd said faster and faster until they got me down for good and choked me with it. If you want any beer you can damned well get up and get it yourselves, Hubert said, for the people had risen from the tables on the roof-garden of the German pavilion whether to see the fireworks better or to ask for drink. I've been trying to put weight on all spring, said Hubert. We were standing so close together that there was no need to move or to embrace each other. After one has burned to death, he said, putting out his thin hands where I could see them, it is impossible to keep the flesh on one's bones.

And then the whole truth of the thing came out and everything else I knew about him might have been something somebody made up. It seems that after he died in the hospital that winter or that May in the Alps then nothing would do but he must get a job on an airship and he wouldn't hear of anything else and he'd get it willy-nilly. He'd get it no matter what, he said, and come what may. And listening to him telling me I suddenly knew and pushed his hand aside in fright and I went running out through the people with my high heels turning sideways in panic with every step I ran. I went crying in terror down the flights of stairs with the heat of the furnace laying waste behind me, the fire after me in pursuit like a crowd of people running fast, some roaring, some whispering through roasted lips, the flames after me relentlessly in truth with the split and the rip of their conflagration pouring in torrents of rushing fire down the cascade of flight to lower flight. At the entrance door below I could not pass, for the skeleton stood there waiting. The rose I had given him was in his fingers still, the petals charred and the leaves ash-white and ready to dissolve in dust. After much difficulty I finally succeeded, he said, in getting a place as steward on the *Hindenburg*. The trip over the sea was beautiful. I wish you had been there.

The *Hindenburg* Disaster

On one evening about half-past four,
The *Hindenburg* was coming along,
But it was running awful slow.
Just a little while, just before night,
The *Hindenburg* had burnt clean out of sight.
Oh, Lord, burnt clean out of sight,
The *Hindenburg* burnt clean out of sight.

The people all thought the *Hindenburg* was supposed to begin
    to roll,
The people in New York City, they all begin to stroll.
The *Hindenburg* when it caught afire,
It was up in the world just a little bit too high.
Oh, Lord, little bit too high,
Just up in the world a little bit too high.

Oh, the *Hindenburg*, the *Hindenburg*,
Whole town's talkin' 'bout the *Hindenburg*,
On one evening 'bout half-past four,
The *Hindenburg* come runnin' slow.

Oh, the *Hindenburg*, oh, the *Hindenburg*,
Largest ship was, in this world,
Whole town's talkin' 'bout the *Hindenburg*,
Largest ship was in this world.

The people saw the boat, when it begin to roll,
The people on the ground begin to stroll.
Whole town's talkin' 'bout the *Hindenburg*,
Largest ship afloat in this world.

Oh, when it caught afire,
Up in the world a little bit too high.
Oh, the *Hindenburg* down on the ground,
Woman kept throwin' her li'l chillun down.

Oh, chillun down, chillun down,
Woman kept throwin' her chillun down.
Whole town's talkin' 'bout the *Hindenburg*.
Largest ship it was in this world.

It's a sin and a shame,
A sin and a shame,
Just look at that *Hindenburg*'s frame.
Sin and a shame, sin and a shame,
The *Hindenburg* burnt up to her frame.

Nancy Nowak

Ascension Day, 1937:
Pictures of an Actual Disaster

How beautiful, but for
the broken
cross on its tail, *sign*

of the sun
made by the ancients
conquered. Its bent hands insist:
it is time. Mark of the raptor

that cruised to Rio, blanketed
the Rhenish countryside with Goebbels' harmonies,

now sails above New York. The ship's

prop blades stroke the air:
this is no eagle, but a vessel
bearing a volatile
offering, lofted not by

the helium America
won't license for export—

> *How do I know*
> *it won't ultimately be used*
> *for war purposes?*

but by hydrogen, abundant
in the sun, lightest, hottest-
burning,

so paying passengers smoke their pipes
in a fire-proofed room
and without the benefit of flash
snap photos through slanting
isinglass windows. The acrobat

Ben Dova, fresh from Berlin's Wintergarden,
trains his Bell and Howell
on the Empire State
observatory, sees himself

taken in by
aperture, iris.
                The ship's skin

like the sky-
scraper's walls and windows
is hung on a rigid

framework no one man
could have made.

Both wonders rival

sunlight, casting steep,
willed shadows. On the ground
people follow under

the vessel's dark hand
while in the harbor, a concert of frantic ship whistles
calls out.

LZ-129 has triumphed again, as last season
it flew above a hurricane
battering New England
and felt nothing, *part of the stream*

of wind. This afternoon
there are squalls westward
and no one is afraid

although Captain Lehmann, aboard
as observer, carries in his flight jacket pocket

a note warning
of sabotage: *do not go
to Lakehurst.* But all luggage examined
found free of pistols, dry cells,
carrier pigeons, he tells no one.

Father to his men, hero
who commanded Zeppelin raids on England and won
the Iron Cross: if Lehmann is worried,

no one knows. Those who have traveled
hours above seas, beacons,
cities, find the ship
the one safe place
as it moves changeless through its element.

But to tear away from earth, say the necessary
farewells! Waiting strangers
soon more alike
than those loved ones left behind,
the passengers
milled in the great darkness of the *Halle* at Frankfurt.
There was melancholy, someone's
furtive look, a man with a package
held too tightly under one arm;
a muscular Alsatian strained at its lead.

As mild rain fell, the spot-lit airship bade
them. They climbed the gang,

the hatches sealed. With the ship
rose brutal

music; as if to haul them back,
Hitler Youth ran across the field beneath
the upward vanishing hull.

Calm days at sea presided over
by the glassy visage of the ship's namesake,
his bust in its niche near the dining room
where stewards served Rhine salmon
on blue and gold porcelain. Not a
drop of wine spilled. In the cocktail bar
Ben Dova amused himself by balancing
a fountain pen on its flat end.

Heaps of soiled linens in the hallways.
The voyage is ending, passengers
redeem their postcard chits.
But unsettled

weather delays landing, when
can they leave the sky?
Captain Pruss cruises from Barnegat to Cape May and back
while black clouds drench Lakehurst.
At last they're clear, passengers wave

as the Navy ground crew
struggles with the lines.

The unbalanced ship fights the wind.

Three blasts of the landing station siren,
and three, and three;

the ship holds still, *a framed,
populated cloud,* then

just as one may experience the longest dream
in but a few seconds

was there smoke
from the engines like a backfire   *a noise*
like bullets coming out of the engine gondolas

did the ship's belly glow pink, lit from within
like a Japanese lantern,

> *the glow spread and a ribbon of fire*
> *raced along the belly to the bow,* was the

brilliant flame
> *yellow,* or

dark red, a mushroom-shaped
flower speedily bursting into bloom

The concussion
could have been the big guns at Fort Dix
except how *the explosions gave way*
> *to sounds of screams,* those in

> *the flaming, falling ship*

> the bow reared up, tail
> smashed to the ground

absolutely had no chance

Oh the humanity and all the passengers

on the port side *felt a slight tremor.*
People were just curious,
walking toward the promenade deck.
Starboard passengers saw

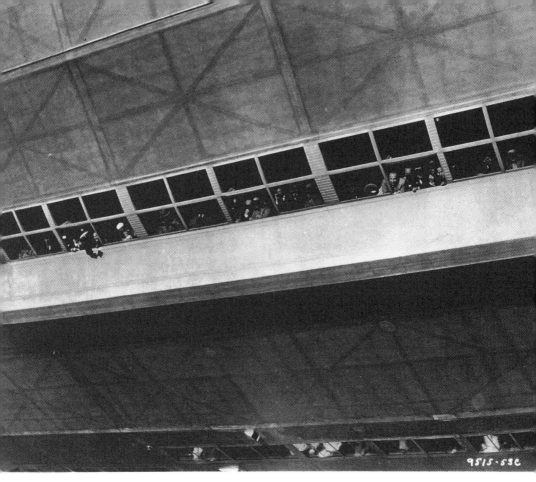

Passengers on the *Hindenburg*'s promenade deck wave to friends on the ground, Lakehurst, New Jersey, 1936. Courtesy of Hepburn Walker.

shocked faces of those on the ground
turned toward *the ship*

    even in breaking up, was gentle
    to its passengers—those who

could, broke through, flung
themselves from the burning, but *some*

    were in flames
    as they plunged to earth

Ben Dova knocked out a pane
with his Bell and Howell.
                    The landing crew watched him

hurl himself from a window,
drop forty feet to the ground, get up
feeling himself
to see if he was really all there

                    before they returned
to the wreck to lead to safety

        Lehmann, his flight jacket on fire:
        I don't understand

the figures burned black or waxen who
stumbled, fell to the sand,
stood again, gesturing for

        the unreserved help of the American airmen
        coming to the rescue of their German comrades

The hangar becomes a morgue

        a beautiful proof of the spirit
        which links airmen of all nations.

After a swastika-decked farewell,
the German dead are freighted home.
An inquiry held in the hangar decides
not *a stroke of war*, not Lehmann's
infernal machine, but *an unfathomable*
Act of God, St. Elmo's fire
killed thirty-one.
                    For its witnesses,
until the next, *this is*
one of the worst catastrophes in the world.

sign . . . ancients. Hans von Schiller, captain of the *Graf Zeppelin.*
How do . . . purposes? Secretary of the Interior Ickes.
part . . . wind. The *Literary Digest,* 1936.

Many of the eyewitness descriptions are taken from newspaper
accounts. Some of the most striking images are from *What
About the Airship?* by Charles Rosendahl, commander of the
U.S. Naval station at Lakehurst at the time of the crash.

the unreserved . . . all nations. Herman Goering.

Richard Brautigan

Your Departure versus the *Hindenburg*

Every time we say good-bye
I see it as an extension of
   the *Hindenburg*:
that great 1937 airship exploding
in medieval flames like a burning castle
   above New Jersey.
When you leave the house, the
shadow of the *Hindenburg* enters
   to take your place.

Jack Stewart

If the *Hindenburg* Had Left from Las Vegas

Almost natural its monochrome,
the Latin, "cumulonimbus,"
an indication of that to come,
how certain syllables contain
disaster, fear.
And yet we point with joy at these:
in Fuji green, Goodyear blue,
the black and white of Sea World,
their ironies erased in neon.
At home beneath a threat
that's almost biblical,
a marquee message in the sky,
what desire lets us forget
that Sodom was a boom town,
with dancers, lights, and splendid coins,
when heaven rained down fire?

Paul Zimmer

Zimmer and the Age of Zeppelins

There was the faint sound
Of a piano playing ragtime
And then an abrupt eclipse.
Zimmer looked up and saw the zeppelin
Like a giant okra ponderously
Sliding over trees and rooftops,
Its girders creaking, echoing.

It took all day to pass over
As the sound of idle laughter
Drifted down from the promenade
And Zimmer heard tinkle of
Ice and glasses from the lounge.
At dusk he watched its fins
Cross over into the night.

It had been such an awesome day
That Zimmer could not comprehend
A sudden astonishing fireball
And thunder over the horizon,
The end of the age of zeppelins.

He ran to see the great craft
Roaring in its own air and fire,
Bodies dropping like blackened tentworms
From a torched nest and then
The whole thing down in a blazing heap,
Cries of the injured amongst the debris,
The old moon sailing on above the agony.

The Afterlives of Count Zeppelin

Inflated, yet elliptical, of epic size,
What great Teutonic riddle hangs there in the skies?
It is the *Graf von Himmel,* bearing from Jews
And postwar debt true Germans on eternal cruise:
Teachers of counterpoint, and, wives in braided locks,
Cherubic manufacturers of cuckoo clocks:
Ex-Kaiserin, Big Bertha, other Krupps, and—*echt*—
A mid-air cellar tanker planes refill with *Sekt.*
For cabin class, a *Turnverein,* a skating rink,
And fourteen cabin boys, to hum them Humperdinck.
Moreover, in the steering gondola, her odd,
Stiff navigator may, conceivably, be God.

Below him there? The flaming skeleton he passed?
That is the *Graf von Hölle*, burning at the mast:
Our instant crematorium, Zigeuner, Slav,
Observe that transportation of the do-not-have;
The gas-fed *Götterdämmerung* of such as die
Unsuited for the great Bayreuth there in the sky;
Who, in the framework of the blazing hull, burned dark,
Pursue the buckling doors; who end as hurried sparks,
And know that in the dummy gondola, ramrod
To the end, hand on the valves, their fellow spark is God.

Acknowledgments

I am most grateful to Tammy Wadley for her generous assistance in the preparation of the manuscript and to the Bush Foundation for a 1997 Bush Artist Fellowship which aided in the completion of the book. I also wish to thank the following for providing valuable help with either text or illustrations: Wendy Amundson, Night Owl Graphics; Eric Brothers, Lighter-Than-Air Society; Lucy Shelton Caswell, Cartoon, Graphic, and Photographic Arts Research Library, Ohio State University; Dawn Dewey, Paul Lawrence Dunbar Library, Wright State University; John Hawk and Duffy Knaus, the Cole Zeppelin Collection and Lighter-Than-Air Library, University of Oregon; Friederike von Schwerin-High and Jeffrey L. High; Bill Hill, ESTIS, Wilson Library, University of Minnesota; Allan Janus, National Air & Space Museum, Smithsonian Institution; James Leasor; Paul K. McCutcheon, National Air & Space Museum, Smithsonian Institution; John Miller, University of Akron Library; William Parsons, Music Division, Library of Congress; Richard Peuser, National Archives; Tom Riis, American Music Research Center, College of Music, University of Colorado at Boulder; Robert Schmelzer, National Geographic Society; Nigel Steel, Imperial War Museum, London, England; Gorden Vaeth; and Hepburn Walker.

In order to obtain current copyright information, I have attempted in every instance to contact the author, publisher, or copyright holder of the material included in this collection. In some cases, such information may still be incomplete. The copyright to each individual work remains with the author or other copyright holder as designated by the author.

Index

DATE DUE